NAPOLEON CONQUERS
AUSTRIA
The 1809 Campaign for Vienna

Major Theater of Operations
(Danube Valley and Italy)

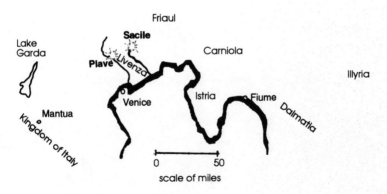

scale of miles

NAPOLEON CONQUERS AUSTRIA

The 1809 Campaign for Vienna

James R. Arnold

ARMS AND
ARMOUR

First published in Great Britain 1995 by
Arms and Armour
Wellington House, 125 Strand, London WC2R 0BB, England
An imprint of the Cassell Group

British Library Cataloguing in Publication Data
A catalogue record for this book is available
from the British Library.

ISBN 1 85409 316 9

First published 1995 in the United States of America
by Praeger Publishers, 88 Post Road West, Westport, CT 06881
An imprint of Greenwood Publishing Group, Inc.

Printed in the United States of America

The paper used in this book complies with the
Permanent Paper Standard issued by the National
Information Standards Organization (Z39.48-1984).

10 9 8 7 6 5 4 3 2 1

CONTENTS

Illustrations follow page 93.

MAPS

ACKNOWLEDGMENTS

I thank Joyce Arnold for her research mission to Florida State University; Dan Eades and Penny Sippel, my editors, for their professional skill and support for this project; Miriam Bergamini for her meticulous proofreading; Jack Gill for providing information about the role of Napoleon's German allies in the 1809 campaign; Peter Harrington and the staff at the Anne K. Brown Library, Providence, Rhode Island; Jean Lochet for providing a translated copy of the Exner manuscript; Ralph Reinertsen for translating German source material; John Slonaker and the staff of the U.S. Army Military History Institute; and Carl Teger for his photography. Special thanks to David Chandler for his enthusiastic encouragement to carry the campaign to conclusion.

Roberta Wiener provided editing, proofreading, and business acumen in the midst of a difficult Virginia farm winter. She is the model chief of staff.

INTRODUCTION

The sun rose on April 24, 1809, illuminating a continent at war. From Poland to Spain some 600,000 soldiers awakened to duty. Rising to the bugle's call and the tap of the drum was a routine that the oldest veterans had performed nearly without pause for 17 years. So huge were the issues at stake that national leaders from emperor, kaiser, prime minister, and king to the minor rulers of the smallest German principality continued to send their young men to far-flung battlefields to resolve, by fire and sword, intractable problems that seemed to defy any other solution. With varying degrees of willingness—17 years of slaughter had taken the bloom off patriotism for many—their subjects answered their call. Because they did, and would continue to do so for most of the next six years, Europe's generals commanded forces of unprecedented size. Nowhere was the concentration of force greater in this spring of 1809 than in the Danube valley, for it was here that the world's undisputed military genius had determined to launch his blow. Armies mobilized, soldiers marched, and men died throughout the continent, but it was on central Europe that men of power focused. Here would be decided the greatest issue of all: Could the Hapsburg Empire finally, on this its fourth try, defeat the French Empire? More precisely, could the Austrian generalissimus, Erzherzog (Archduke) Karl, vanquish on a field of battle the heretofore invincible French led by Napoleon?

Before the French Revolution, European heads of state had warred for limited objectives: the possession of a province or the capture of a fortress. They did not seek to overthrow a fellow monarch. The revolution, and the subsequent rise of Napoleon, changed the nature of warfare. "With me," Napoleon reflected, "the stake is always my existence and that of the whole Empire."[1] So it was in 1809 when Austria attacked France. Consequently, in cabinet rooms, palaces, and salons from London to St. Petersburg, diplomats and military men alike awaited battle's resolution. If Karl could triumph, most of Europe stood poised to pounce on a wounded, overly extended French giant. If Karl failed, all except England and perhaps Portugal and Spain would make whatever accommodations necessary to survive under Napoleonic hegemony.

The Bavarian town of Regensburg, known to the French as Ratisbonne, was the hub around which events whirled, for it was here that the 40-year-old Emperor Napoleon Bonaparte had established the headquarters for his Army of Germany. The previous day, in an audacious display of naked courage, French soldiers had scaled Ratisbonne's ancient walls to capture the town. During the action, the emperor himself had been wounded. News of his wound spread with electrifying suddenness as thousands of soldiers broke ranks to flock to Napoleon's side to see for themselves if the great man still lived. In fact the wound was minor, if painful. Hobbling to his horse, a beautiful and conspicuous white charger, Napoleon had coursed the field so his entire army could see that he was unharmed. Amid thunderous cries of "Vive l'empereur," his army returned to the business of driving the Austrians through Ratisbonne and over the Danube.

On April 24, the town became much more than a mere army headquarters because Napoleon was much more than the army commander in chief. With the title emperor came the demands of being the head of state for a vast territory bordered by the Atlantic, the Mediterranean, the Pyrenees, and the Rhine. Moreover, rulers handpicked by Napoleon, along with sovereigns who opted to side with the French because of fear or respect, or both, controlled the affairs of state in Holland, Germany, Italy, Illyria, and Poland. It was an empire the likes of which had not been seen in Europe since Roman times, and it was all incredibly centralized in one person, Napoleon. Field command coupled with national leadership was a crushing dual responsibility that only a man of immense mental powers could undertake.

Even in the midst of a life-and-death campaign struggle against Austria, Napoleon continued to make nearly every decision of state. Often, during his bath, while being shaved, when eating his meals, aides present petitions and requests for his tireless attention: a second lieutenant asks to retain his French citizenship while serving in the Dutch army. Granted. Emperor Alexander I of Russia asks that an English prisoner of war who is a relative of his personal surgeon be released. Granted. It is proposed that a certain General Cambacérès be employed in the Army of Germany. No. He is good for nothing. The foundry in Turin proposes to transport bronze from distant regions to complete the manufacture of certain armaments. Refused. The emperor identifies six closer, less-costly locations from which to obtain the bronze. The minister of war in Paris proposes to send 25 foot and 15 mounted gendarmes into the upper Loire to bring back deserting conscripts. Approved.[2]

Petitions dealt with, next comes a torrent of orders as perspiring secretaries work in relays to keep pace with the emperor's fervid mind. The Poles just captured while serving in the Hapsburg ranks should be collected and sent to Spain where they can reinforce the Vistula Legion that fights in the French service.

The 200 men of the 15th Légère coming from Portugal should hasten to Bavaria to make good recent losses. The Duke of Valmy shall proceed to Mayence to command a newly assembled corps of observation that is needed to overawe Prussia while the emperor completes his campaign against Austria. General Dejean must dispatch his 12th Battalion of military equipments to the front because its 240 caissons will be very useful for the Army of Germany's continuing campaign. The laborers and marine gunners at Brest are sufficient to protect the port against amphibious attack by the English, but six provisional dragoon regiments must be relocated to serve as a mobile reserve for the entire Breton coast.[3] If genius lies in the attention to detail, here was genius at work.

Since becoming emperor in 1804 Napoleon has never lost a campaign, let alone a battle. The past five days has witnessed another dazzling campaign. Because his crisis on the Danube had come as a strategic surprise, he had been forced to improvise a hastily concocted counterstroke to Karl's invasion of Bavaria. The resultant campaign displayed flashes of military genius but had not included a war-ending stroke. Although Napoleon's counteroffensive failed to destroy the enemy army, he did inflict a series of defeats that split the Austrian army in two. One wing, commanded by Karl himself, is retiring from Ratisbonne into the Bohemian mountains. The other wing, commanded by Feldmarschall-Leutenant Johann Hiller, is also in retreat south of the Danube where it blocks a direct advance on Vienna. Having achieved a central position with his army interposed between the two Austrian wings, the emperor must decide what to do next. A direct pursuit against the recently defeated Karl, the classic military solution, has much to recommend it: Defeat the enemy's main army, and all else will follow. But Napoleon is not yet sure if Karl has taken the majority of the Austrian army with him into Bohemia. Alternatively, a drive to the east against Hiller leads to the glittering objective of the enemy's capital. Weighing the choices, as yet without accurate intelligence informing him of the relative strengths of the two enemy wings, Napoleon hints at his predilection when he announces to his army: "In less than a month, we will be in Vienna."[4]

While the emperor attended to affairs of state in Ratisbonne, the main body of the Austrian army was staggering into Cham on the edge of the Bohemian mountains some 32 miles to the northeast. Having been bested on consecutive battlefields for the past five days, everyone, from private to general, felt considerable discouragement. No one was more despairing than the man at the top, the 38-year old Erzherzog Karl. Although he had not favored this war, he had labored long and hard to reform the Hapsburg military and prepare it for contesting the mighty French war machine. For the first time, the Hapsburg Empire had summoned the latent nationalism of its people—at least of the German majority; the government feared that the ethnic minorities, the Czechs, Poles, Croats, and Serbs, could not be trusted with the fiery spirit of nationalism—and the people, in turn, had marched to war with uplifting thoughts of liberating the German peoples from the French yoke. National morale had soared to unmatched heights. In Karl's eyes, all of this spirit, all of the associated efforts at military reform, appeared to have been for naught.

In fact, the situation was not as bleak as Karl believed. Although his army had suffered defeats, they had been the defeat of detachments. Isolated units, from brigade up to corps size, had engaged and been overwhelmed; never had Karl's entire host, or even a majority of his men, been united on the field. Moreover, most formations had fought well and maintained their integrity as they withdrew from the field. Karl had retreated over the Ratisbonne bridge into Bohemia with most of four army corps, including one that had barely fought. North of the Danube he had joined up with General der Cavalerie Heinrich Bellegarde's entirely fresh I Corps. Twenty-seven thousand men strong, Bellegarde's corps comprised some of the best formations in the Austrian army. In sum, Karl still commanded over 90,000 men, nearly half of whom had yet to engage.

Yet so demoralized was the Austrian generalissimus that he wrote to his brother, Franz I, that his ranks numbered a mere 50,000. Furthermore, he advised him to sue for peace. It would take time for a courier to ride around the French army and deliver this bleak message to Franz. In the meantime, Karl decided to continue his retreat deeper into the shelter of the Bohemian mountains. His army would not reappear for nearly a month. Meanwhile, the army's other wing, Hiller's command of at least 50,000 men, would have to fend for itself as it tried to block a direct French march on Vienna. This then was the consequence of the Ratisbonne campaign: Napoleon had seized his cherished central position and driven his main opponent from the strategic chessboard.

Napoleon does not ponder long about what to do next. His only fear is that the two Austrian wings might somehow reunite. Consequently, he decides to press hard on Hiller's heels. Napoleon misapprehends Austrian intentions, thereby committing a strategic error uncharacteristic of his previous performance. In the false belief that a sizable enemy host stands between him and the Hapsburg capital, he resolves to follow the waters of the mighty Danube and march on Vienna. Downstream of the Hapsburg capital, the Danube rushes by the Marchfeld, the longtime parade ground of the Austrian Army. On its flat plain will come the battles that Europe awaits. On the Marchfeld the heretofore invincible Emperor Napoleon will exhibit his growing self-delusion, an overweening confidence that leads to his first battlefield defeat. A restive Europe will quake in sympathetic opposition to French rule, but before it can overthrow its shackles, Napoleon will rally his forces. He will return to the Marchfeld for a second and decisive encounter.

What follows is the story of genius on the wane, how one of history's great captains suffers his first defeat while French emperor and then rallies to earn the last strategic victory of his career.

Note: The following German spellings are used for Austrian names and ranks.

Erzherzog	Archduke
Kaiser	Emperor
Generalissimus	Commander in chief of field armies
FM (Feldmarschall)	Field Marshal
FZM (Feldzeugmeister)	Full General (Infantry)
GdK (General der Cavalerie)	Full General (Cavalry)
FML (Feldmarschall-Leutenant)	Lieutenant General
GM (General-Feldwachtmeister)	Major General

Chapter 1

STRATEGIC DELUSION

The strength of an army, like the power in mechanics, is estimated by multiplying the mass by the rapidity; a rapid march augments the morale of an army, and increases all the chances of victory.[1]

CARNAGE IN THE STREETS

The day after the storming of Ratisbonne, Napoleon had told his army that within a month they would occupy Vienna. The third day of May 1809 found the French in hot pursuit of Feldmarschall-Leutenant (Lieutenant General, or FML) Johann Hiller and his men. Alarmed by the French pressure, Hiller resolved to defend the crossing of the Traun River at the town of Ebelsberg, some 90 miles due east of Vienna. After trouncing the Austrians during the Ratisbonne campaign, Napoleon believed that the capture of Vienna and the final defeat of the Austrians, would be a mere matter of marching. The slaughter at Ebelsberg removed the scales from his eyes.

The first indication the French received that Austrian resolve had stiffened came when General Jacob-Françoise Marulaz's division of light cavalry encountered an Austrian force blocking a narrow defile on the route to Ebelsberg. It is the quintessential role of light cavalry to pursue the enemy vigorously. Napoleon's light cavalry officers excelled in this role. Aggressively Marulaz sent his leading troopers of the 14th Chasseurs à Cheval against the Hapsburg rear guard. The 14th's van platoons charged the defile, uncovered an Austrian infantry battalion, and fell back before its fire. At the price of a captain killed and several troopers wounded, the chasseurs had performed the time-honored tactic of the scout: sacrificing blood for information. French infantry hastened forward, and the Austrian rear guard withdrew. More of the same occurred farther along the road when a skillfully positioned Hapsburg force hidden in the woods fired from ambush and thus forced Marulaz into the time-consuming necessity of fully deploying his men. Still, as he neared Ebelsberg, the cavalry brigadier correctly sensed that he was encountering delaying actions designed to cover an Austrian retreat over the Traun River.

The Hapsburg Army was not at its best while in motion. The Ratisbonne campaign had demonstrated that unless the Austrians had time to prepare for battle, they fought at a severe disadvantage. The opening of the Battle of Ebelsberg reconfirmed this point. FML Hiller hoped that his substantial rear guard would delay the French approach to the Traun River bridge leading to Ebelsberg. This rear guard comprised a mixed arms force of sufficient strength to hold the stout villages lining the bridge road. Yet the men assigned this mission understood that there was an unfordable river to their rear. They had observed their comrades fleeing in mounting disorder through a defile leading to the safety of the bridge over the Traun River, and now they saw a fast-approaching, confident French force. The Austrian rear guard were sacrificial troops, and they knew it.

Across the lines, Marshal André Massena joined Marulaz to survey the situation. The prematurely aging marshal had exhibited a certain indolence so far in the campaign, preferring to ride with the rear echelon troops while his able chief of staff, General Beker, attended to the details of running his IV Corps. But his name was renowned throughout Europe as a great fighting general, and now the marshal displayed some of the energy that had characterized his behavior in the glory days of the past. Massena saw that Marulaz's troopers could do little more since the enemy could shelter themselves from flashing French sabers by retiring inside the village. The situation called for infantry. Massena personally directed his leading infantry brigade to clear the village at the bayonet.

As had been the case since Napoleon's counteroffensive began 14 days ago, the Austrian rear guard failed when facing a French bayonet charge. While the Hapsburg horse galloped to safety over the Traun bridge, the hapless Spleny and Benjowsky Infantry Regiments were overrun by the rapidly advancing French. Penned against an unfordable river, some 500 surrendered. Their feeble resistance did not buy the time necessary for the main body to get set in Ebelsberg. Instead, the Austrian horse, foot, and artillery all intermixed in the defile leading to the bridge and created a panic as they fled toward the town. Hard on their heels came two Italian units that served in the French Army, the celebrated Tirailleurs Corse and Tirailleurs du Pô.

On the far bank some of Ebelsberg's defenders tried to rescue the intrepid Austrian handful who refused to surrender and preferred to risk the fast-flowing river. One of these was Private Joseph Uhlandicki. Using both his lance and his sword, Uhlandicki fought his way toward the Traun bridge. With one party of French cavalry in close pursuit and another group blocking egress to the bridge, the determined uhlan rode his horse down the steep bank and into the river.[2] The infantry on the far shore lent a hand to Uhlandicki and to a squadron of uhlans who likewise swam their horses to safety. Better still, they helped ashore an officer and 107 soldiers of the Gradiskaner Grenzer—muddy, bedraggled, spewing water but alive—who had seized hold of the horses' tails and been towed to safety.

An Austrian aide de camp also got caught up in the confused panic as the French bore in against the disorganized Austrian rear guard. He saw a dismounted Hapsburg staff officer desperately fending off enemy soldiers while trying to escape the melee. Nobly he dismounted himself and offered his mount to the major. As a contemporary Austrian historian observed, "By this act he found himself in the same situation as the Major."[3] Concealing his uniform with an overcoat, the orderly picked up a French shako and joined the ranks of the French infantry marching toward Ebelsberg. Once he gained the town, he found a side street leading back to his general's headquarters. But only a handful showed such fortitude. Hussar Lieutenant-Colonel Bubna and 500 others surrendered to the pursuing French.[4] Whether their sacrifice was to mean anything depended on their comrades' performance in Ebelsberg proper.

A 550-yard-long wooden bridge spanned the Traun River to Ebelsberg. Both the bridge and the town presented a formidable spectacle to Marshal Massena as he examined the scene. Alpine snowmelt had swollen the Traun to an unfordable torrent. At the bridge's far end sat Ebelsberg, a solidly built medieval village situated in a natural amphitheater dominated by a two-tier ridge. Upon a knoll overlooking the village was a stone chateau built for defense. Massena saw "every window crowded with troops, whilst the terraces of the castle bristled with artillery."[5] The marshal could also see Austrian infantry massed on the heights behind Ebelsberg with artillery deployed in the intervals. The only way to cross to the far side was to storm the bridge, but it clearly was not something that could be done easily. Moreover, it was something that did not have to be done at all if Massena followed orders. Two days earlier he had received a directive from the emperor to seize a crossing over the Traun only if the Austrians made no serious effort to oppose the crossing. Perhaps frustrated that his command had yet to perform any great feat, with his troops already in hot pursuit of the disorganized Austrians, the audacious marshal resolved to allow events to run their course regardless of his orders.

What he first saw were his brown-clad Italian and Corsican light infantry eagerly surging across the Traun bridge. These men had earned a reputation for gallantry beginning with their defense of Napoleon's right flank at Austerlitz four years earlier. At Ebelsberg they again fought aggressively and with courage. The tirailleurs crossed the bridge in open order under a barrage of indiscriminate Austrian artillery fire that sent both retiring Hapsburg soldiers and pursuing French plunging into the chasm below. Led by the fiery General Cöehorn, a descendant of the famous French engineer who invented a type of siege mortar, the light infantry cast the wagons blocking the bridge into the ravine and charged on. An Austrian lieutenant tried to slam closed the bridge gate in their faces, but they shouldered their way through and entered the village.

Their sudden eruption into Ebelsberg took the defenders by surprise. Austrian pioneers had prepared the bridge for firing by piling up faggots and smearing them with tar but had not had time to ignite the material before the tirailleurs' arrival. Yet it soon became apparent that Cöehorn's soldiers had overreached. Arrayed in two lines on the heights overlooking the town was the bulk of two Austrian corps. Three companies garrisoned the chateau while three battalions of Viennese volunteers, men who had never before faced enemy fire, stood in support in the adjacent cemetery and park. Below the chateau was a 6-pound battery sited to deliver flanking fire against the bridge. Grenzers, hardy Slavic light infantry who lived along the militarized eastern border of the Hapsburg Empire, manned the riverside buildings from where their fire swept the bridge. A howitzer at the base of a stone tower controlled the bridge's exit. Initially, Cöehorn's impetuous pursuit overmatched these preparations. This solid accomplishment aside, the Tirailleurs Corse and Tirailleurs du Pô found themselves in the midst of a vastly superior defender who fired from rooftop, window, and doorway and whose artillery on the heights bombarded them with ceaseless fury. One gun in particular, directed by a brave cannoneer named Karl Lenk, proved deadly. After firing directly at the bridge, Lenk moved his piece back to the marketplace square from where he fired canister at the charging tirailleurs. When his infantry supports abandoned him, Lenk retreated to the slopes overlooking Ebelsberg and continued to pour punishing flanking fire into the masses below.

Although hurt by Lenk's fire, Cöehorn still managed to lead a column in an uphill charge against the chateau. The defender's fire leveled his leading platoon and killed Cöehorn's horse. Cöehorn's brigade could advance no more. They milled about in some confusion while the town about them began to burn. A more prudent officer might have recalled Cöehorn's brigade, but this was not Massena's way. As soon as more troops arrived, he sent Division General Claparède's two remaining brigades along with a section of artillery and the elite company of the 19th Chasseurs à Cheval across the river to succor Cöehorn.

The fight escalated into a bloody house-to-house combat pitting French tactical ingenuity against Austrian numbers. Slowly Claparède's men advanced up the village streets toward the main line of defense resting on the heights overlooking Ebelsberg and anchored on the stout chateau. Here they encountered two battalions of Vienna Volunteers, new to war but enthusiastic, defending a large cemetery. They fired two volleys that halted the French advance. Seeing their enemy waver, their battalion commanders ordered a bayonet charge. Meanwhile, a third battalion worked its way via back streets and alleyways to take the French in the rear. FML Hiller, who until now had provided no useful direction of the fight, recognized that the French advance was nearing the point where it could threaten his withdrawal. Capitalizing on the inspired charge of the Viennese Volunteers, he ordered heavy columns of fresh troops down the streets toward the bridge to drive the French from Ebelsberg. Then his pioneers would destroy the bridge to secure an unmolested retreat.

To pave the way for the counterattack, the Austrians pushed their cannon to the front so their fire could clear the streets. So great was the slaughter that they could not advance beyond the top of the streets because the dead and wounded jammed under their equipment's wheels. Then the Austrians began a series of concentric assaults down the streets toward the river. Lieutenant Colonel Baumgarten, a brave and intrepid staff officer, placed himself at the head of a battalion of the Lindenau Infantry and led a bayonet charge that reached the bridge's approach. On his left, a corporal of the 5th Battalion of Vienna Volunteers encouraged his comrades by shouting: "Remember you are Viennese! Only as brave soldiers can we show ourselves to our fellow citizens. We fight for wives and children."[6] Inspired, the 5th Battalion drove the French all the way back to the bridge. Meanwhile, near the chateau a third counterattacking column bested Cöehorn's men and sent them reeling as well. Among many, an Austrian hussar had helped inspire the volunteers during their charge by lending his veteran experience. He marched at their front, turning from time to time to say, "Comrades do not be afraid; look, I am safe." Then French bullets proved his position was anything but safe, and the hussar staggered with multiple wounds. The volunteers implored him to go to the aid station to have his wounds dressed. He replied, "Who would desert such brave comrades. I will not leave the battlefield" until the enemy is driven back to the market square. Likewise, a Captain Heinrich von Sigler from a line infantry regiment joined the charge shouting, "Follow me, comrades."[7]

As was frequently the case in the musketry era, control of the streets demoralized the bypassed defenders who sheltered inside the buildings. Consequently the Austrians scooped up prisoners as their columns advanced toward the bridge. In this manner a captain of the 4th Vienna Volunteers captured the commander of the Tirailleurs du Pô while other Austrians seized two French battalion fanions.

Faced with disaster, Cöehorn exposed himself recklessly and managed to rally his men. The two French artillery pieces that had managed to cross the bridge took up a position in the market square while Claparède's remnants occupied the adjacent buildings. After the canister-firing artillery repulsed the Vienna Volunteers, a murderous close-range firefight engulfed the bridge's approach as officers on both sides fell. One canister fragment wounded Baumgarten in the shoulder, and on the French side two colonels were killed and three wounded. Mindful of his own failure of initiative earlier in the campaign, Claparède spurred his division to near-suicidal intensity.[8] A series of bitter house-to-house combats ensued as the opponents hunted one another from attic to cellar. A Frenchman later told his parents that it "was the most terrible battle one could imagine."[9]

One Austrian soldier who made it so was Sergeant Major Johan Wade of the Viennese Volunteers. Wade entered one building to bayonet two enemy soldiers. His fury prompted the surviving three, including one officer, to surrender. Returning to the street, Wade entered a barn where a blow to the head from a swinging musket knocked him senseless. Upon reviving, he returned to battle to capture two more enemy soldiers. Another Austrian soldier, Frederic Nagl, joined four comrades to fight their way through a bakery window and drive the defenders into the cellar. Nagl then lit a fire whose smoke brought ten wheezing Frenchmen up the stairs to surrender. So it continued for three hours as both sides fought ferociously amid frightful chaos.

Angered by what had transpired and unwilling to accept any personal blame, on the opposite bank Massena snapped at his staff, "Why did he [Claparède] put himself in such a mess?"[10] Even as he spoke, the situation worsened as Austrian sappers set fire to the bridge's far end. Fortunately for the French cause, a strong west wind put out the blaze. Massena was no stranger to desperate fighting and set himself to bringing order to a combat that can only be characterized as a lethal street brawl. He summoned his remaining effective reserves, the artillery, and built up a 20-piece gun line to counterbattery the Austrian artillery firing from the opposing heights. Heretofore the Hapsburg weapons had been delivering a deadly plunging fire into Claparède's troops, who packed Ebelsberg's narrow streets. Moreover, Hapsburg howitzer shells periodically set the wooden buildings afire, and the blaze threatened to spread to the bridge itself. Massena's gun line relieved some of this pressure.

When the marshal saw Claparède's division losing ground to Hiller's ponderous counterattacks, he had sent couriers spurring to hasten the arrival of reinforcements. Colonel the Baron Pouget's men, who belonged to Legrand's brigade, were already marching hard when one of Massena's aides-de-camp delivered the request for more speed. Unperturbed, Pouget responded that he was not going to force his men to trot since he wanted to arrive with his regiment intact. Ten minutes passed, and along came another courier conveying the same request. Pouget lost his temper: "You can see . . . that we cannot march any faster; I will not force the pace, regardless of your orders; go tell Monsieur the Marshal that I am about to arrive with my entire regiment."[11] And Pouget did just that.

As soon as Massena saw the reinforcements approach, he ordered them to go to Claparède's aid. While the men quaffed a bracing gulp of brandy, a staff officer galloped up to Division General Claude Legrand to inform him of the situation. Legrand cut the briefing short: "I do not ask you for advice, except where to place the head of my column."[12] Given one of Cöehorn's sergeants as a guide, Legrand rode to the head of Pouget's 26th Légère to lead the advance. Then the 26th Légère set out across the Traun bridge to begin one of the celebrated assaults in French Napoleonic history.

Again passage over the bridge looked forbidding. An Austrian battery, sited on a rise behind the village, had acquired the range during prior French crossings and now dominated the scene. Musket fire flailed the bridge's exit. Pouget, a veteran warrior, knew that speed was everything. He ordered his men to open their ranks and sprint across the bridge, thereby reducing the time spent in the lethal beaten zone of flying metal. Gaining the far side, the 26th Légère re-formed under the shelter of buildings, counted noses, and found that miraculously only five or six soldiers had been hit during the crossing.

Brigadier General Cöehorn rode up to Pouget, gestured toward a narrow village street, and said: "You are going to follow this street to a chateau occupied by the enemy. You will attack it."[13] By now it was apparent that whoever held the chateau controlled the village below. From the village square where Pouget received his orders, the chateau could not be seen. Undaunted, the colonel dismounted, placed his sappers to the fore, and marched his men up the winding, cobbled street. So narrow was the passage that in places his column had to shrink to a six-rank frontage. After a stiff climb, Pouget sighted his objective 40 paces away. Although sounds of firing about the village could be heard, here at the top of the alleyway an eerie silence prevailed. Pouget could see no one and wondered whether the Austrians were inside. As his leading company of carabiniers reached the small square outside the chateau, muskets suddenly appeared from window and turret, the first small explosions of igniting primer gave an all-too-brief warning, and the resultant discharge of noise, smoke, and lead arrived before the French could react.

It had been neatly done. The disciplined defenders of the Jordis Infantry Regiment, supported by sharpshooting grenzers, had waited until enough French soldiers massed at the top of the alleyway before firing, thus ensuring that each of their shots counted. Ignoring the casualties, when the smoke cleared Pouget studied the chateau's entrance. He saw that a vaulted stone archway framing a stout wooden gate guarded the entrance. Above it was a window, loopholed and mullioned with iron bars, from which came a steady fire. Pouget perceived that only one ground-level window could be approached without suffering a murderous crossfire. Sheltering himself behind an archway, Pouget called out his orders. He had his best marksmen, the carabiniers, engage the defenders in a musketry duel. It was an unequal contest: the Austrians were well protected while the carabiniers found meager cover around the entryway. In the first ten minutes, 3 carabinier officers and 53 men, more than a third of their strength, fell here. The combat proved harder still on the légère companies jammed motionless in the alleyway at the rear. Slowly but surely the Austrian fire winnowed their ranks as intrepid Austrian marksmen entered adjacent buildings to rain fire down upon the French. Unable to retaliate they could only stand and endure.[14]

Although there was no lack of will on the part of the assailants, their casualties mounted. Pouget acknowledged to a small knot of carabiniers that in spite of all efforts, the defender's fire did not diminish. He summoned a certain Lieutenant Guyot, a well-known marksman, and told him to silence the enemy's fire. Guyot strode four paces out into the open, aimed his rifled carbine carefully, fired, and demanded another loaded and primed weapon. Inspired by his example, more carabiniers joined Guyot. By having men from the rear pass forward loaded weapons, they managed to build a continuously discharging fire line against the concealed enemy. Although they fell in heaps—some chasseurs clambered atop their fallen comrades to obtain a level shot against the window—slowly they silenced the Austrian fire. As the sappers charged forward to axe their way through the wooden door, other French soldiers found an unprotected cellar entrance and began to clear the chateau room by room. When the sappers burst through the front door, the garrison laid down their weapons and surrendered.

Meanwhile, the 18th Ligne, composing Legrand's second brigade, had also traversed the Traun bridge. One battalion marched to clear out the buildings still housing Austrian marksmen. The two remaining battalions followed a footpath to turn the village from the right. They pressed on to the heights where they encountered the balance of Hiller's units who had not been committed into the battle below. The 18th formed line and advanced, but Austrian cavalry checked the French egress from Ebelsberg. And so it was all along the front. The fighting at the top of the streets leading out of Ebelsberg matched the intensity of the earlier action around the village square.

Fighting now centered on the Vienna gate. Here the Vienna road passed beneath several vaulted arcades wide enough only for a single carriage before continuing out into the countryside. Once through the gate, it proceeded through a series of gardens enclosed with hedges defended by Austrian infantry. Massena rode across the bridge and up the heights to inspire his soldiers with his presence. There was nothing for it but a naked charge. Cöehorn "ordered the head of his column to keep together, fix bayonets, and charge for the gardens, trampling down all the unfortunate wretches in the way."[15] Austrian fire toppled the entire front rank of men who first emerged through the arcade. The following ranks clambered over the fallen and drove the defenders from the gardens. Even so, lacking cavalry, the French could not make further progress. Cöehorn's voltigeur companies closed to within 80 paces of the enemy line from where they managed to inflict serious losses on the unwavering Austrian ranks. Even when reinforced by the remainder of Legrand's division, including a hard-fighting Baden brigade, Hiller's men maintained their position.

Having failed by main force to recapture the bridge, Hiller ordered the village set afire to prevent the French from passing additional troops through its streets. Although parts of the village had already burned, and at one point the fire had spread to the bridge itself until French sappers put it out, there was not yet a general conflagration sufficient to block all French movement. Artillery Corporal Jean Gabella, one of the many Italians who chanced to live in Hapsburg territory and thus fought for an Austrian kaiser instead of a French emperor, received the assignment. He took a grenade from the munitions wagon and worked his way through the village until reaching the bridge's approaches. Lighting the grenade, Gabella tossed it into a wooden house to set it afire. Whether it was Gabella's grenade or the howitzer fire, a fierce blaze swept through Ebelsberg, burning down three-quarters of the town and incinerating numerous wounded who were unable to flee. Under cover of the fire, Hiller began his withdrawal. Since the French light cavalry could not pass through the blazing streets, there was no effective pursuit.

Even in retreat the Viennese Volunteers continued to distinguish themselves. Seeing an abandoned Austrian cannon, a Lieutenant Zaunmuller from the 6th Battalion organized a party to hand-haul the gun to safety. Such conduct was infectious. In an adjacent lane, a line sergeant organized a small counterattack to protect a group of men who were working to save two more guns.[16] In this fashion the Austrian Army continued its retreat toward Vienna.

Except for the Italian contingent, most of Massena's men who fought at Ebels-berg were young conscripts new to war. This accounts for the high officer casualty list experienced by the French. The officers clearly believed that they had to set an inspirational example for their young soldiers. Only their gallant, and at times reckless, front line leadership had held units together. Claparède himself received a wound, two of his three brigadiers had their horses shot out from under them, and the third had his hat creased by a bullet. Losses were so severe that Cöehorn had to consolidate survivors from four battalions to form a battle-worthy unit for the march on Vienna. Although it is impossible to state French casualties ex-actly—French battle accounting was seldom precise, particularly in the midst of a rapid advance—the Austrians did capture close to 700 men along with the two battalion fanions. Certainly the French lost in excess of 4,000 officers and men, three-quarters of whom came from Claparède's division.[17] Austrian losses can be more closely specified at 4,495: 29 officers and 537 men killed; 56 officers and 1,657 wounded; and 31 officers and 2,185 captured.[18] Emergent German nation-alism was evident in the selfless conduct of the Vienna Volunteers, who had fought as well as any other troops on the field. They lost 305 of their men killed or seriously wounded.[19] Yet they and their comrades had only another discour-aging retreat to show for their sacrifice.

Massena's order committing Claparède's soldiers to the assault was far worse than ill advised. His decision sent hundreds of brave young soldiers to unnec-essary death and maiming; on the balance sheet of martial leadership it dem-onstrated the extent of this once-great leader's decline. That his men had prevailed—if the modest success of capturing a minor river crossing and retaining a gutted Austrian village constituted victory—was a tribute to the still great reservoir of French valor and a censure of bumbling Hapsburg generalship. Aus-trian infantry had exhibited bravery equal to that of their adversaries. But yet again something was amiss at the top. In the words of one critic of Hiller's less than sterling leadership: "A man who could fail so hopelessly in such a posi-tion . . . is not worthy of the name of a general."[20]

The strong wind that had fortuitously kept the fire from repeatedly spreading to the Ebelsberg bridge had also prevented the noise of battle from reaching Napo-leon's headquarters, although it was within easy riding distance of Ebelsberg. Ig-norant that a battle was ongoing, not until dusk did Napoleon enter the charnel house that was Ebelsberg. Many of the wounded on both sides had been con-sumed by the flames. Although the emperor was inured to war's horrors, the frightful spectacle of blackened, prostrate forms lining the market square and ad-jacent alleys affected even him. This awful sight shocked war-hardened generals and privates, leaving them speechless in their horror.[21] So thickly pressed toge-ther were the fallen that the carefully stepping horses of Napoleon's entourage could not avoid trampling them. After issuing orders to rescue the surviving wounded from the still advancing flames, he established his headquarters on Ebel-sberg's outskirts. Reputedly shaken by what he had seen, Napoleon was still able to dictate orders from 10 P.M. until 3 A.M. before retiring for a few hours' sleep.

The next morning the emperor emerged from his tent fit, recovered, and remorseful. He wrote a candid letter to II Corps Commander Marshal Jean Lannes criticizing the foolishness of Massena's attack, particularly when other French units were crossing the Traun elsewhere unopposed.[22] Still, he understood how much he relied on future displays of gallantry and so put a brave face on the unnecessary slaughter. He did not publicly censure Massena and had his generals publish casualty figures that typically understated the real losses. Then he reviewed the survivors and while so doing again showed that above all other generals of his era he understood how to manipulate officers and privates alike.

He commended General Cöehorn's conduct and bestowed upon him the Bavarian Order of Max-Joseph. He mingled with the Tirailleurs Corse, addressing them in Italian, paying particular attention to those hailing from his native Ajaccio, pinching ears as a sign of affection and esteem. He did all of this to assess their mood. A man in the ranks assured him that the unit had enough men left for two such attacks. Napoleon continued on to the 26th Légère and asked that the sapper who had struck the first ax blow against the chateau gate come forward to receive the Légion d'honneur. He inquired who was the bravest officer in the regiment. The question took Pouget by surprise. Impatiently, Napoleon snapped, "Well! Have you heard me?"

Pouget responded, "Yes, Sire; but I know many who . . . "

Napoleon interrupted, "No pretty phrases, answer."[23]

Pouget nominated Lieutenant Guyot, the officer who had stood exposed to enemy fire before the chateau's entrance. Napoleon named him a baron of the empire and gave him a handsome gratuity. He then asked Pouget who was the regiment's bravest soldier.

Nearly unhinged by the emperor's presence, Pouget's mind went blank. One of his majors helpfully suggested a name, Carabinier Corporal Bayonnette. The name delighted Napoleon, who made Bayonnette a Chevalier in the Légion d'honneur with a handsome pension. As Napoleon had intended, his actions made a tremendously favorable impression on officers and men alike. They fought with the knowledge that their valor could be rewarded on a colossal scale. In Corporal Bayonnette's case, Napoleon's munificence had an unintended consequence. Henceforth, Bayonnette avoided all combat exposure. As his comrades remarked, he was not so stupid as to go get himself killed now that "his bread was baked."[24]

The 26th's most cherished award came the next day when it presented arms to the Imperial Guard's Chasseurs à Pied as they passed along the route. The Chasseurs' commander strode forward to Colonel Pouget and in front of everyone seized his arm to compliment the colonel by jokingly complaining, "So, you did not want to leave us anything to do."[25]

The dead buried, wounded left in the uncertain hands of the surgeons, and the emperor's favors received, the Army of Germany continued east through the Danube valley toward the enemy capital.

THE FALL OF VIENNA

On the day the rival armies contested Ebelsberg's streets, Austrian officials in Vienna, 90 miles to the east, convened their first council of war to discuss the defense of their capital. Among the notables attending were the minister of war, assorted lieutenant generals, and Karl's brother, the young Erzherzog Maximilian, who chaired the proceedings. Maximilian had little experience of war, yet among them all it was only he who suggested that the time had come to prepare the city's fortifications to resist the French. Erzherzog Maximilian's query produced a litany of excuses why this would be difficult to do. Vienna's fortifications were in deplorable condition, observed one general. The French could easily set fire to the suburbs, and the conflagration would spread to the city itself, protested another. Maximilian responded that the city would be defended regardless.

The next day the council reconvened to establish the practical basis for the city's defense. They agreed where to quarter the garrison, how much to pay workers to build the defenses, the method to obtain the wood required, and rules to govern the conduct of the city's firefighters. With wonderful bureaucratic pedantry, Maximilian's council worked out the details for everything that mattered least. On May 5 work finally began.

It was the same day that found Karl and his army deeply committed to the second of what would become three days of rest at the city of Budweis. Here Karl found time to write to Maximilian that he would begin a march to Vienna the very next day (in fact, he would not depart until May 7) and hoped to arrive on May 17 or thereabouts. Then, Karl continued, he would cross the Danube to meet the enemy. Therefore, his brother would have to hold the capital at all costs until Karl arrived. However, if forced to evacuate the capital, Maximilian should burn the Danube bridges and defend the north bank. Here was command vacillation equal to that exhibited by Maximilian's council of war: defend, dear brother, the capital at all costs; alternatively, retreat! It was hardly the stuff of inspiration. In contrast, Napoleon displayed single-minded determination by leading a driving advance on Vienna.

After the rival armies broke contact with the Danube River separating them, the light cavalry could no longer produce intelligence about the foe. Leaders on both sides turned to special means to try to acquire information by asking for volunteers to cross the river and visit the enemy's camps. For Napoleon, the question requiring resolution was the whereabouts of Hiller's corps after the Battle of Ebelsberg. Marshal Lannes presented one of his aides-de-camp, young Captain Marcellin Marbot, for the mission. The near fearless Marbot took a small boat across the swollen Danube at night toward the Austrian camp. Dodging waterborne debris and Hapsburg sentinels alike, he captured a handful of prisoners and returned. The prisoners confirmed that Hiller had passed over the river. Marbot's success delighted the emperor. After interrogating the captain he said,

"I am very well pleased with you, 'Major' Marbot." As Marbot relates, "These words were equivalent to a commission, and my joy was full."[26]

At about the same time, Erzherzog Ludwig, another of Karl's brothers who commanded the Austrian V Corps, requested a similar expedition. One major difference was that Ludwig offered hard currency up front: 300 florins to any volunteer who would cross the Danube and spy on the French. Cavalry Corporal Zubow volunteered. He passed himself off as a deserter who wanted to enlist in the French ranks. Such men were not uncommon, and Zubow managed to circulate through the French camp collecting information about the enemy order of battle and its morale. The problem was how to return to deliver a report because suspicious French guards watched him closely. Zubow hit upon the time-honored means of rendering one's guards unwary: he took them drinking. When their vigilance relaxed, the corporal took off for the river, plunged in, managed to survive a few musket shots sent his way by his besotted former captors, and returned to Ludwig's headquarters. The kaiser himself offered Zubow the agreed reward, but Zubow declined, explaining that he was content to have performed his duty. Franz rewarded his noble conduct with a gold medal and a gift of 1,000 florins while his captain promoted him to sergeant.[27]

Marbot and Zubow, two different men, united by their quick wits, bravery, and zeal.

A French Napoleonic army in full cry advanced with blitzkrieg-like speed. Few surpassed the emperor himself. On May 7 he traveled some 45 miles from Enns to Moelk, where that night Marbot performed his mission. Realizing that little now stood between his army and Vienna, the emperor journeyed another 25 miles from Moelk to Saint-Polten the next day. On May 9 he concentrated his forces and on May 10 marched them 34 miles to Vienna's suburbs. For the second time in less than four years Napoleon stood before Vienna's gates. Since his last visit, French soldiers had been busy capturing, in turn, Berlin, Warsaw, Madrid, and Lisbon. With the enemy present, Maximilian examined his order of battle. At Karl's command, after the Battle of Ebelsberg, Hiller had abandoned his blocking position and marched to the Danube's left bank. This left Maximilian with a motley collection of Ebelsberg survivors, hastily assembled depot battalions, half-trained recruits, raw volunteers, and landwehr, the German national militia. Maximilian's first call for volunteers had yielded an enthusiastic response: "The enthusiasm of the mob was so great that even disinterested passers-by were forced to accept weapons and man the walls."[28] However, as the French drew nearer, spirits waned. On May 10 Maximilian deemed the defense of the suburbs impossible and retired to Vienna proper. That night Napoleon slept in the Austrian Imperial Palace of Schönbrunn. Just to make sure he felt at home, there to present arms in his honor were 25 Old Guard grenadiers, men who had volunteered to march an extra 50 miles for this purpose.

While Napoleon slept, Erzherzog Maximilian issued a proclamation to his 12,000 or so men imploring them to defend their capital with determination.

They were understandably nervous about the prospects of holding Vienna's crumbling walls against the vaunted soldiers of Napoleon's army. On the night of the tenth, anxious patriots belonging to a unit of university students opened a rattling fire against an imagined French assault and managed to wound three Austrian infantryman and one gunner. Elsewhere along the walls, groups of armed civilians protested about their prospects and slipped away from the positions at every opportunity. Austrian officers circulated among the defenders and concluded that they were not likely to stand up to a determined bayonet attack.

At dawn Napoleon sent Maximilian a summons to surrender. When the French emperor failed to receive an answer, he spent the balance of May 11 reconnoitering Vienna's defenses and siting batteries to breach the city's walls. The imperatives of military science being what they are, the place he chose for the main breaching battery had once been occupied by a Turkish battery during the great siege of 1683. The emperor did not intend to rely on naked might alone. In order to turn the city's defenses, he designed a clever amphibious assault against an undefended island located in the Danube behind Vienna.

At 9 P.M. that night the French breaching battery opened fire. To the inexperienced Maximilian, the four-hour-long bombardment seemed terrible. French shells set numerous fires that overwhelmed the city's firefighting capacity. Panic-stricken inhabitants ran amok through the streets. Amid the chaos, Maximilian held another council of war. Ignoring Karl's desire to defend Vienna at all costs, the council chose the generalissimus's second alternative: retreat. The young erzherzog escaped with his best troops but still managed to abandon 13 generals and 17 staff officers along with a more useful force of 153 junior officers and 2,044 men. Worst of all he abandoned intact Vienna's entire arsenal. Somehow, in spite of all their councils and preparations, Austrian military authorities managed to overlook how extremely useful this arsenal would be in replenishing Napoleon's depleted supply trains. The arsenal's contents provided a welcome windfall to French ordnance officers, who found 145 cannon, 8 howitzers, 21 small mortars, tons of gunpowder, more than 370,000 cartridges for small arms, 75,662 rations, vast quantities of flour and wheat, uniform material, equipment, camp utensils, and much more, including money chests with 4.5 million gulden: a treasure perfectly designed to restore Napoleon's army to fighting trim.

For the men in the ranks, Vienna and its 300,000 inhabitants offered unprecedented opportunities for looting. Their march to the Austrian capital had been fast and hard, with food distribution infrequent. A conscript in the 63d Ligne wrote to his parents, "We have not been paid nor received bread. We are nourished by the peasants, who furnish all."[29] Maurice de Tascher, the empress's cousin, observed that one-quarter of the army left the ranks to engage in "highway robbery" during the march to Vienna.[30] Indeed, one of the ways Napoleon achieved strategic mobility was by not burdening his soldiers with such unessential impedimenta as supply wagons with food. He relied on his men's ability to live off the land, which in practice meant that they plundered farmhouses and peasants' hovels. At the end of the day's march, each company sent out its best foragers to scrounge wood, straw, and supplies. When those who remained in camp saw the foragers return, the cry would go up, "The market will be good, the dealers are coming . . . from all sides, we see hurrying forward our fearless freebooters loaded down with sacks full of poultry, baskets of eggs and loaves of bread stuck one after the other on ramrods. Some push before them sheep and cows, oxen and pigs; others make peasants . . . carry the straw and wood."[31]

Hard as this was on the inhabitants, from a military standpoint it worked well as long as the columns could fan out along parallel roads to steal from a wide area. On the other hand, when, as was the case in May 1809, the advance was along a narrow front with many units sharing the same road, those troops who had the misfortune to march in the middle or the back of the column found thin pickings. Although there was an army-wide distribution of meat and bread, once the soldiers reached Vienna, better still were the city's famous cafés, beer gardens, and bars serving *apfelwein* (hard apple cider) as well as the densely packed dwellings with their easily grabbed plunder. A drummer in the 93d Ligne recalls how the French camps soon resembled "a street fair" with soldiers displaying their pillaged merchandise.[32] The soft days in Vienna helped the men forget recent privations.

And so 27 days after departing Paris, and for the eighth time in 13 years, Napoleon and his army occupied an enemy capital. As impressive as this triumph appeared, it was in fact a hollow achievement. Napoleon partially recognized this when he commented, "I arrived in Vienna, alone with my little conscripts, my name, and my big boots."[33] In 1805 Austria had not capitulated when Napoleon captured Vienna. It was the same in 1809. Worse, extending back toward France was a line of communications insecure at best. From the north, across the Danube, an Austrian corps commanded by Feldzeugmeister (FZM) Karl Kollowrath threatened a march that would sever Napoleon's lifeline. In the south the entire Tyrol was in rebellion. The experience of Spanish patriots' conducting a guerrilla war against the French occupation army had taught Europe that the struggle need not end with the defeat of a field army. The Hapsburg monarchy had taken notice and for the first time had mobilized its people's latent nationalism against the invader. Nowhere was the response more fervent than in the Tyrol, a mountainous region populated by devout Catholics.

It was a region that Napoleon had unwisely subtracted from the Hapsburg Empire as part of Austria's penalty for losing the 1805 war. He had rewarded his Bavarian ally with the Tyrol, only to see heavy-handed Bavarian administration violate pledges to respect Tyrolese liberties. The introduction of the Bavarian legal code and conscription along with the elimination of many Tyrolese social and religious rights produced a flammable situation. The 1809 war provided the tinder. Tyrolese guerrilla leaders met in the capital at Innsbruck to plot rebellion. Bankrolled by Austrian money, they appealed for recruits to overthrow Napoleon the anti-Christ, and the people turned out by the thousands. Under the messianic leadership of a simple innkeeper named Andreas Hofer, the Tyrolese caught a column of French conscripts marching through a mountain valley en route to

Italy. The conscripts' defense was not helped by the fact that their leader, a certain General Bisson, was better known for his prodigious drinking capacity than for his tactical abilities. The Tyrolese bagged Bisson's entire 1,700-man column along with the eagle, the cherished French national emblem that adorned a unit's flagpole, belonging to the 3d Ligne. Hofer proceeded to conduct a skillful guerrilla campaign against the Franco-Bavarians, capturing 6,000 more men, 7 cannon, and 800 horses. The guerrillas managed to tie down an entire Bavarian infantry corps and sever direct French communications with Napoleon's Franco-Italian Army operating in northern Italy. Moreover, Hofer's spreading influence squeezed the French supply line to a narrow corridor along the Danube River, a corridor that could be blocked completely if Kollowrath managed his affairs competently.

This double menace to his supply line impelled Napoleon to seek conclusions quickly with the main Austrian field army. But Maximilian had managed to burn the Danube bridges when he evacuated Vienna. Consequently, the emperor realized that he had to make an assault crossing of the river, build a bridgehead on the far bank, and then fight the decisive battle.

His first attempt was a disaster. Back in 1805 Napoleon had observed an island upstream of Vienna opposite Nussdorf that seemed to present a ready-made stepping-stone to the far bank. On May 13 a body of voltigeurs belonging to the 72d and 105th Ligne rowed across to the island. They operated under the command of two separate officers. In the absence of command unity, the voltigeurs failed to coordinate their actions. When Napoleon arrived to supervise the action, he sent an entire battalion numbering about 800 men to support the voltigeurs. It proved an error. Napoleon did not know that since he had last been this way, a jetty had been built linking the island with the far bank, thus allowing the Austrians a march directly against the "island." General-Feldwachtermeister (GM) Armand Nordmann, one of several French émigré officers in Hapsburg service, led an overwhelming Austrian counterattack featuring a fierce combination of grenzers and Viennese Volunteers.[34] Nordmann's troops steadily drove the French back to a corner of the island. After massing all available artillery to support his infantry, the emperor could only watch helplessly while his men surrendered. Overconfidence, coupled with poor reconnaissance, had lost 700 to 800 men. Napoleon learned nothing from this affair. Instead, he cast his gaze elsewhere and found a similar situation downstream where another island provided a stepping-stone across the Danube.

Whatever he accomplished there would have to be done in the face of the entire Austrian Army, for on May 16 Erzherzog Karl had arrived opposite Vienna. With his reunited force, numbering about 114,000 men, Karl was determined to use them to crush the next French attempt to cross the Danube. Karl's resolve set the stage for the first defeat Napoleon would suffer since becoming emperor.

Chapter 2

THE ARMIES OF 1809

I give myself only half the credit for the battles I have won . . . for the fact is that a battle is won by the army.[1]

THE FRENCH WAR MACHINE

A Napoleonic troop review was unlike any other. Throughout military history, most such affairs feature a pro forma inspection conducted by functionaries or superior officers who have little time and less of an idea about what they are looking at. Not so a review attended by the emperor. Because a successful review could lead to the next step on the promotion ladder and a less than stellar review could end a career, these occasions were times of considerable anxiety for the officers. The troops formed up, and then the great man appeared:

He wore a grey riding coat of the plainest appearance; a little hat looped with black, with no ornament but the cockade; the riding coat was unbuttoned and just allowed the colonel's epaulets to be seen on the undress uniform of the Chasseurs of the Guard, the only uniform he ever wore on a campaign after he became Emperor. He had white breeches and waistcoat, and soft riding boots. He was mounted on a beautiful bright grey Arab horse; the housings of the saddle were fringed with a rich trimming of large bullion, and the stirrups were plated with gold, as were the bit and buckles of the bridle.

On his first pass Napoleon would ride at a walk across the unit's front. Next he might put the unit through some basic maneuvers. Then came the dreaded interrogations. Beginning with the senior officers and continuing down through the captains' ranks, the quick barrage of questions came: "What is your effective strength? How many men in hospital? At the small depots? Sick in cantonments? Absent from any other cause?"

Woe to the officers who did not have the answers pat, stammered, or became confused. Among many, the hapless Colonel Merlin of the 8th Cuirassiers became so rattled during one review that there was an enormous difference between the total of his effectives and the amount made up by summing the subtotals. Merlin received "words of reproof and looks that did not bespeak the near approach of favours." Napoleon clearly believed that if a man could not withstand the pressure of his interrogation, he would not be able to maintain his composure on a battlefield.

Interviews completed, the unit would defile past Napoleon one more time. If they were cavalry, they passed at the trot, swords raised in the air. Repeated shouts of "Vive l'empereur" (expressed with varying degrees of feeling) sometimes might evoke a reply directed to the unit's commander: "Colonel, on the first action a bullet or a General's stars."[2]

Napoleon's veterans, and in particular his Imperial Guard, were known as *les grognards* ("the grumblers"). A line captain recalls that during reviews the men only occasionally shouted "Vive l'empereur" with great enthusiasm. Ordered to cheer by their officers, more commonly they muttered, "Let him give me my discharge, and I'll cheer as much as they please!" or "We have no bread; when my stomach is empty, I can not cheer."[3]

The infantry battalion was the Napoleonic period's tactical building brick. A typical French infantry battalion numbered 840 men divided into six companies. Four were fusilier (conventional infantry) companies. The voltigeur company comprised specially trained skirmishers who fought in front of the battalion in open order. The voltigeurs operated in two-man teams utilizing all available cover and employing modern fire and movement tactics. The bravest and biggest men in the battalion formed a grenadier company. Napoleon believed that these grenadiers should not be converged into elite units (the way the Austrians did) because to remove them from the line would be to remove the "cream" that gave the unit its quality. The grenadier's role was to provide a solid and inspirational core for the entire battalion. In the assault they should lead the way.[4]

Battalions maneuvered and changed formation within the larger framework of regiment/brigade/division/corps. Two to four battalions comprised a French regiment. The inefficiencies of the infantry musket forced the foot soldiers to stand in battle shoulder to shoulder, three ranks deep, a mere 22 inches between men, in order to generate adequate firepower. From this imperative all else flowed.

To maneuver hundreds of infantry in close order was not easy and required extensive practice. Whereas in modern times repetitive close-order drill is intended merely to instill the habit of obedience, in Napoleon's era soldiers' survival depended on their ability to perform the many maneuvers described by the drill manuals. There were three basic infantry formations, each with a specific purpose. A line permitted the greatest number of men to fire their muskets. A column, wherein individual companies massed one behind the other, allowed rapid marching across a battlefield and was the preferred order for attacking narrow defiles or assaulting through a village's streets. A column had much reduced firepower because anyone standing more than three ranks deep could not use his weapon. The third formation was the square. Since it took even well-trained soldiers some 30 seconds to load and fire their muskets, soldiers could not unleash enough volleys to stop a determined cavalry charge before the horsemen reached their front. Therefore, infantry formed battalion squares—boxlike formations that presented four short, bayonet-bristling sides—to repel cavalry charges.

Within these generalities were numerous tactical permutations that required good judgment on the part of battalion and regimental leaders. For example, if advancing when there was a threat of a cavalry charge, the column should have sufficient intervals between companies to permit it to deploy rapidly into square. If fighting when there was little threat of a sudden enemy cavalry charge, a veteran unit could safely remain in line and send some or all of its companies forward to reinforce the skirmish line, where soldiers fought in small groups and took advantage of all available cover. There were no hard-and-fast rules. As Napoleon wrote, "the circumstances of the attack or defense require the troops to be in line or in column," and the "successive passage from the one order to the other . . . requires a rapid and experienced coup d'oeil."[5] Units that had trained six years earlier with the Grande Armée demonstrated this ability. Consider the experience of the 23d Légère at Wagram. At 8 A.M. it formed in line to support the army's right flank. It shifted to serried column followed by square to resist a cavalry charge. By 10 A.M. it had reformed into column to advance 300 paces to support the front line. The regiment's three voltigeur companies deployed in skirmish order across the regiment's front. Under heavy fire, the 23d retired slowly, halted, faced to the right, and maintained its position in support of an artillery battery. In sum, the 23d maneuvered during an entire day of battle while under artillery fire, exhibiting, in the words of its colonel, characteristic "precision, silence, and calm."[6] This was the hallmark of a veteran French infantry unit.

In 1806 the emperor told his stepson, "It is not sufficient for the soldiers to shoot, it is necessary that they shoot well."[7] This was not so easy given the technical characteristics of the era's muskets. Although the .69- to .71-caliber musket could send a ball to a distance of more than 1,000 yards, effective range against formed enemy troops was under 250 yards. After repeated firings, muskets became encrusted with unburned powder, flints became worn, and troops tired. These factors, coupled with the difficulty of seeing a target clearly through the thick smoke of the black powder period, meant that most lethal firing took place at under 50 yards. Experienced units tried to reserve their fire for a handful of close-range volleys. Illustrative of the accuracy of the musket is the experience of Captain Desboeuf during the Battle of Znaim. In the smoke and confusion of battle he thought a nearby unit was Bavarian. Desboeuf approached to within five or six paces when he realized that they were Austrian. Seven or eight soldiers raised their muskets and fired, but Desboeuf dodged at the last instant and escaped unharmed.[8]

While moving individuals could escape even close-range fire, a closely packed elbow-to-elbow formation presented a vulnerable target. Reliance on close-order formations accounts for the horrific casualties characteristic of the 1809 battles. Infantry was the only arm that could capture and hold ground. Charging foot soldiers advancing in shoulder-to-shoulder formation moved at a rate of about 70 yards per minute.[9] Under near-ideal conditions, a waiting defender could fire eight volleys starting at long range and shatter the attackers before the charge struck home. More typically, the issue was decided within the final 50 yards. If the defenders stood firm, their last point-blank volley dropped scores of attackers and discouraged all but the bravest from carrying on. On the other hand, if the attackers had received support from their artillery and skirmishers such that the defender had grown anxious and discouraged, the unnerving sight of an advancing wall of gleaming bayonets would cause the defenders' last volley to be poorly aimed. In this event, the attackers would continue, and the defenders would break and flee. Only occasionally did the defenders' fire stop but not break a charge. Then a close-range firefight took place, with both sides loading and squeezing trigger as fast as possible. Except when engaging in house-to-house combat, infantry almost never fought one another with bayonets.

Within a tactical sector, an infantry charge brought matters to a head. Either the defender or the attacker would break from the encounter. Seeing his front ranks yield, a general would then send in the reserves, and the whole process would be repeated. In this manner, once fighting began, it tended to suck in adjacent troops. Even a small reserve could tilt the balance in dramatic fashion, a fact reflected in Napoleon's famous aphorism that "there is a moment in engagaements when the least maneuver is decisive and gives victory; it is the one drop of water that makes the vessel run over."[10] Good officers were known to maintain their balance amid the confusing shock of combat and to commit their reserves at a finely calculated moment. This talent required an instinct for battle and could not be acquired by textbook learning.

At all times, except when the rival battle lines were at close quarters, distant artillery would be sending cannonballs into the fray that literally bowled over file after file. Amid a near-deafening roar of discharging weapons, front-line officers' commands could barely be heard. Senses numbed, wreathed in clinging smoke, soldiers mechanically shuffled inward to replace losses as their ranks thinned. Noncommissioned officers (file closers) shouted and prodded their men to close toward the center where the battalion and regimental flags loomed above the smoke to serve as a rallying point. Under the trying circumstances of Napoleonic combat, training, discipline, morale, and tradition told.

By 1809, artillery was becoming the dominant weapon in Napoleon's battles. Back in 1785, the then 16-year-old Napoleon Bonaparte had passed the artillery exam and been commissioned a second lieutenant in the artillery. With such a background, it is unsurprising that he devoted great attention to the artillery, the most scientific of the three arms. A telling incident occurred before the Battle of Aspern-Essling. Two batteries of Imperial Guard foot artillery presented themselves for inspection. While chatting with the gunners, Napoleon learned that one of the 12-pound pieces fired erratically. Four days after the battle, Napoleon again reviewed the guard artillery. He asked the battery commanders the customary questions: How many men and horses did you lose in the battle? How many cartridges do you have left? And then, "Your erratic cannon, did it shoot true?"[11] Years later, the amazed battery commander still marveled at Napoleon's memory for detail and concern for his artillery's efficiency.

In broadest outline, the smoothbore artillery of the Napoleonic era were line-of-sight weapons firing solid shot out to a maximum distance of 820 yards for the light artillery and 1,050 yards for the "Emperor's daughters," the big 12-pound guns. Six-inch howitzers, which composed about one-quarter of the artillery, lobbed explosive shells out to a distance of 1,300 yards. In 1809, the French artillery was still implementing reforms begun in 1803 that involved the substitution of lighter-weight, more mobile 6-pound guns for older 4- and 8-pound weapons. Because of technical advances, these 6-pound guns almost matched the 8-pounder's range and punch while having nearly the same mobility as the 4-pounder. Similarly, improved howitzers were replacing the older Gribeauval model weapons.

A French battery consisted of six guns and two howitzers. Ideally, Napoleon wanted a ratio of two guns and howitzers per 1,000 soldiers. Such an arsenal would provide each infantry division with one 6-pound foot and one 6-pound horse battery and each cavalry division with a 6-pound horse battery. The surprise Austrian spring offensive interceded before this goal could be met. Consequently, French gunners entered battle with an array of 4-, 6-, 8-, and 12-pound weapons along with two types of howitzers.[12] In addition to his divisional artillery, the emperor possessed corps artillery intended for a reserve role. Napoleon liked to retain the corps artillery, with their hard-hitting 12-pounders, until the situation ripened. Then, committed at the decisive point, they could form a massed battery to batter a hole in the enemy's line.

As with the infantry, the gunners' accuracy depended on being able to see the target. Unlike the infantry, gunners could continue to inflict significant losses by merely firing into a roiling, surging mass of smoke that identified the enemy position. Only natural obstacles—particularly hillsides but including minor undulations in the ground—or a stoutly constructed stone structure slowed or deflected the cannonball's path. Otherwise it continued bounding along the ground until running out of kinetic energy. If a cannonball encountered human flesh during its passage, it tore off limbs and crushed internal organs. The more densely packed the target was, the more damage it inflicted by striking multiple ranks. A cannonball could carve a furrow in a column or enter one side of a square and exit the side opposite, killing and maiming the whole way. At closer ranges, 700 yards on in, cannon and howitzers fired canister, a tin can filled with musket balls that ruptured upon firing, causing the balls to spread out in a shotgun-like pattern. Because of their canister firing capability, generals judged that a battery could defend its front from all comers. A successful assault against a battery would typically approach the guns from the flanks.

The two keys to artillery's effectiveness were positioning the guns in a good firing position and employing them in mass. Good firing positions allowed cannon to fire obliquely at their target. A ball colliding straight into a three-deep line could strike three men at most. The same ball striking at an angle could hit more targets. Moreover, if the gunners misestimated the range, a ball or shell fired directly at its target would miss. Fired obliquely, a long shot still could strike home. On Saint Helena, Napoleon reflected that it would seem that a good officer could easily master the challenge of learning to site a battery favorably. He noted that the opposite was true; it was an all-too-rare skill.[13]

Back in his first battles in Italy, Napoleon had recognized that massed artillery could create an impact greater than the sum of its parts. During his first effort to cross the Danube, he did not have enough guns to implement this insight. His second effort would feature the most successful massed employment of artillery in history up to that time.

Infantry units under artillery fire preferred to be in line or, better still, in a village, because this reduced their losses to artillery ball and shell. However, when maneuvering in the presence of cavalry, they had no choice but to assume a denser formation because to remain in extended formation risked near-instant annihilation. If cavalry managed to contact men on foot, they would ride them down, kill with saber and lance, or compel the foot soldiers to surrender. Consequently, when confronting hostile cavalry, infantry invariably deployed into square or, if they were Austrian, battalion mass. Either formation presented a wall of unassailable bristling bayonets to the charging cavalry.

Regardless of valor, cavalry versus an infantry square reduced to a simple equation: if the infantry remained steady, they could not be broken. Veterans understood this. In 1809 an Austrian sergeant encouraged his square by gesturing toward the French cavalry and saying, "Those men there will not harm us. All they can have are bloody heads and even more if they are brave enough to charge home."[14] Battlefield experience proved the sergeant's contention. There were no more gallant troopers than those belonging to the French Imperial Guard cavalry. Yet at Wagram, when the Guard light cavalry charged an Austrian square, they were repulsed after losing ten men and ten horses. The fact that such light casualties could deter one of the world's most formidable fighting bodies underscores the nature of a cavalry versus square encounter.

When a unit formed square it tended to remain in that formation until the officers were sure that no enemy cavalry continued to lurk within striking distance, perhaps hidden by smoke or by a small fold in the ground. Soldiers in square were safe from enemy cavalry but vulnerable to firearms. Attacking foot soldiers could approach in line or skirmish order and shoot the hapless square apart. Worse, the artillery could stand off at a safe distance and ply cannonballs through the square, carving great gaps. Since only one side of a square faced the cannon, it was very hard for a unit in square to close ranks. If the artillery advanced to canister range—a specialty of the horse artillery—they could erase a square's entire side by firing canister. One of the true horrors of Napoleonic combat was having to endure an artillery bombardment while standing in square. The artillery fire often threw a square into disorder. A subsequent cavalry charge could mark its doom.

While the contest between infantry in square and charging cavalry was an extreme test of nerves, nowhere did morale factors play a larger role than in cavalry versus cavalry combats. Whereas some men will sacrifice their lives in a death or glory charge, horses instinctively shy away from collisions. When op-posing mounted forces charged at one another, it would seem as if a tremendous collision was inevitable. In fact, one of three things would occur: one contestant would falter and turn about (a failure of nerve brought on by the trooper's fear and enthusiastically seconded by his mount), the rival lines would pass through each other (the least common occurrence), or the foes would halt on contact and begin a hack-and-thrust melee. The physical and psychological factors influ-encing a cavalry charge account for Lasalle's comment, "there are lost men," whenever he saw a rival force charging at a gallop. A galloping line could not maintain order. It was full of gaps that encouraged the horses to turn about before contact while simultaneously encouraging the foe to advance confidently because rider and horse alike could see that they could avoid the shock by entering the intervals between enemy riders. Lasalle tried to keep his men restrained at the trot. The formidable appearance of a compact line at the trot caused opposing troopers who were galloping ahead to pause and consider: there are not intervals before me to allow avoidance of the collision, the shock is certain; if these trotting troopers advance at such a steady gait it is because their resolution is firm and they do not require a wild gallop to steady their nerves. Galloping troopers did not reason this out but instinctively understood it and bowed to the superior moral force of the trotting charge. The description of a cavalry skirmish on May 20 contains the elements of cavalry combat:

At about 7 P.M., after a fierce cannonade, the Austrians launched a ferocious cavalry attack on us. Enemy hussars made a vigorous frontal attack . . . while a regiment of uhlans attacked the left flank. The enemy hussars had reached only 200 to 250 paces away from us, and were cantering along with shouts and hurrahs, when General Lasalle began to advance at a walk [to counter an enemy charge that had drawn so near with a maneuver that begins at a walk is an exhibition of supreme confidence in his troopers], then trot, and finally at a gallop so he hit the hussars at full tilt. [Even Lasalle could not restrain his troopers though the entire charge.] A regiment of the second line wheeled to the left to engage the uhlan regiment. [This ability to change front to flank in the face of an enemy charge underscores the abilities of the Grande Armée.] The opposing sides got as mixed up together as shredded cabbage.[15]

A cavalry officer who examined the ground after this skirmish was surprised to note how few men had been killed in spite of prolonged hand-to-hand fighting. The explanation is that cavalry-versus-cavalry encounters were nine parts psychological to one part physical. In addition, unless they are among a skilled handful, men on horseback must attend to the mechanics of controlling their mounts before all else. Once the melee began, individual sword play told all. To kill a man with a long and heavy length of steel required both strength (one light cavalry officer relates that after a cavalry melee he was so tired from delivering saber blows that he could barely raise his right arm) and dexterity. Far more common than the lethal death blow was the glancing strike that drew blood but did not prove fatal. In addition to fatigue, the aforementioned light cavalry officer endured five or six saber cuts, and his horse received one cut to the face. Yet these blows failed to prevent the trooper and his horse from being ready to go out again the next day.[16]

Technique also entered the calculus of close combat. Troopers trained to use the point of the sword instead of slashing with the blade inflicted far more serious losses. In the just-described combat, an eyewitness counted twice as many dead Hungarians as French and attributes this to "the fact that the Hungarians brandish their sabers about a great deal, whereas the French thrust with the point."[17] However, cavalry melees tended to feature a disproportionate number of officer casualties. Officers believed it their duty to lead a charge. As a dragoon officer wrote, being "always at the front, they found themselves naturally the most exposed."[18]

The protective equipment the cavalry wore was unequal to battlefield stress. An eyewitness recalls that at Aspern-Essling he saw many cuirassiers killed when Austrian saber blows split through helmets.[19] The cuirasses protected against sword thrusts but did little to stop musket or canister fire. The light cavalry shakos had metal-reinforced bands to help ward off sword blows that proved worse than useless since they directed the blow down the neck. Compared to the infantry, the cavalry on the 1809 Danube battlefields faced greater risk. A mounted man presented a bigger target and, because of the near-universal tendency to fire high, was more likely to be hit by enemy fire. Unlike the infantry, they could not open their ranks or avail themselves of cover. Once cavalry entered a melee, they faced the dangers of cold steel. The range of injuries among seven distinguished troopers in one French light cavalry regiment after a series of charges at Wagram illustrates this point: a captain wounded by a lance thrust to the chest; a lieutenant with a saber wound to the head; another lieutenant with a shot wound to the head; a second lieutenant with a shot wound to the knee; three chasseurs with saber wounds to the head and arms.[20]

In sum, a Napoleonic cavalry battle began with rival commanders' making important tactical judgments that required a fine sense of timing, terrain, maneuver, and morale. Once opposing forces engaged, the battle quickly degenerated into the crudest sort of fighting, featuring individuals hacking and thrusting, a type of fighting totally familiar to soldiers from time immemorial. The Napoleonic Wars were the last battles in Western history to feature significant losses caused by edged weapons.

On the Napoleonic battlefield, the interplay of the three arms was crucial for both attacker and defender. An attacking general employing a combined arms assault—infantry, artillery, cavalry—put enormous stress on the defender. The tactical problem this sort of assault posed to a defending battalion commander reduced to a conundrum: to remain in line would allow the opposing cavalry to overrun him; to form square permitted the attacker's infantry and cannon to shoot his unit into red ruin. In an era where command and control extended only as far a general's voice carried, orchestrating a combined-arms assault amid the chaos of battle was extremely difficult. However, a general using a properly managed combined arms assault possessed a tactical trump to any defensive ma-neuver.

The campaigns around Vienna in 1809 saw the full participation of one of history's renowned military formations. Even in its own era, Napoleon's elite Imperial Guard possessed a legendary reputation. The emperor lavished great attention on the guard's every detail, and the result was units without equal. The qualifications to enter the Guard were rigorous in the extreme. At a minimum, a soldier had to have five years' service with participation in two campaigns and to have exhibited battlefield heroism, as evidenced by multiple wounds, to be considered for the Old Guard, the elite of the elite. Once a man made it to the Imperial Guard, his exalted status was reflected by a tremendous material im-provement in his life. Extra pay, the best quarters, magnificent uniforms, a rank equivalency superior to that of the line units, and first call on rations and medical care were some of the rewards. In 1809 (before dilution through expansion) the Imperial Guard was still a relatively small force comprising all three arms.

Napoleonic-era soldiers wore resplendent uniforms. Napoleon believed that such dress cemented a soldier's attachment to his country and helped him endure a heavy fire on the battlefield.[21] The best foot soldiers in the army were the four battalions of grenadiers and chasseurs of the Old Guard who wore impressive blue uniforms with red or green trim. The surpassing symbol of their elite status was their tall bearskin helmet. During battle, the mere sight of the bearskins of the guard caused many foes to waver. Beneath them in status were four fusilier battalions who wore uniforms similar to the grenadiers and chasseurs in every way except for the substitution of the shako for the bearskin. These eight su-premely experienced battalions were both a priceless collection of combat ex-perience and extremely expensive to maintain. Even a fusilier cost twice as much as a line soldier. Far worse, their existence had a debilitating effect on the army by draining off the best men. For example, after the Battle of Wagram the Guard absorbed 456 select noncommissioned officers from the line infantry and 410 from the cavalry. This draft came at exactly the time—after a bloody battle when discipline decayed and raw troops needed to be trained—that the regular for-mations most needed their best men. The consequences of removing the best soldiers in order to create elite units were something Napoleon well understood. In 1807 he wrote to Marshal Joachim Murat to castigate him for drawing off his best men to form guard formations. The emperor predicted that absent their elite companies, Murat's line units would be lost.[22] Still, Napoleon persisted in expanding his guard. It was an expense unmatched by its battlefield worth because Napoleon was always loath to commit them to battle. "Being so precious, one fears to expose them," he observed.[23] From top to bottom, the Guard did provide a manpower pool that Napoleon drew on when he needed to bolster some battle-weakened line unit. For example, to make good the losses in Espagne's cuirassier division after Aspern-Essling, the emperor promoted a colonel from his Guard dragoons to replace a fallen brigadier general. Likewise, he drew on noncommissioned officers in his Young Guard infantry to fill the gaps in certain shattered line infantry units.[24]

At the beginning of 1809, the emperor created a new formation composed from 3,200 of the strongest, best educated conscripts. In order to avoid the word *conscript*'s unpleasant connotation, Napoleon styled the new units *tirailleurs* (literally, "skirmishers" or "sharpshooters"). These junior units—the tirailleur-grenadiers and tirailleur-chasseurs—entered the Imperial Guard with the title Young Guard. Their officers and noncommissioned officers were either former Old Guardsmen or graduates from the military academy at Saint-Cyr. The Battle of Aspern-Essling would witness their first exposure to combat.

For the 1809 campaign Napoleon fielded four six-gun companies of Old Guard foot artillery. Like their infantry counterparts, these gunners wore the prized bearskin helmet to symbolize their vast experience. Three companies possessed 12-pounders, guns Napoleon affectionately called his "cherished daughters." Of even more exalted status were the six six-gun Guard horse artillery companies. Crewing the skilled positions in the horse artillery were veterans with 15 to 20 years of experience. The demanding entrance requirements for the Guard horse artillery allowed it to boast that it had Europe's finest gunners.

The mounted Imperial Guard formations included four splendid cavalry regiments of four squadrons each. Wearing the bearskin helmet were the troopers of the Grenadiers à Cheval. Equal in status was the light cavalry in the Chasseurs à Cheval, whose green uniform the emperor wore while on campaign. The Empress Dragoons provided another regiment of heavy cavalry. They, like the line dragoons, could never quite overcome the pedestrian reputation associated with dragoon service. Two squadrons of large men mounted on black horses composed the Gendarmes d'Élite, a unit that could trace its lineage back to the armored knights who guarded French kings. Newest in service was the Chevaulégers Polonais, saber-armed Polish troopers who seemed to believe that if they could exhibit enough zeal, the emperor would restore Poland to its ancient glories. Like the other two branches, the Imperial Guard cavalry were distinguished combat veterans. Unlike the infantry, Napoleon made freer use of his Guard cavalry. Still, as their nicknames indicated ("The Gods," the "Cherished Children," and the "Immortals"), they were not subjected to the brutal attrition experienced by line cavalry. The outbreak of the war against Austria had found the Imperial Guard in Valladolid, Spain. By foot and by wagon convoy, they marched frantically to catch up with Napoleon, and most would arrive near Vienna on the eve of Napoleon's first effort to cross the Danube. None would surpass the performance of the Imperial Guard Dragoons who completed the 2,800-kilometer journey in 63 days without loss of a man or horse.

The Guard's privileges excited much jealousy among line soldiers. One line captain recalls how his comrades encountered an Imperial Guard wagon and delighted in obstructing its march. In bantering tones a soldier said, "Come soldiers of the line, make way for the mules of the Guard."

"Bah!" replied another, "they are donkeys."

"I tell you they are mules."

"And I, that they are donkeys."

"Well! suppose they are, what difference does it make? Do you not know that in the Guards donkeys have the rank of mules."[25]

At the opposite end of the spectrum of military prestige were the lowly conscripts. To fight the 1809 campaign, the emperor ramrodded a measure through the French Senate that conscripted 80,000 men who had been passed over in previous years. This had never happened before and amounted to an extremely unpopular double jeopardy. It was no longer enough to be lucky just once; henceforth the long arm of the conscription service could reach back to pluck those who had thought themselves safe from military service. In addition, the emperor called another 80,000 immature youths from the class of 1810, nearly two years in advance of their time. Conscription had never been popular, but such extraordinary measures as these went far toward producing a nationwide war weariness. Consequently, to an increasing extent the rich hired substitutes, and the poor fled into the mountains and forests to escape. Among those hapless conscripts who actually entered the ranks, desertion rates were high. A veteran officer recalls marching his conscripts under guard and shutting them up every night behind "bolt and bar."[26] Although conscription applied to all classes of society, since this was a French army, conscripted cooks received exceptional attention. They became chefs to high-ranking officers and, recalls one envious soldier, "the greatest care was taken that the lives of these gentlemen should not be exposed to the hazards of war, nor their precious healths endangered by the inclemencies of sentry duty."[27]

While everyone recognized the considerable benefits that accrued when a unit drilled together for months at a time, French method believed that a raw recruit could acquire the necessary basics in a mere one month of instruction.[28] Because Napoleon needed additional manpower quickly to replenish his army, he maintained a constant flow of minimally trained replacements heading from depots in France toward Vienna. They marched in ad hoc formations, *marches de colonnes*, that provided discipline and administrative convenience as well as an emergency fighting formation should they encounter guerrillas while en route.

Some entire divisions, such as those in Oudinot's Corps, comprised entirely raw conscripts. Other formations, particularly units in Davout's Corps, could trace their lineage back to the camps of instruction on the channel coast in 1803. At that time the French army and its commanders had an unequaled opportunity to drill in all aspects of tactics. Officers and men alike honed their skills on everything from individual marksmanship to corps-sized exercises featuring live musket and cannon fire. Soldiers who trained here became part of the Grande Armée and proved nearly invincible over the period 1805 to 1808. By 1809 the Grande Armée, Napoleon's finest army, was no more. Attrition combined with unwise dispersion, particularly in Spain, to force Napoleon to create a new army to fight Austria. During the Ratisbonne campaign, veteran units, such as the 10th Légère and 57th Ligne, had shown that they remained capable of amazing feats. But such exploits were no longer the norm. Their ranks diluted by conscripts and allied forces, the Army of Germany would prove to be of uneven quality.

Discipline in the French army was far less brutal than in the armies of its contemporaries. Napoleon believed that a French soldier was "not a machine to be put in motion but a reasonable being that must be directed."[29] What motivated Napoleon's soldiers to fight? The prospect of promotion and other rewards stimulated many officers to prodigies of valor. The emperor lavishly showered favors on those whom he regarded as being devoted to him heart and soul. Of course, he also felt free to treat these men with "those extremely offensive snubs" that could bring a general to near tears.[30] Although soldiers marched with the prospect of a marshal's baton in their knapsack, in fact, no man in the ranks rose to command level during Napoleon's reign as emperor. The common soldier responded to some basic stimuli. Some quite simply enjoyed war. "I like to fight," wrote one cavalry trooper. Conscripted at a young age, many had never known an alternative. "It is deadly play, a game that might kill, but this is the life of a soldier and it is as good as any other," concluded another.[31] Napoleon brilliantly encouraged the pursuit of glory. In 1804 he had instituted the Légion d'honneur, an order that rewarded loyalty to his person or to achievement that benefited France. The Legion d'honneur came with a lifetime annuity. More prized by the soldiers was the five-pointed white enamel double-clefted star surmounted with an imperial crown. The cross, as it was known, inspired men to display surpassing courage. Although wearied of war, in 1809 most French soldiers retained a spirit of martial patriotism. This, combined with loyalty to comrades, served as their lodestar for the coming ordeal.

Throughout military history, state leaders and generals alike have recognized that the receipt of timely intelligence can translate to battlefield victory. Before the French Revolution, a dispatch typically took two weeks to move roughly 330 miles from Paris to Bordeaux. This changed in 1793 with the installation of Claude Chappe's semaphore system that linked Paris with the frontiers. By the next year the system, contemporarily described as a telegraph, was in military use, bringing the welcome news from the Swiss border that the Russian Marshal Suvorov's army was in retreat, shedding cannon and prisoners as it went. By 1809 the telegraph had been perfected to the point that in good visibility a message could move 20 miles in a mere seven minutes and require only one and a half hours to pass from Bayonne, near the Spanish border, to Paris. While Chappe's invention gave the emperor a powerful technology with which to direct affairs from a considerable distance, the surprise Austrian invasion of Bavaria had also demonstrated the telegraph's pitfalls.

Complementing the telegraph was a superb courier system. In 1805, Napoleon had charged Postmaster General Lavalette with its thorough reorganization. Lavalette created an army postal system featuring the famous Estafettes, dedicated dispatch riders renowned for their speed and fidelity. In guerrilla-invested regions like the Tyrol, the Estafettes were prime targets. In recognition of sterling service performed amid hazard, Napoleon would reward one of them in 1810 with a saber of honor.

Last, Napoleon had at his beck and call young, vigorous aides-de-camp who could travel endless hours through conditions fair and foul to deliver a report from a distant general. The combination of the telegraph, the Estafettes, and select aides-de-camp coupled with the fact that compared to his foes, Napoleon enjoyed interior lines of communication. As we will see, a scheme hatched in London in 1808, the descent on the Dutch coast at Walcheran, had to travel around the empire's periphery in order for British agents to coordinate with Prussian partisans (Schill), Westphalian patriots (Dornberg), and Tyrolese guerrillas (Hofer). It made for difficult planning, easily interrupted by unforeseen developments. In contrast, when a garrison officer on Walcheran Island spied the British fleet in the early afternoon of July 29, 1809, he could transmit his report via courier and telegraph to Paris so that authorities at the Ministry of War could quickly devise countermeasures. Because of 16 years spent building an excellent communications system, during the 1809 war Napoleon profited from superior strategic intelligence.[32]

THE AUSTRIAN WAR MACHINE

Napoleon marveled that the German soldier (a class he understood to include Austrians) was "almost indifferent to defeat."[33] Their sense of duty caused them to rally after a battle to fight again. This was all the more remarkable in the light of the fact that the Hapsburg Empire consisted of a favored German majority with large (and unfavored) Czech, Polish, Croatian, and Serbian minorities. Before the 1809 war, authorities had stimulated patriotic zeal by appealing to Germanic nationalism. However, such were the empire's ethnic schisms that the government restricted appeals to the German majority and did not even bother to translate inspirational broadsides into Czech. Conscripted from the lowest in society, the line privates, most of their corporals and sergeants, and a fair number of their junior officers were illiterate.

The army fielded 46 German and 15 Hungarian regiments of regular infantry. When placed on a war footing, an Austrian or Hungarian infantry regiment had three battalions with six companies per battalion and two grenadier companies. By tradition the Hungarian units were slightly stronger than their Austrian counterparts. When war began, an Austrian infantry company numbered 180 men and a Hungarian company 200 men.[34] Thus, with officers included, an Austrian regiment fielded 3,732 and a Hungarian regiment 4,092 men. A six-company chasseur battalion had 720 men.

Hapsburg uniforms were characterized by a simple elegance. In an era when camouflage was nearly unheard of, the infantry wore bright white uniforms trimmed in distinctive regimental colors. Hungarian and grenzer regiments stood out in their cornflower-blue pants and half boots; the German regiments wore white breeches with knee-length black gaiters. In 1809, the shako began to replace the more ornate helmet, but, as with so many other prewar Austrian preparations, the transition was incomplete. Most Hungarian regiments went to war with the shako; most Austrian regiments wore helmets.

They fought in lines three ranks deep, formed square when pressured by cavalry, and maneuvered in march column outside of combat range. On the level Danube plain outside Vienna, the Austrian infantry was able to demonstrate a tactical innovation developed in 1807. This was the division and battalion mass, an attempt to merge a column's maneuverability with a square's strength against cavalry. The division mass comprised two three-company-deep columns that operated adjacent to each other separated by a 60-pace gap. The success of the division mass required company-grade initiative, something that was quite beyond the Hapsburg Army, and thus this formation was seldom used. The battalion mass, a formation with a one-company frontage and a six-company depth, was much handier. It operated in either open or closed order, the latter requiring individual soldiers to pack together so they literally could touch the man in front of them. The virtue of the battalion mass was that it could stand up to a cavalry charge from the front or either flank and in contrast to the inert square, maneuver, albeit with considerably difficulty. Karl particularly favored this formation and urged his subordinates to employ it. He recognized that the mass formation was extremely vulnerable to artillery fire so prescribed that the units in mass utilize all existing cover—a rather silly order because the only places the masses could maneuver were places devoid of cover. In the event, at Aspern-Essling the infantry in battalion mass successfully repelled numerous cavalry charges and (in the absence of French artillery and unimpeded by natural obstacles) then resumed their advance. Having acquired confidence in the formation, they used it at Wagram, where it proved less successful because of its extreme vulnerability to artillery fire.

There were several other noteworthy differences between the Austrian and French infantry. Hapsburg soldiers did not have the habit of self-direction. They were not expected to live off the land. Instead, they relied for subsistence on a tremendous wagon train to carry rations and bread ovens. The presence of these wagons placed a substantial brake on Austrian march mobility. In battle, the Austrian infantry maneuvered by a system that was slightly slower and less supple than the French method. More important, the Austrians were not adept at skirmish tactics. Skirmishing called for quick-thinking individuals, something the French showed a genius for and something that the Austrians could not quite grasp. The army's designated light infantry, the jagers, volunteers, and grenzers, partially filled the void, but the jagers had only recently been raised and were untried in combat; the volunteers had patriotic enthusiasm and little else, and the grenzers—originally hardy Slavic peoples inhabiting the empire's militarized eastern border—had been in decline ever since the Turkish threat that had forged them had receded.

The Austrian infantry had fought valiantly during the Ratisbonne phase of the campaign and would continue to do so throughout the 1809 campaign. But like any other army that experiences repeated setback—in the American Civil War, the Army of the Potomac comes to mind—there was a certain something, perhaps a fatalistic expectation, that contributed to defeat. A French soldier observed that many captured Austrians complained that their efforts had been undone by their generals.[35]

The campaigns around Vienna prominently featured the landwehr, the German national militia. Outside Hungary, militia service was compulsory for all trusted males (a category that did not include Galicia, where many pro-French Poles lived) between the ages of 18 and 45 unless they had an exempt status. Karl took a keen interest in organizing the landwehr. He intended them to form in provincial groupings where they would serve as a frontier guard and a reserve force. The unexpected setback early in the campaign forced Karl to summon his landwehr to join the main army. It was a role for which they were ill prepared. Only those who belonged to the lower Austria landwehr were remotely ready for active service.

Shortly before the war began, Karl conceived the idea of taking the cream of the landwehr and forming volunteer units that could serve with the field army. Bohemian landwehr volunteered for service in the Archduke Karl Legion. Moravian volunteers formed their own ethnic units (Mahrische Freiwilligers). Citizens of the nation's capital enlisted in six battalions of Wiener Freiwilliger. In this manner, about 20,000 dedicated patriots joined the volunteer service.

The empire was an unwilling grouping of restive people, and nowhere was this more true than in Hungary. The Hungarian nobility possessed a touchy pride and had to be handled gingerly by the Viennese government. Accordingly, instead of contributing to the landwehr, Hungarian authorities raised "insurrection" soldiers. They were supposed to be members of the minor nobility, but the practice of hiring substitutes meant that only the truly down and out entered the ranks of the insurrection. A total of 20,810 infantry and 15,107 cavalry mustered for the 1809 campaign. Croatia also had an insurrection force of 11,387 infantry and 1,627 cavalry, while Esclavonie furnished another 5,000 men. They were not reliable soldiers. Erzherzog Johann wrote of his insurrection cavalry, "One cannot count upon much from these men."[36]

The German landwehr tended to be raised amid great patriotic fervor. Typical was the "Call of the Styrian Landwehr":

> Come along! Come along!
> Whoever still can carry arms,
> Whoever has German blood in his veins,
> Whoever is possessed of noble strains.
> In Styria let the cry ring out:
> Come along and join in the glorious bout!

Inspired by such patriotic odes, some 70 of the 150 authorized battalions did indeed "come along" into armed service. The landwehr had second claim on weapons and were usually poorly trained. The monarchy had decidedly mixed feelings about arming its populace and thus insisted that the landwehr officers be either nobles or landowners. This restriction meant that the landwehr often had poor officers. Consequently, during the Ratisbonne campaign, Karl had not trusted them with important assignments. So heavy had been his losses that at Aspern-Essling and again at Wagram he had no choice but to commit them to battle. On these fields they would exhibit little offensive talent but would demonstrate that they could perform with the best as cannon fodder while defending a position.

The Austrian cavalry had a tradition of excellence that had become tainted by lackluster conduct in recent years. Its heavy cavalry comprised cuirassiers and dragoons; the light included chevaulegers, hussars, and uhlans. Cuirassier and dragoon regiments featured three divisions of two squadrons each, with each squadron numbering 133 horse; complete with officers and noncommissioned officers, these heavy regiments numbered 798 men. Light cavalry regiments had four two-squadron divisions, with each squadron containing 149 horse, and the regiment numbered 1,192 horse.

Theoretically, commanders reserved the heavy cavalry for decisive battlefield strokes, while the light cavalry served as scouts, performed outpost duty, and operated on the flanks during battle. Battle doctrine emphasized shock action. Regulations strictly warned the cavalry not to receive an enemy charge at the standstill but rather to countercharge. All charges utilized flanks guards and retained a reserve. While some cavalry maneuvers took place in column, the basic fighting formation was the line. In a regimental charge, pairs of squadrons would attack with each wave separated by twelve-pace intervals. All of this was not greatly different from French practice.

In 1809, Austrian cavalry mounts included a large number of partially trained horses. Like the French troopers, Austrian cavaliers who had their horses shot out from under them had standing orders to remove their saddle and carry it with them to the rear. This was asking quite a bit of a man who at a minimum had just had a close brush with death and a nasty fall. Von Thielen relates the story of how one cuirassier had his horse killed during the Battle of Aspern-Essling. He dutifully took his saddle and headed for friendly lines. Several French bullets passed over his head and unnerved this trooper. He became disoriented and in spite of helpful shouts from his comrades ran the wrong way into a hail of bullets and fell dead.[37] Unlike their French counterparts, the cuirassiers wore only armored breastplates, although, these were somewhat musket proof. Von Thielen describes a charge at Wagram during which seven or eight musket balls clanged against his armor but did not penetrate.

There were significant differences between the Hapsburg and French mounted arms. Whenever a unit finds that the formal doctrine by which it has trained is unsuited to combat reality, it suffers in battlefield effectiveness. This was the case with the Hapsburg horse. Austrian cavalry regiments were roughly twice as large as their French counterparts. Because this size proved awkward to maneuver, they tended to be split into two divisions on the battlefield and operate independently. Equally important, cavalry doctrine had no precise instructions for coordinating charges by several regiments at once. Consequently, too often individual Austrian squadron, division, and regimental charges would be overwhelmed by larger, multi-unit French charges.

The Austrian artillery comprised trained artillerists and semiskilled laborers drawn from the Handlanger corps who performed the brute-strength chores of laying and reloading the guns. Foot artillery included brigade and position batteries. On average, 170 men served in each battery. Direct fire support for the infantry came from the brigade batteries, the Hapsburg Army's light and medium field artillery. The brigade commander controlled these batteries, which composed either eight 3-pound or eight 6-pound guns. The heavier position batteries had either four 6-pound or four 12-pound guns and two howitzers. The division commander positioned these batteries wherever they could most usefully be employed. It was a flawed system. What usually occurs when an infantry officer is in charge of artillery is that in the heat of combat, he leaves the artillery to fend for itself or at best shoves them into position as an afterthought. They neither achieve the best firing position nor are used in mass. In partial compensation for the organizational weakness of the Austrian artillery was the corps artillery reserve. Each infantry corps possessed two or three 12-pound position batteries and an extra 6-pound battery. Unlike the brigade and divisional guns, this force provided a powerful, independent striking force.

Unlike the French, the Austrian army lacked true horse artillery. Instead it had cavalry batteries composed of four 3-pound or four 6-pound guns and two howitzers. The crew of the cavalry batteries were not fully mounted. Most gunners sat on padded seats atop the long ammunition chest fixed atop specially elongated trails. The bulging, sausage-like shape of these unique seats gave rise to the nickname "wurst" guns. The advantage of this system was that most of the crew merely had to hop off their seats to serve their weapons rather than first dismount and secure their horses. They required a brief 10 seconds to halt and open fire, a speed unequaled in Europe. However, the "wurst" batteries lacked cross-country maneuverability and, due to their weapons' lightweight construction, fired reduced powder charges, with a consequent reduction in range and penetration. A canister round from an Austrian gun had only four-sevenths the number of balls a comparable French round held.

Overall, there were 2.8 guns or howitzers for every 1,000 soldiers in the army. The 6-pound gun was by far the most common weapon, comprising 60 percent of the total artillery force. Howitzers provided 17 percent of the artillery arm, with the balance approximately equally shared by the 3-pound and 12-pound weapons.[38]

Erzherzog Karl's top subordinates received their postings based on seniority and birth rather than ability. They tended to be elderly warriors (the average age of all Austrian generals was 63) brought up in the school of Maria Theresa and that era's out dated tactical methods. Karl was neither free to choose his corps commanders nor empowered to dismiss any generals for incompetence or insubordination. Consequently, he had to tolerate having his bitter rival, Johann Hiller, lead the VI Corps. Two of Karl's best fighting lieutenants were Karl Stutterheim and the 43-year-old Joseph Radetzky. Stutterheim had exhibited energy and drive during the Ratisbonne campaign while commanding an advanced guard brigade. In keeping with his aggressive reputation, at Aspern-Essling and Wagram he led a mixed unit of foot, horse, and artillery. Radetzky was one of the comers in the Hapsburg Army, a staff officer who happened to be one of the handful of forward-thinking reformers who had real influence with the military bureaucracy and with the monarchy. He had joined the army at age 18 and become a combat veteran three years later in the wars against the Turks. He had been in the thick of the fighting ever since, exhibiting a conspicuous blend of courage and enterprise. Over time he would rise far, serving as a successful field marshal at age 83 in the war against Italy, and become idealized by the rank and file who called him "Vater [Father] Radetzky." Absent at Aspern-Essling, Radetzky at Wagram commanded an extraordinary mixed division of regular and light infantry, landwehr, cavalry and foot artillery, freicorps cavalry, and hussars.

Like Napoleon, Karl tried to heighten morale by issuing orders of the day that complimented particularly gallant units and by handing out medals and awarding pensions to the most deserving. His men responded with displays of tenacity and devotion to both the man and their country. By this behavior, Karl had shown himself to be the most Napoleon-like of any Austrian leaders. Unlike his rival, Karl had developed an explicit doctrine for waging war. In 1806 he had coauthored *The Fundamentals of the Higher Art of War for the Generals of the Austrian Army*. This contained a doctrine that did not promote command initiative while emphasizing careful planning, logistics, and precise battle alignments. In the campaign to date, few of Karl's lieutenants had displayed an ability to think on their own once the inevitable friction of war upset high command planning. But the Ratisbonne campaign had featured encounter battles fought over wide expanses of covered terrain. The next test of Karl's meticulous approach to war would take place on much more favorable ground. Indeed, it would take place on the very fields where Austrian doctrine had been developed, the dead-level and open parade ground called the Marchfeld.

Chapter 3

DAY OF BATTLE

In war nothing can be gained except by calculation. Whatever has not been profoundly meditated in all its details is totally ineffectual.[1]

BRIDGEHEAD

To cross a river in the face of enemy resistance is a tricky operation, but Napoleon appreciated that the elusive campaign-ending victory required such a crossing. He believed he could not linger because he was at the end of a tenuous line of communications with an enemy to the front (Karl), flank (Erzherzog Johann in Italy and the rebellious Tyrolese in the mountains of upper Austria), and rear (England). Therefore, he had to come to grips soon with his main adversary, and this required a combat crossing of the mighty Danube. So much hinged on the pending battle that Napoleon personally supervised the details of the river assault, right down to the construction of the bridges. He chose a crossing point where a narrow band of trees screened the bridging site from prying Hapsburg eyes. Here, near the village of Kaiser-Ebersdorf, the French established a work area. Eyewitnesses report seeing Napoleon visit this area at dawn, circulating among his bridge builders to encourage, cajole, and even lend a hand with the work. He slept in their midst, waking at odd moments to ask how the work progressed. His energy, and his manifest impatience to have the bridge completed, inspired the *pontonniers* to labor hard and undoubtedly also produced a fair amount of slapdash construction.

The crossing came in stages. On the night of May 18 French light infantry (voltigeurs) rowed across the Danube's main branch carrying a cable that would support the bridge to the island of Lobau. In Napoleon's mind, the island would serve as a staging area, a place of arms, for his entire offensive. While the voltigeurs performed this duty, pontonniers and a detachment of Imperial Guard Marines in small boats probed the river bottom with poles in order to locate places to anchor the pontoon bridge. After the voltigeurs cleared the island, construction began, carefully supervised by the emperor himself. When finally completed late the next night, the painstakingly built bridge spanned an 825-yard-wide channel and was built atop 68 assorted fishing boats and 9 rafts. Because there were not enough anchors, workers sank open boxes filled with stones, cannonballs, and crates of canister. They even tied obsolete cannon barrels taken from Vienna's armory to the bridge to try to secure it against the Danube's fast-flowing current. By noon on May 20 the first bridge was complete, and French soldiers began filing across to Lobau.

Lobau itself was a large, wooded island bisected by many small drainage canals. On Lobau Napoleon could mass his forces while remaining hidden from enemy eyes. The next challenge was to cross the 100-yard-wide channel separating Lobau from the Austrian-held left bank.[2] Napoleon chose a place where the island formed a reentrant angle to build a second bridge leading to the far bank. This position permitted French artillery to dominate the area that would become the *tête de pont* (bridgehead). To protect the construction of the bridge that would lead to the Austrian-held shore, one of Massena's aides, a certain Major Charles Sainte-Croix, who was to play a prominent role later in the campaign, led 200 voltigeurs across to the right bank. Although Sainte-Croix concealed his men in a band of trees, watchful Hapsburg cavalry pickets reported this activity to Karl. By 6 P.M. pontonniers had completed the second bridge. It barely reached to the far shore, and it too was a rickety structure, precariously supported on three trestles and 15 captured pontoons that had been reserved for an important task. The lack of time and materials prevented the construction of an upstream barrier to deflect objects propelled by the current. As soon as the pontonniers completed the second bridge, Molitor's division crossed over to the tête de pont and began digging an earthwork to defend the position. Anyone who had taken the time to notice would have seen that although the Danube was swollen and flowing fast, it was still well below previous flood marks and thus could be expected to rise even higher.[3]

Molitor's men encountered troublesome opposition from an Austrian horse battery near Essling. A French horse battery arrived to cannonade and drive off this foe. Then French light cavalry pushed to the front and established outposts in front of Aspern and Essling in the fading light. Ominously, the quick passage of the cavalry overstrained the second bridge, causing it to break. Not until 3 A.M. the next morning could the balance of Massena's corps reach the right bank. Meanwhile, more men crossed to Lobau. Aware that Napoleon was somewhere nearby, some young conscripts in the 93d Ligne asked, "Has anyone seen *le tondu?* Had anyone seen *le petit caporal?*" A veteran drummer replied, "He is taking his toilette in preparation for the grand ball he will hold tomorrow for the Austrians."[4] While his words still hung on the air, the drummer felt someone nudging him aside. He turned to see the emperor, smiling at his words and then hurrying on to supervise the buildup. From Napoleon's perspective, things had proceeded swimmingly. His army had completed a potentially perilous crossing over one of Europe's major rivers without significant loss. In his mind what remained—to funnel the balance of his forces across the bridge, find the enemy, and defeat him—would be easier.

That night the Army of Germany was in good spirits. Around their campfires on Lobau they joked, laughed, and sang in the manner of heedless youth. The young men attached to Marshal Lannes's staff sang the latest popular song attributed to Queen Hortense:

> You leave me, dear, to search for glory
> My loving heart will follow your steps[5]

During the pending battle, their pursuit of glory would find one aide-de-camp killed, one mortally wounded, and four more hit by hostile fire. Worse, their beloved marshal would receive his death wound.

Napoleon rose before dawn on May 21 and, accompanied by his staff, rode to the right bank. Immediately his trained eye detected a flaw in the fortifications protecting the crossing site, and he paused to trace a new line complete with an earthen lunette. This precaution was to prove very useful in the coming battle. He proceeded on and met with his principal lieutenants. The question of the moment was whether Karl would offer battle.

The light of the moon illuminated an assembly comprising most of Europe's foremost military leaders. The center of attention was, of course, Napoleon, who remained mounted on his horse. Gathered around were his marshals who had come to report on the enemy's dispositions. Typically Berthier, downtrodden by years of clerical staff work, chose to remain silent. But then there was little opportunity for comment since the voluble Lannes waxed enthusiastic with his claims that a mere 6,000- or 8,000-man Austrian rear guard was on the field. Bessières, the cavalry soldier, had received reports from his questing troopers. He relayed their claims that there were no substantial enemy formations within three or four miles of the bridgehead. Massena disagreed. He had climbed the Aspern church tower and observed a lengthy chain of campfires extending off to the northwest. This, coupled with his long experience of war against the Austrians, led him to suspect that the enemy's entire army stood just beyond the French outpost line. Given this mixed counsel, Napoleon resolved to conduct a personal scout. He rode to the forward French outposts only to find that a shroud of Hapsburg light horse blocked effective reconnaissance. Napoleon commented he would need his heavy cavalry to pierce their veil.

The emperor coursed the field behind his outposts in order to learn the lay of the land. The French bridgehead debouched into a thin band of woods on the fringe of which he had designed the protective earthworks. Beyond the trees was a small plain extending to the village of Aspern on the left and Essling on the right. In Napoleon's mind, the position was like an entrenched camp, with Aspern and Essling serving as bastions, and the connecting elevated and ditched

Aspern-Essling
(the Tactical Battlefield)

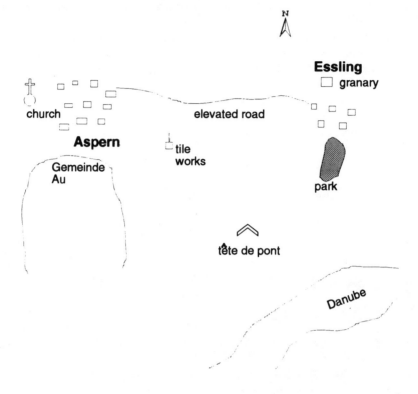

road, 2,000 yards long, acting as a curtain to unite the whole. Aspern, a large village of some 1,500 inhabitants, was 2,000 yards from the bridges, Essling 3,000 yards distant. Both villages contained numerous stoutly constructed buildings surrounded by a network of small dikes designed to keep at bay the Danube floodwaters. Another 2,000 yards to the right of Essling was the village of Enzersdorf, which, in turn, was 600 yards from the Danube. The combination of villages and the elevated road provided a good defensive position. It was most vulnerable to attacks from the wings, but difficult, marshy terrain partially protected the area between Aspern and the Danube on the left flank, while an enemy advancing against the right flank between Essling and the river would confront flanking fire from Enzersdorf.

Napoleon was less interested in his means of defense than in what stood beyond his bridgehead out on the Marchfeld, for it was here that he intended to fight any battle. The Marchfeld was remarkably flat, rising only slightly to the north in the direction of Raasdorf and Breitenlee. It well lent itself to ricochet fire, the tactic preferred by artillerists. Verdant fields of grain separated the small villages dotting the land. Napoleon could see that many of the villages contained

substantial buildings, shining white in the gathering morning light. Several included towers, notably Breitenlee's gleaming turret and the large, square tower
at Markgrafneusiedl. Finally, off on the northwest horizon, Napoleon could dis-
cern the wooded heights of the Bisamberg. Nothing he saw during his reconnaissance discouraged him from the plan forming in his mind. He would debouch
from his bridgehead onto the Marchfeld while refusing his left and leading with
his right.

The emperor issued a flurry of orders: Lannes would cross the bridge behind
Massena, followed by Marshal Louis Davout's III Corps, the cuirassiers, the guard,
and the trains. It quickly became apparent that implementing these orders was
going to require more time than anticipated. The fragile pontoon bridges, rocked
by the Danube's fast-flowing currents, forced all who crossed to proceed cautiously. Moreover, the river had risen 3 feet overnight. At 10 A.M., a heavily
laden boat crashed through the second bridge. Like an opening gate, the two
bridge sections separated as the water forced them apart. The French army stood
riven in two. Until nearly evening, Massena's three division, numbering some
20,603 soldiers, supported by 8,554 troopers belonging to Marulaz's and Lasalle's
light cavalry, Espagne's cuirassiers, and Nansouty's 1st Brigade, and 58 cannon
would have to stand alone.[6]

Hussar trumpeter Phillippe Girault had crossed to the tête de pont shortly
before the bridge behind him broke. He happened to come across Napoleon and
his staff. He saw Marshal Berthier gesture toward the Marchfeld and say, "Here
is a magnificent ballroom. We will make the Austrians dance!" Girault afterward
noted that this time the marshal was mistaken: "They made us dance, and we
had to pay the violinist."[7]

Erzherzog Karl had assembled his forces on the commanding Bisamberg heights
on May 18. The Bisamberg overlooked the old, well-used Hapsburg drill ground
known as the Marchfeld. It was historic ground. Here in 1277 Rudolph of Hapsburg had defeated the king of Bohemia. The next day Karl's lookouts reported
the French concentration opposite Lobau. On the morning of the twentieth,
Karl ordered a reconnaissance in force to verify the French intent to cross. The
cavalry battery that had annoyed Molitor's men during the evening had been
part of this mission. In midafternoon, once he became convinced that the Lobau
crossing was Napoleon's main effort, Karl shifted his army onto the slopes overlooking the Marchfeld. Massena had seen these men's campfires in the early hours
of May 21. Karl then issued an eve-of-battle proclamation to his army:

Tomorrow, or the following day, there will be a great battle. The result of it will . . . decide
the fate of the monarchy and of the freedom of every one of you. Between eternal disgrace
on the one hand, and undying fame on the other, there is no middle way. I count on the
bravery of the army, on the example and spirit of enterprise of the officers."[8]

As had been the case in 1277, the fate of Vienna and the Hapsburg dynasty
would be determined on the Marchfeld. Because the Austrians had held periodic

The Grand Tactical Battlefield
(Danube Crossing Sites and Marchfeld)

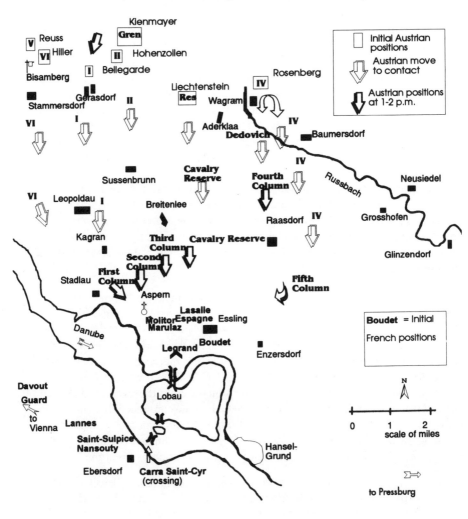

army maneuvers on this field, Karl and his staff knew the ground well. Yet the lingering inefficiency that characterized Austrian staff work showed itself again when Karl requested a map of the battlefield. After considerable fumbling, a breathless staff officer raced up with a map. Karl unfolded it, only to see it was for an entirely different region!

On the night of May 20–21, the Hapsburg generalissimus drew up his battle plan. Karl divided his army into five attack columns, a cavalry corps, and a reserve of grenadiers. The French position described a shallow arc with the left, anchored on Aspern, lying closer to the Austrian overnight encampment. At precisely noon the movement would begin with the infantry marching by "demidivision," with each column having "a proper advance guard." The First Column, composing Hiller's VI Corps, would march to the Danube, deploy with its left flank solidly resting on the river, and advance through Stadlau toward Aspern "with all possible vigor." Hiller was to use his artillery to counter any French guns located on Lobau that interfered with this maneuver. The Second Column, Bellegarde's I Corps accompanied by Karl himself, would maintain contact with Hiller, march to Hirschstatten where it would join with the Third Column (Hohenzollern's II Corps), and jointly proceed toward Aspern. The Fourth Column, with half of Rosenberg's IV Corps, would move by Aderklaa and Raasdorf toward Essling. The Fifth Column, with the balance of Rosenberg's Corps, would pass east of Raasdorf, pivot on Enzersdorf, and advance on Essling from the east. The grenadiers remained in distant reserve behind Gerasdorf while the cavalry screened the Third and Fourth columns from any French cavalry charges.

This entire array composed about 70,000 infantry distributed among 103 infantry battalions, 12,000 cavalry distributed among 148 cavalry squadrons, and 288 artillery pieces divided into 42 batteries.[9] Their objective was to throw the French back onto Lobau, destroy the bridge, and then line the Danube with numerous artillery, particularly howitzers, and pummel the enemy. Karl conceived of a series of feint crossings upstream to hold as many French as possible in place.[10] In sum, Karl's orders specified a ponderous attack order wholly characteristic of the Austrian way of war. In their first encounters in 1796 against a young general named Bonaparte, the Austrians had frittered away their numerical advantage by devising an overly complex attack plan composing numerous columns and detachments. So it had been on the eve of Austerlitz in 1805, when an Austrian staff officer had dictated an unwieldy allied plan of attack involving no fewer than seven major groupings. And so it was in 1809: another complex maneuver contrary, in Napoleon's words, "to the true principles of war."[11]

There were two other flaws. The attack began in the afternoon. Although it would remain light until close to 11 P.M., this reduced the time available to exploit any success. The plan also committed an undue strength directly against Aspern while ignoring the less easily defended ground between the two villages. Although Aspern was the key to the battle, the space required for troops to deploy meant that only a portion of the Austrian might could assault at any one time.

Around 1 P.M., a staff officer galloped to Napoleon's field headquarters near the Aspern tile works to announce that not only did Karl intend to offer battle but that the entire Austrian army was advancing against the French position. The fact that the emperor did not know this up to this time highlights the colossal failure of his cavalry to provide timely warning. Napoleon had just learned of another rupture in the bridge, and his first instinct was to retreat to the safety of Lobau while leaving a force on the right bank sufficient to hold his bridgehead. It was difficult for him to contemplate a withdrawal against a foe whom he had routinely trounced since his earliest days as a general. Moreover, aides advised that the bridge would soon be repaired. Accordingly, Napoleon resolved to stay and fight. He hastily improvised a command structure: Massena with two divisions would defend Aspern; Lannes, whose own corps remained stranded on the far bank, would supervise the defense of Essling. Then came the first assaults on what proved to be an extremely trying day.

"A NUMEROUS ARTILLERY RAVAGED OUR LINES"

They began with the French émigré General Nordmann who conducted an advance guard against Aspern from the west. Simultaneously, a special force commanded by Count Colloredo pressed in along the Danube's bank southwest of Aspern. Colloredo's thrust composed a battalion of the St. George Grenz, a battalion of Viennese volunteers, and a landwehr battalion. Operating as light infantry, this force tried to work its way over the marshy Gemeinde Au. Potentially, this was the most dangerous thrust of all, for should the attackers prevail here, they would have but a short advance to capture the bridgehead itself. But the heavily wooded, marshy terrain well favored French skirmisher tactics. A few companies belonging to the 16th Ligne initially yielded some ground until retiring behind a wide moatlike ditch (once the main river channel) that bisected the Gemeinde Au. Here the Austrians tried halfheartedly to storm a bridge over the ditch, only to fail before French musket fire. The entire action underscored the continuing inability of the Hapsburg military to develop an effective light infantry skirmishing capability.

Meanwhile, Nordmann's drive against Aspern itself was enjoying considerably more success. So surprised were the French that the initial Hapsburg assault found the village garrisoned by only a few companies of infantry. Spearheaded by the Giulay Regiment, the Austrians overran Aspern. Division General Gabriel Molitor responded to the battle's first crisis with great verve by immediately counterattacking with the 37th and 67th Ligne. The Austrians resisted stoutly, the Giulay Regiment lost 700 men during this action, but the French column forced its way through the entire village and had begun to pursue into the open ground when recalled by Massena. With its division battery posted between the church and the river, Molitor awaited the next Austrian attack.

Aspern comprised two parallel streets, each one wide enough to permit a full infantry platoon to deploy. Along both sides of the streets were stoutly built two-story masonry buildings. Behind these houses were gardens surrounded by diffi-

Defense of Aspern
(2:00 P.M., May 21, 1809)

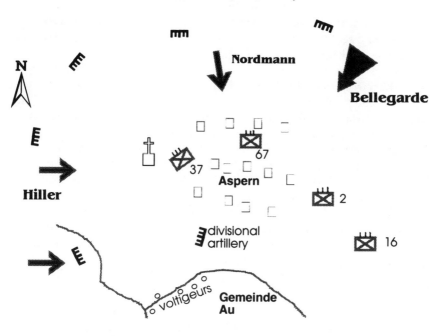

cult-to-climb walls. The streets met at a small square on the western edge of the village where stood a large church and adjacent cemetery. A masonry wall, musket proof but vulnerable to cannon fire, surrounded the cemetery. The church and cemetery were the tactical keys to Aspern. Whoever held them could sweep the open field to the west and northwest or pour enfilade fire against anyone in the streets to the east.

Exhibiting the kind of energy that had been altogether lacking at Ebelsberg, Hiller re-formed his corps and at about 2 P.M. sent them in against Aspern's western face. Molitor's battery severely punished the packed Austrian formation, but the white-coated infantry closed ranks and bore in toward the church and its adjacent cemetery. Sheltered behind the cemetery walls, a battalion of the 67th Ligne rose up and delivered a point-blank volley that broke the back of Hiller's attack and sent his infantry stumbling to the rear. For Aspern's defenders, this success proved but a momentary reprieve. The retreat of Hiller's men cleared the front to reveal an even more formidable foe deploying for an attack. They were the 20,000 or so infantry belonging to General der Cavalerie (GdK) Heinrich Graf Bellegarde's column.

Bellegarde had hurried his artillery to the fore to begin a preparatory bombardment while he formed his infantry in three lines. These guns joined with

Hiller's artillery to compose a 90-gun battery that opened a furious fire against Aspern's northwestern face. Its effect was terrible. Molitor's after-action report would recount how "numerous artillery ravaged our lines and dismounted our artillery" during this phase of the battle.[12] Driven into shelter, the 37th and 67th dispersed into self-sufficient fighting groups with an officer taking command in each house and barn. Then came Bellegarde's first assault.

Austrian officers from corps level on down had harangued their men, stimulating them to a fevered battle pitch. Full of enthusiasm, on marched the white-coated infantry with bands playing and soldiers singing patriotic songs and religious hymns. At the front of their columns came sappers who wielded hatchets to breach Aspern's garden walls. A cannonball took off the feet of Captain Komadina of the Reuss-Plauen Infantry. When soldiers tried to help him to the rear, he spurned their offers, telling them to "follow the path shown with the blood of your brave comrades."[13] As had occurred at Ebelsberg, "each street, each house, each barn" became the scene of fearful fighting as the battle degenerated into a series of small unit encounters and personal combats.[14] The French tried to blockade the streets with overturned wagons, carts, and farm equipment. Sappers began to loophole the walls to provide protected firing positions for the infantry.[15] The defenders held, only to confront a second and then a third attack. After each assault, the Austrian artillery renewed its bombardment, and soon the village was ablaze.

Three large trees shaded the Aspern cemetery. Beneath them, Massena established his headquarters, disregarding the canister fire that rattled through the leaves and frequently caused branches to fall. It took terrific presence to maintain composure when subjected to such fire, and no one surpassed the marshal. He mounted his horse and asked a soldier to adjust his stirrup. No sooner had Massena lifted his leg up to his horse's neck to permit the adjustment when a cannon carried away both the stirrup and the soldier. Massena calmly looked at his staff and said, "Let's get going, I'll do without the stirrup."[16]

Erzherzog Karl had particularly enjoined his infantry to "form on the plain in battalion mass."[17] The paucity of French artillery permitted Bellegarde to do just this. Had more French guns been available, the dense column formations would have been fearfully ravaged. Still, there simply was not enough space for the Austrian masses to utilize their superior strength against Aspern. The grinding battle of attrition wore on.

While Hiller and Bellegarde's men engaged, Hohenzollern's Third Column found it difficult to deploy and advance against Aspern from the north because of aggressive maneuvering by Brigadier General Marulaz's light cavalry. This delay revealed another flaw in Karl's combinations. He had concentrated most of his mounted force in GdK Johannes Liechtenstein's cavalry reserve and instructed that general to counter any French cavalry movement against the Third and Fourth Columns. Toward this end, the Hapsburg cavalier had stationed his reserve between Hohenzollern and the Fourth column. Here he was on the opposite flank and too far away to protect Hohenzollern from Marulaz. Hohenzollern had only eight squadrons attached to his own corps, and they proved insufficient to ward off Marulaz.

Finally, around 3 P.M., Hohenzollern managed to reach his attack position. He formed his corps in two lines, with the units in the front forming battalion masses. His powerful artillery opened fire, striking particularly hard at Legrand's division, which lay exposed in the open ground southeast of Aspern. Hohenzollern's advance placed Aspern in grave peril. Answering this emergency was the duke of Istria, Marshal Jean-Baptiste Bessières, who commanded the army's reserve cavalry. He was one of the army's notable eccentrics, a devout Catholic in an army of agnostics, a man who fastidiously powdered his hair in the old style while his peers relentlessly pursued the latest Parisian fashion. That he was brave went without saying; all Napoleonic marshals displayed great personal bravery. For reasons having more to do with his personality than his ability, he was one of Napoleon's favorites. Future campaigns would expose his inadequacies while on independent command. But he understood the power of a cavalry charge. When he saw Hohenzollern's column advance toward Aspern, he ordered Marulaz to charge. That general's five light cavalry units— three French chasseur à cheval regiments and two small allied regiments, one of Baden light dragoons, the other the Hessian Garde-Chevaulégers—numbered about 1,500 troopers.[18] Their target numbered in excess of 17,000 infantry and 50 guns. Undaunted by the odds, Marulaz's troopers advanced.

When Karl saw Marulaz surge forward, he shifted two regiments from Bellegarde's adjacent column to buttress Hohenzollern. Then he rode to the scene of the action. Encouraged by his presence, the Zach, Colloredo, Zettwitz, and Froon Infantries held firm. Close-range musketry fire from their mutually supporting battalion masses coupled with effective crossfire from the brigade batteries prevented Marulaz from pushing his charges home. During the action Marulaz himself had three horses shot out from under him, and his promising chief of staff fell dead at his side.

Napoleon saw Marulaz's distress and ordered Lasalle to join the action to succor his disordered troopers. This Lasalle could not do because Liechtenstein anticipated the maneuver. Liechtenstein belatedly realized that he had failed to protect Bellegarde's infantry from opposing horsemen. Accordingly, he sent nine regiments, spearheaded by the O'Reilly Chevaulégers, to drive off the French light horse. This they did by engaging Lasalle frontally with four regiments and using the remaining five to charge Lasalle's flank. Still, albeit at a stiff price, the French light cavalry had made amends for its failure to detect the Austrian presence by forcing the Austrian Third Column to grind to a halt and thereby buying time for the hard-pressed infantry in Aspern.

By 3 P.M., all of Karl's army had reached its assault positions. The emperor literally had his back up against a wall, the battlefield reduced to a narrow triangle bounded by Aspern, Essling, and the Danube. Because the Austrian artillery formed a semicircle around the French position, there was no safe place within the entire defensive perimeter. Cannonballs aimed at Essling bounded into the reserve positions behind Aspern to strike men in the back. Shots fired against Aspern killed men stationed near Essling. At his field headquarters in a small depression beneath the Aspern tile works (Tuilerie d'Aspern), Napoleon remained calm. He sat on a drum listening to a staff officer who had climbed the tile works to obtain a better view describe what was taking place. Couriers departed at the gallop carrying Napoleon's orders to Massena and to Lannes, to whom he had assigned Boudet's division at Essling in order to free Massena to concentrate on Aspern. His orders were clear: defend to the last extremity.

After Marulaz finished his fight against Hohenzollern, Napoleon's lookout spied the emergence of another threat to the French position. When the Austrian Fourth and Fifth columns continued to march laboriously toward their assigned positions, Liechtenstein had deployed his formidable cavalry reserve opposite the French center. Protected by their presence, a long line of artillery began to unlimber. Under normal circumstances it would have been a major error to use cavalry to hold the center of a defensive position. Because of the break in the bridge, on this field Napoleon had no choice but to station Espagne's cavalry division between Aspern and Essling. Here they presented a vulnerable target to the Hapsburg artillery. When the Austrian gun line began its fire, it proved so punishing that the emperor ordered Bessières to do something about it. Once before, in the snows of Poland at Eylau, Napoleon had required his cavalry to rescue him from an untenable position. Here again he requested the same.

Bessières ordered Espagne's cuirassiers to advance onto the plain. The four cuirassier regiments advanced at a trot, breaking into a gallop only when drawing near the guns. So far, GdK Liechtenstein's formidable 9,000-man cavalry force had barely participated in the battle. However, the same flat terrain that enabled the Austrian artillery to ravage Napoleon's army also allowed the French guns to fire effectively. According to an Austrian cuirassier, although his unit remained in reserve most of the day, it still suffered substantial losses from the French guns.[19] Ignoring this fire, Liechtenstein prepared carefully for the French charge. Just behind the artillery he positioned four cavalry regiments in line. At an oblique angle to the French advance he stationed GM Kroyher's two regiments of heavy cavalry. Then he waited for the French to draw near.

Espagne's 2,500 troopers had to pass through shot and shell that furrowed their ranks. Next they encountered a hail of canister as the brown-coated gunners switched to the lethal, close-range, antipersonnel ammunition that easily penetrated armored breastplates. Closing ranks and accelerating the pace, Espagne encountered Liechtenstein's four deployed regiments who, instead of countercharging, remained stationary. Their impassive stance communicated great resolve, and the French wavered. Then, the Kaiser and Liechtenstein Cuirassiers, with nearly 1,100 armored troopers, crashed into Espagne's flank and sent his troopers reeling backward in a swirling mix of individual combats. Major Berret, a squadron leader in the 9th Cuirassier, received two lance wounds and had his horse killed beneath him. A Belgian cuirassier corporal, Englebert Brahy, saw his captain desperately defending himself against a host of enemy cavalry. Brahy faced about with his section and hacked his way through the Austrian ranks to disengage his captain, thereby earning the coveted Légion d'honneur. While exhibiting great valor, Espagne's first charge had been a costly failure. Among the losses was General Durosnel, one of Napoleon's aides-de-camp and the Empress Josephine's riding master, who was wounded and captured in the charge.

Bessières withdrew his men and re-formed. Across the field, FML Dedovich's Fourth Column began to advance against Essling. Napoleon worried that they would overrun Lannes's defenders and ordered the cuirassier to mount another attack. Espagne placed himself at the front of his first brigade and charged. Once again, intense canister fire subtracted a heavy toll, and the Cobourg, Erzherzog Louis, and Czartorisky regiments formed square to repulse the French heavy horse. Espagne tried again with his second brigade. He reminded them of their great success earlier in the campaign at Eckmuhl and demanded they do the same here. This time his cuirassiers approached to within 20 paces of the Austrian battalion masses before dissolving under their fire. They left the ground in front of the Austrian squares littered with downed horses and fallen men. In spite of Espagne's troopers' self-sacrificing valor—about 400 of them fell during this series of charges—Dedovich's advance resumed.

By now Marshal Jean Lannes was feeling very hard-pressed in nearby Essling. The long approach march Karl prescribed for FML Franz Fürst von Rosenberg's Fifth Column meant that it engaged hours after the attacks against Aspern began. FML Dedovich, the leader of the Fourth Column, in turn, had waited passively outside Raasdorf until Rosenberg's men reached their assault positions. This gave Marshal Lannes, who commanded Boudet's division in Essling, opportunity to examine his sector. Lannes saw that the tree-lined main road from Aspern entered Essling's western quadrant, known as the upper village, and then narrowed to a width capable of permitting a single infantry section to deploy. The road continued between the same kind of masonry buildings that composed Aspern until reaching a dominating, three-story brick building that served as a public granary. The granary itself jutted slightly north into the plain, where stood Dedovich's inert column. Lannes realized that the granary thereby served as a breakwater against assault from the north. Nearby was a large farm with a walled garden. The road continued east along a dike and through a belt of trees, past a small pond and adjacent park, and entered the lower village before debouching onto a plain leading to Enzersdorf. Thus Essling was a smaller version of Aspern, having only one main street. But the village's core, with its granary, walled farm, and park, provided an easily defended redoubt. Essling's greatest vulnerability lay to the south between the park and the Danube.

Lannes appreciated that he lacked the manpower to defend both Essling and Enzersdorf. He stationed a mere outpost in the latter village, backstopped by an artillery battery sited to sweep the ground east of Essling. He positioned his infantry in Essling itself with a second battery sited on the western outskirts where it could cross its fire with Bessières's horse batteries. He assigned a picked company to defend the granary. Unlike the defenders in Aspern, the French in Essling

Essling

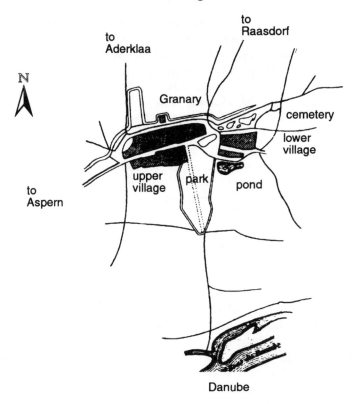

had ample time to prepare their defense by loopholing the walls and blockading the streets and alleyways.

Spearheaded by an impetuous grenzer battalion, the Fifth Column swept through Enzersdorf and moved against the Essling park around 4:30 P.M. This was when Dedovich also began to advance. Both Dedovich and Rosenberg had received an order from Erzherzog Karl, who was frustrated with his men's inability to capture Aspern, demanding that they take Essling. The ensuing assault engulfed the village. The 3d Légère, drawn up in line in the park, slowly yielded ground against a vastly superior force. Pursuing Austrian cavalry swept toward the bridgehead, threatening to outflank Lannes's defenders. French artillery, massed on Lobau and screened behind a belt of poplars, opened an unexpected fire. The hail of canister that struck the surprised Hapsburg horse in flank and rear proved more than they could endure. What had begun as a easy charge into the vulnerable French rear disintegrated into slaughter, and the shocked, disordered horsemen withdrew. For the remainder of the battle, no Austrian soldiers essayed an advance across this fireswept ground.

In Essling itself, Rosenberg's artillery methodically pulverized the outlying buildings. Lannes and his staff experienced the power of the Hapsburg bombardment. From his field headquarters near Essling, Marshal Lannes had been receiving and dispatching a steady stream of couriers. While three of his young aides were reporting on their various missions, a cannonball struck one aide, flinging him over his horse's head. It was the Spaniard, Captain d'Albuquerque, a young and carefree fellow who had led the singing the night before on Lobau and who reveled in war's glory. Lannes commented sadly, "There is the end of the poor lad's romance."[20] A second ball smashed into the saddle horn of another aide. One of General Boudet's aides-de-camp appeared to report on the fighting in Essling, but before he could say a word, a cannonball decapitated him. Convinced that the position was untenable (it had to have been directly in line with a distant Austrian artillery battery) Lannes shifted his headquarters. This was a marshal's prerogative. The men in the ranks had to stand and take it. Against an overwhelming Austrian assault, Boudet's men reluctantly retired from the lower village.

Glancing toward the center, Lannes saw Bessières's troopers seemingly idle and confused. Jean Lannes had been looking for an opportunity to revenge himself upon Bessières ever since that marshal had foiled his attempt to woo Napoleon's sister a decade ago. Because Napoleon had placed him in command over Bessières, Lannes saw his chance. Cooperation among Napoleon's marshals was always a touchy issue, requiring tact and goodwill to succeed. Quite deliberately, Lannes took the opposite approach. Ignoring the din of battle, he carefully instructed an aide-de-camp to convey an order to Bessières instructing that marshal "to charge home."[21] This emphasis suggested that heretofore Bessières had been unwilling to attack with vigor, which was, of course, untrue. It was a calculated slight sure to rile Bessières, and it did.

For the moment Bessières had no choice but to obey. He maneuvered Espagne's troopers carefully to approach the right flank of the Hapsburg horse. His second charge overthrew two lines of Austrian horse consisting of more than 1,000 cuirassiers belonging to the Erzherzog Albert and Erzherzog Franz regiments and 640 some troopers of the Knesevich Dragoons. Espagne's exultant cuirassiers encountered a third line composed of the mounted regiments belonging to the Hungarian insurrection. These units were unused to war and broke before the terrifying sight of the veteran cuirassiers. The French horse found itself deep in Karl's center. But they were without supports, for there were no spare troops on the entire field. Fresh Austrian cavalry advanced against them, and fire from the adjacent infantry ravaged their ranks. During this action, General Espagne fell dead, the victim of a canister round that struck him in the face. Three of his four colonels died in this combat. The cuirassiers had to abandon a dangerously wounded Brigadier Fouler who became a Hapsburg prisoner. Marshal Bessières himself got caught up in the melee and had to discharge both his pistols and

Aspern-Essling
(4:00–5:00 P.M., May 21)

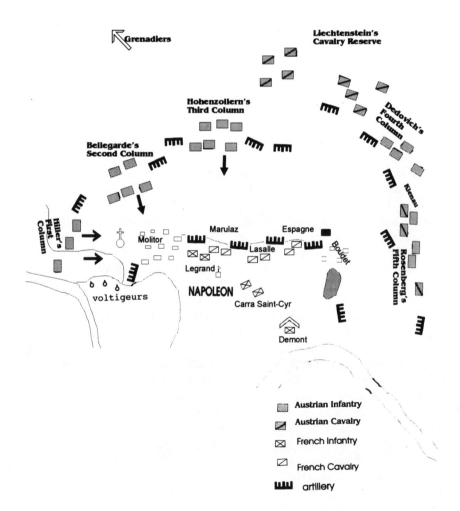

draw his sword to defend himself. In sum, four of the seven highest-ranking French officers in the division died, and one was captured during this action.

Back at the Aspern tile works, at about 5 P.M., Napoleon rode to the tête de pont to appraise how the work progressed. He saw his chief engineers, generals Bertrand and Pernetty, supervising hard-laboring French pontonniers and sappers as they tried to reattach the army's lifeline. Ever since it had broken, the two bridges had endured a barrage of waterborne projectiles, both natural and man-made, the latter resulting from the efforts of Austrian engineers who had launched a succession of floating mills and boats laden with rock into the current. An intrepid handful actually boarded these unwieldy craft in an effort to steer them.

The work to fend off these projectiles and to restore the bridge focused attention on the sapper/engineer and pontonnier companies. They typically performed useful but not noticeable service. On May 21, 1809, Napoleon was fortunate that Massena's Corps had a relatively large number of these specialists. The one pontonnier and three sapper companies belonging to the IV Corps, along with Oudinot's sappers and engineers, now entered center stage in the battle against the Austrians and the mighty Danube. Out in the raging current, they rowed some of the few remaining boats in an attempt to deflect the objects pushed out into the upstream waters by equally hard-working Austrians. The Austrians had set fire to some of the projectiles, making the French labor doubly difficult as the sapper/engineers and pontonniers fought against fast-moving water and hot flame. Napoleon's presence undoubtedly stimulated renewed zeal, but the workers hardly needed any additional reminder of the vital importance of their task. They could see for themselves that the cloud of smoke encircling the French position was steadily closing upon the tête de pont.

Satisfied that all was being done that could be done, the emperor returned to his headquarters. At last, around 7 P.M., about the time he heard that Espagne had been killed, General Anne Jean Savary brought the welcome news that the bridge was restored and the first squadrons of reinforcing cuirassiers had reached the tête de pont. Behind them came Carra Saint-Cyr's 6,916-man division. They were most welcome, because during the time Napoleon had been inspecting the bridging work, the Aspern church had finally fallen.

While the rival cavalries contested the center and Lannes's men retired before Austrian pressure at Essling, Karl had remained fixated on the fight for Aspern. It was here that he continued to feed in reinforcements. Much of the town changed hands five or six times. During the intervals between Austrian attacks, Molitor's men rebuilt their barricades and scraped shallow trenches behind them. One of Massena's aides describes the scene as the combat continued into the evening: "Aspern was erased by a hail of balls, burned by howitzer shells, choked by the intermingled dead of the contestants. . . . We fought without letup, inside, outside; we disputed every foot of the church, the church tower, each street, each house, each wall. . . . The furious combat continued along the streets, driven out of one alleyway, we awaited them from the next."[22] After one particularly heroic defense by soldiers of the 67th Ligne, Molitor embraced the unit's colonel and gave him his own Légion d'honneur. All the while Molitor's surviving artillery vied manfully against the overwhelming Austrian fire. Among many, artillery colonel Aubry fell. Nearby, Massena continued to inspire by his imperturbable conduct.

At 6 P.M., Karl completed his new dispositions for a general assault. He told Hiller and Bellegarde to capture Aspern regardless of the cost while Hohenzollern and the cavalry reserve supported them on their left. To date during the campaign, Bellegarde's corps had failed to fulfill its potential. Their repulse of Marulaz's cavalry had been the first time many had fired their muskets. Yet included in their ranks were some of the finest units in the entire army. Bellegarde selected GM Vacquant and his brigade to lead the attack. Eager to prove themselves, they advanced with great vigor joined by units from the First and Third columns. No one surpassed the courage of Captain Komadina of the Reuss-Plauen Infantry Regiment. A French cannonball took off his feet while he marched at the front of his regiment. The captain shouted, "Long live Austria! Advance comrades, the enemy is escaping, the victory is ours!" When soldiers tried to assist Komadina to an aid station, he sternly reminded them of their duty, telling them to leave him alone and keep up with the assault troops.[23] Supported by an enormous artillery, the terrific Austrian assault in which the 3,000 some men of the Vogelsang Infantry Regiment particularly distinguished themselves, drove Molitor out of Aspern.

Most generals would have committed their reserves to rectify any of the number of earlier crises. Massena had exhibited masterful tactical feel, drawing the last ounce of strength from his front-line soldiers in Molitor's division. These men had conducted an epic five-hour defense and lost nearly half their strength in the process.[24] Now, around 8 P.M. in this final emergency, Massena summoned his reserve, two regiments of General Legrand's division. He massed all of his available artillery to deliver a preparatory shock bombardment. Fifteen minutes before their assault, Napoleon and Berthier inspected Legrand's men. As intended, this put them on fighting edge. Then Legrand hurled his 4,000 men in a counterattack against Aspern.

The redoubtable Colonel Pouget's 26th Légère advanced in line on the village outskirts. Pouget saw an Austrian column marching obliquely across his front toward the village. French musketry fire took the Austrians in flank and caused frightful losses. To Pouget's amazement, the enemy column neither broke nor turned to confront his fire. Instead it kept marching to reinforce its comrades in Aspern.[25] Legrand's other regiment, the 18th Ligne, confronted similar Austrian tenacity. The 18th advanced in column up the street until it reached the cemetery. Here, withering fire drove it back to shelter in the nearby houses.

As the battle faded, Hapsburg canister fire knocked Colonel Pouget from his saddle. His regiment's surgeon and its music chief carried him back to the tête de pont, where Surgeon Dominique Larrey, the army's senior medical officer, had established a field hospital. Larrey took one glance at Pouget's wound and said,

"Well my dear colonel, there is a leg for me!" Napoleon's soldiers considered Larrey infallible. The army's medical community did not share this opinion. As soon as his porters conveyed Pouget out of Larrey's hearing, his regimental surgeon said that although he could not question his superior to his face, he believed Pouget could recover without amputation. So they carried the wounded colonel across the bridge to Lobau. Although Pouget would contract lockjaw and fever and the wound would continue to pain him for the next 30 years, he recovered without losing his leg.

Encouraged by the capture of Aspern, at 7 P.M. Karl ordered Hohenzollern and the cavalry to advance against the French center and complete the victory. To counter this advance, Bessières demanded that Espagne's weary men charge again. So fearfully had the enemy's canister ravaged their ranks that Espagne's men could form but a single rank for the charge. The men of iron battled heroically but were bested. To their aid came Marulaz's light cavalry, spearheaded by the only uncommitted French cavalry unit on the field, the 23d Chasseurs à Cheval. Marulaz's troopers overcame Hohenzollern's cavalry screen only to become enmeshed in the solid Austrian battalion masses. Marulaz tumbled to the ground with another horse shot out from under him. While the balance of his troopers withdrew, a handful rallied to his calls for help. Although Marulaz lay nearly under the bayonets of the enemy masses, a gallant chasseur lieutenant rode to him, dismounted, and gave the general his horse, thereby allowing Marulaz to escape. Nearby, Lasalle mustered his troopers for a charge as well. Lasalle managed to defeat the first Hapsburg line, but the Blankenstein Hussars and Riesch Dragoons took Bruyère's brigade in flank, drove them back in fearful disorder, and captured numerous chasseurs of the 24th Regiment.

Displaying great tenacity, Bessières rallied the remnants of his cavalry reserve and prepared to charge again. Fortunately, at this point, around 7 P.M., elements of Saint-Germain's fresh cuirassier brigade—the first men to cross the repaired bridge—arrived to join him. Napoleon ordered his cavalry marshal to take all the surviving horsemen, form them into three columns, and charge. Bessières used Saint-Germain's units to spearhead the effort. As had occurred repeatedly, this final charge overcame the first two Austrian lines only to run into the invincible Austrian battalion masses. Brought up short before the solid infantry masses, the French horse presented vulnerable flanks to Liechtenstein's troopers. The Austrian cavalry took advantage and sent the French reeling once more. Although defeated, Bessières's charge had accomplished the task of checking the Austrian advance against the French middle.

Several hours of twilight remained, but both sides were fought out. Slowly the firing dwindled. Hardly had the fighting ceased than Bessières sought out Lannes to demand satisfaction for the Gascon's insult. Lannes reiterated his position: "I gave you the order [to charge home] because you did not do it, and because all the morning you were parading before the enemy without approaching him boldly." Bessières responded, "That's an insult, you shall give me satisfaction!" Putting his hand on his sword, the hot-tempered Lannes showed he was only too

happy to oblige immediately. Fortunately Marshal Massena interposed: "I am
your senior, gentlemen . . . I shall not permit you to give my troops the scandalous
spectacle of seeing two marshals draw on each other, and that in the presence
of the enemy."[26]

And so the first day's conflicts ended with Legrand holding the lower portion
of Aspern while GM Wacquant's three regiments held the church and cemetery.
In Essling, Lannes's men had repulsed three more Austrian attacks and managed
to cling to the upper village. All along the front, both sides withdrew a slight
distance to cook rations and re-form. So close were the rival positions in the two
towns that fitful musket fire between outposts, and annoying Austrian howitzer
fire, kept most from resting well.

It had been an extraordinary day, the greatest battlefield peril Napoleon had
encountered since the desperate battle on the Italian plains of Marengo in 1800.
During the day's fighting, Napoleon had exhibited signs of both genius and a
leader past his prime. He attended to important details, such as personally cor-
recting the line of the bridgehead's fortifications, that lesser men would have
overlooked. Yet he recklessly sent his army across a single insecure bridge and
compounded this error by allowing it to be caught by a surprise assault in broad
daylight. At Marengo, as on the Marchfeld, overconfidence had placed the army
in a near untenable position, a situation narrowly retrieved by his men's devoted,
tenacious fighting. On May 21, as on that distant June day in Italy, Napoleon's
soldiers had bought just enough time for reinforcements to arrive and save the
day.

The comparison to Marengo applies to the Austrians as well. During that
battle, as on this first day of Aspern-Essling, the inability of the Austrian high
command to coordinate its attacks robbed the Hapsburg soldiers of the victory
their gallant conduct deserved. Much of the blame was due to Karl's overly
detailed attack plan, with its five columns and five advance guards. Moreover,
there was little tradition of subordinate initiative in Karl's army. Thus, while the
infantry battered away against Aspern and Essling, Liechtenstein performed his
duty of linking the Austrian Third and Fourth columns and fending off Bessières's
periodic eruptions but otherwise sat passive with his great cavalry reserve. Had
he charged the French middle at the same time the infantry attacked the wings,
the French could not have withstood the onslaught. As Karl retired to his headquarters at Breitenlee, he did not dwell on what might have been. Instead, he
was well pleased with the day's effort. Surely tomorrow would complete the victory. He issued orders to restock ammunition and bring up food and forage,
demanded that his cavalry remain alert (the troopers were not to unsaddle their
mounts, a painfully fatiguing experience for the horses), and told his scouts to
watch carefully for the expected French retreat back to Lobau.

Unbeknown to Karl, Napoleon had no intention of retiring from the field.
Overnight, substantial French reinforcements joined their battered comrades on
the far shore: Lannes's 13,150-man corps, commanded by General Nicolas Oudinot, consisting of Ebelsberg survivors and Saint-Hilaire's magnificent division;

Demont's 4,264-man conscript division; Saint-Sulpice's cuirassier division with 2,462 men; another 86 artillery pieces; and best of all, the 7,800 infantry of the Imperial Guard. Napoleon had hoped for more, but during the night the bridge had again broken, leaving Davout's Corps, half of Nansouty's division, most of the Imperial Guard horse, and the allied formations stranded on the right bank. Still, these reinforcements gave the emperor a total strength of about 58,000 infantry and cavalry and 144 artillery pieces.[27] He judged that this would be enough. Allowing his men a mere three hours of repose before their sergeants dragged them back to the ranks, Napoleon ordered the Army of Germany to prepare a battle-winning offensive.

Chapter 4

"A COMBAT OF GIANTS"[1]

War is a serious game in which one can compromise one's reputation and country.[2]

LANNES'S ASSAULT

At 10 P.M. the erzherzog issued orders for May 22. He anticipated that Napoleon would conduct an overnight withdrawal back to Lobau, surely his opponent's most logical course of action, but Karl underestimated Napoleon's resolve. Consequently he merely instructed his men to remain alert and ordered a renewed effort to float fireships and the like out into the Danube current. He would rely on the river to complete the discomfiture of his enemy. The emperor had, in turn, prepared a battle-winning assault but did not want it to begin until his entire army had crossed to the right bank. What took place was at odds with both leaders' expectations.

The fatigued soldiers experienced a short night of interrupted sleep: exploding howitzer shells, a picket's uncertain query followed by an escalating flurry of musket fire, snatches of fitful rest, and then sleepy sergeants kicking even sleepier privates awake in response to the officer's call to arms. The battle resumed at 3 A.M., an inevitable consequence of large numbers of edgy men packed into a small area separated from one another by a musket shot's distance. First, the rival outposts traded shots against targets shrouded by a clinging Danube mist. Then, as the predawn light illuminated the field, the awful cannon gave voice once more. Filtered through the smoke of a still-smoldering Aspern, the sun rose above the horizon to appear like a "blood-red globe of fire."[3] To members of Napoleon's staff, it was an evil omen.

Again it began in Aspern. Here the hero of the first day's action, Marshal

Massena, concentrated three divisions. Opposing him were the same troops who had assailed the village the previous day. The difference was that the Hapsburgs began this day with the tactical key, the church and adjacent cemetery, already in their hands. Overnight the eight Austrian battalions assigned to village defense had fortified the position. At 3:30 A.M., Legrand's 18th Ligne and 26th Légère, supported by the Baden jagers, formed column and attacked up the street toward the church. The mist permitted them to draw close to an Austrian battery before the brown-clad gunners realized the threat. Legrand's men managed to overrun the battery. The conspicuous courage of the 17-year-old son of the Grand Duke of Baden earned the lad the Légion d'honneur. A resourceful 23-year-old private in the 18th Ligne, Joachim Delmarche, turned a loaded cannon toward the Austrian position. Lacking the means to fire it conventionally, Delmarche used his musket to ignite the charge and send the ball flying toward the enemy. General Legrand, who saw this exhibition, said, "Grenadier, I will make sure your gallantry is rewarded when I speak to the Emperor."[4]

Nonetheless, the defenders' fire stopped the French. Then, aided by their overwhelming artillery, the Austrians counterattacked. Working outward from the fortified church, the whitecoats slowly managed to expand their control to encompass the entire village. An Austrian musket ball creased Legrand's hat; another hit the general. In the struggle along Aspern's main street, the 18th Ligne lost 80 men killed and 500 wounded. It required two hours of bitter fighting little different from that of the previous day, but at last, around 5 A.M., Aspern was again in Austrian hands.

They had no chance to consolidate their gain. Showing an excellent sense of tactical timing, Massena hurled the 24th Légère against them. The 24th's brilliant bayonet charge overran a battery, seized 700 prisoners, and recaptured the church. Before the victorious 24th could catch its breath, the Austrian commanders showed that they too had their fingers on the battle's pulse. Supported by an artillery bombardment, fresh infantry belonging to the Benjowski Regiment counterattacked and seized anew the church.[5] Massena responded by committing yet another assault wave comprising the 4th and 46th Ligne into the maelstrom of canister and shell that engulfed Aspern. An officer inspired the 46th Ligne by reminding them that they represented the sacred honor of France's foremost grenadier, la Tour-d'Auvergne. La Tour-d'Auvergne had died while serving in the regiment, and today the unit's oldest grenadier carried his preserved heart in a silver gilt box as an icon to inspire heroism. While the 46th fought to preserve honor, the 4th Ligne fought to redeem itself from a four-year-old disgrace that had cost them their eagle on the field of Austerlitz. The emperor had denied them a new eagle until they proved they deserved it. Revenge was theirs as the two regiments, ably backed by four Hessian battalions, reclaimed the village. So it continued, back and forth at least four times, until finally, around 7 A.M., the French regained the entire village, leaving their opponents too fatigued for the moment to contest it further.

Meanwhile, behind the village an equally important struggle raged for the

Gemeinde Au. The previous day had witnessed halfhearted efforts by poorly trained landwehr to wrest this vital position from French hands. This day saw something altogether more serious. Molitor's shattered division undertook the defense of the Gemeinde Au. So thoroughly had the previous day's fighting disrupted the internal structure of the Austrian army that Molitor confronted an assault composed of an ad hoc mixture drawn from several Austrian corps. Their ranks included the 2d Tyrolean Jagers, the Saint-George Grenzers, three battalions of Viennese Volunteers, and a battalion of Moravian Volunteers. These troops belonged to what passed for the Austrian Army's light infantry and were thus well chosen for operating on the Gemeinde Au's broken terrain. Still, they could not overcome the skirmisher tactics of the more experienced French. Even while the fighting raged, Molitor did not fail to notice that the Austrians were using the adjacent river channel as a conduit for their water-borne missiles directed against the pontoons linking the army with Lobau. The general ordered sappers and artillerists out into the waters. A brave handful plunged into the roiling current, clambered aboard the small boats, and grounded them against the shore before they could break the bridge.

At first light Austrian assaults also began against Essling. Here Baron Dedovich led his fourth column against the village's northern edge while FML Johann Graf Klenau assaulted the eastern edge. Between 3 and 7 A.M., these assaults broke against Essling. Although Erzherzog Karl's own infantry regiment gallantly seized lower Essling, failures on the regiment's flanks caused it to stand isolated. While Austrian infantry battered directly against Essling, the IV Corps, spearheaded by the aggressive Stutterheim's uhlans and hussars, thrust into the gap between Essling's park and the river. This was a potentially deadly stroke but had been fully anticipated by Napoleon. The emperor had sent Espagne and Lasalle to defend this sector. Taking advantage of the fog that still wafted above the Danube's shore, the French horsemen delivered a series of short, sharp charges intended not to break the solid Austrian masses but to impose caution. These tactics worked masterfully as FML Rosenberg failed to press hard his attacks. His inaction allowed Boudet to concentrate on defending the village itself. By 8 A.M., this general had regained control of all of Essling. Boudet's successful defense of Essling was the key to Napoleon's emerging counterstroke.

The emperor coursed the field to assess the situation. An Austrian cannonball that killed the horse of a nearby senior aide underscored the tremendous Austrian artillery superiority. During the two-day battle the Hapsburg gunners fired two artillery shots for every one sent their way by the French.[6] Unperturbed, Napoleon observed that Molitor appeared to have matters under control, although the entire Austrian left wing had entered the fray. Simultaneously, the interminable combat at Aspern seemed to attract most of Karl's reserves from his right wing. The emperor remarked to his staff that with the enemy concentrated against the flanks, the 2-kilometer-wide middle must be stretched thin. Here Napoleon determined to strike. Lannes would conduct the battle-winning advance against the Austrian center with three infantry divisions supported by all available

Aspern-Essling
(7:00–9:00A.M., May 22)

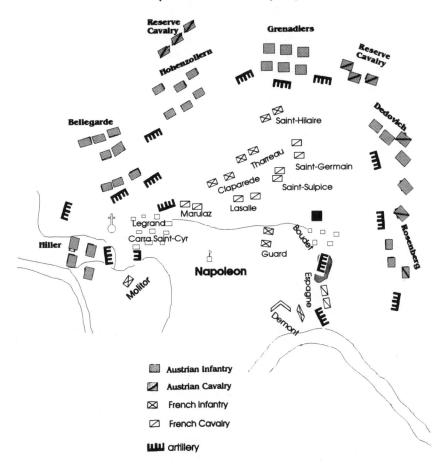

Austrian Infantry

Austrian Cavalry

French Infantry

French Cavalry

artillery

French cavalry. The emperor rode in front of the assault divisions, raised his hat, and brandished it toward the enemy. The soldiers waved their shakos on the end of their bayonets and cheered wildly. With Marshal Jean Lannes at their head, they marched on the enemy.

Gascony-born Lannes was one of those rare officers who combined fearless personal bravery with a desire to improve himself as a general. He took the great military tomes—books about history and strategy, as well as drill manuals—on campaign with him and studied alone in his tent. All of this served him well as he prepared what would become the last assault he would ever lead. Saint-Hilaire's veteran division moved out first, its right flank partially protected by the French defenders in Essling. In echelon slightly behind and to Saint-Hilaire's left were Oudinot's two conscript divisions, the men who had fought at Ebelsberg. All three divisions advanced in a dense formation of mixed columns and squares.[7] Accompanying the advance by filling the gaps between the regimental columns came the artillery. Behind the guns were 20 regiments of cavalry neatly arrayed in columns to charge forward through the intervals between the massed infantry. Placing himself in front of Saint-Hilaire's division, Lannes ordered the movement to commence. To repeated cries of "Vive l'empereur!" the infantry set out in parade formation across the level ground that had long served as their foe's drill field.

The soldiers awaiting them conducted an active defense utilizing all three arms to best advantage. During the French approach march, Austrian horsemen screened the front. Suddenly they retired, thereby unmasking a formidable artillery line that pounded Lannes's columns. Bounding cannonballs furrowed gaps in the French formation. They could do nothing but close ranks and continue. The carnage became worse when they entered canister range. Hundreds of iron balls scythed through their ranks. When the French approached to within 200 yards of the enemy, the Hapsburg infantry columns closed the range and deployed. They presented a checkerboard formation with units drawn up in battalion mass. While the brigade and position batteries continued to deliver canister blasts from the flanks, the infantry waited until the French drew near and then began firing controlled battalion volleys.

Perhaps more experienced attackers, men trained at the famous camps of instruction at Boulogne, could have opened their ranks to limit the artillery's ravages.[8] But two-thirds of the attacking force were conscripts, and they lacked the capacity to perform complex maneuvers when under close-range fire, so it became a battle of attrition and of will. The duke of Rovigo describes the scene:

The cannonade began almost at the very moment of our advance; it was murderous because . . . we presented heavy masses to their artillery. . . . We persisted in our attempts to penetrate their checkered line when the canister and musketry disordered our columns, compelling us to halt and engage in a firefight, with the disadvantage of numbers against us. Every quarter hour that we spent in this position made the disadvantage worse."[9]

Yet veterans and conscripts alike could not be denied. Inexorably they pressed on, but at ever increasing cost. Even in retreat the Austrian gunners exacted a toll by unlimbering and firing a few canister rounds before resuming their withdrawal. Worse, Lannes's advancing divisions were becoming increasingly scattered. They had begun the advance like a clenched fist. Emerging from the protective shelter of their defensive perimeter, they entered onto an open plain where they had to cover an expanding frontage with reduced ranks. Saint-Hilaire in particular confronted a dangerous isolation; no longer did the defenders of

Essling secure his right flank. Then from directly in front came a new menace. The Austrian infantry had retired behind a long, imposing line of Hapsburg horse. Infantry alone could not advance against them. The tactical situation called for a French cavalry charge. Lannes ordered the cavalry to pass his lines and attack.

The French heavy cavalry swept past Saint-Hilaire's men, only to fall in droves before the enemy's massed canister fire. General Defrance led the grenadiers of the cavalry, the elite carabiniers—tall men wearing broad felt hats and a blue uniform trimmed in red, riding large horses—in a series of spirited charges and had three horses shot out from under him. The cuirassiers, the "men of iron," joined the carabiniers to overthrow the first line of Austrian cavalry only to encounter another line, and then another. By the time they had defeated the Austrian mounted troops, the Hapsburg infantry had re-formed. Twice the cuirassiers charged this new infantry line but could make little impression against the battalion masses. A few squadrons penetrated to the outskirts of Breitenlee where Karl had his field headquarters. It was the highwater mark of Lannes's charge. Behind them the French artillery unlimbered to engage, and it too could accomplish little against the enemy's overwhelming firepower. Saint-Hilaire sighted an Austrian cuirassier regiment maneuvering to charge his exposed flank. He reacted with the speed and boldness that had characterized his style of leadership at Eckmuhl.[10]

The normal tactical response was to order the infantry into square, but Saint-Hilaire was a gifted, unorthodox leader who well knew the measure of his men. Instead of losing momentum by ordering a square, he commanded the trusty 105th Ligne to face to the flank, told the drummers to beat the *pas de charge*, and advanced against the enemy horsemen. Infantry charging cavalry was something rarely attempted. It demanded great resolution, for any wavering, any gap in the solid bayonet wall, would provide the cavalry with the opportunity to charge and annihilate the infantry in a flash. The 105th met the challenge and drove off the startled Austrian heavy horse.

During Lannes's advance, Lasalle's and Marulaz's light horse charged at least three times in an effort to support the infantry. Marulaz, like the better-known Lasalle, routinely led from the front. This behavior cost him a serious wound. The troopers had fought hard the previous day and suffered greatly. Again their charges incurred serious losses, and although they frequently overthrew the first Austrian line, it was the same story as the previous day; a second stout line of battalion masses, supported by numerous cavalry, blocked any additional advance.

Covered by these cavalry charges, Lannes's infantry pressed slowly forward. Behind them regimental officers were coursing the field, searching for ammunition to restock the men's near-empty cartridge boxes. There was none to be had; the supply wagons belonging to the grand park remained on the Danube's opposite bank. In French military myth, Lannes's offensive was now on the verge of total triumph. This view is some distance from the truth. The assault was losing momentum, a consequence of heavy losses, stiff Austrian opposition—in particular the resolute conduct of the d'Aspré, Rohan, and Colloredo Infantry—and a loss of tactical coordination after an advance of 3 kilometers onto the Marchfeld's wide plains.

While many of the Austrians directly in front of Lannes's men were indeed retreating, Karl was marching his reserves against Lannes in order to seal off the breach. Legend has it that so desperate was the fighting that Karl himself intervened by seizing the flag of the Zach Infantry Regiment to rally his fleeing soldiers. It is a story carried in most French accounts and memorialized by a fine statue in Vienna. Asked about it, Karl replied shyly, "Do you think a small chap like me could carry such a heavy burden?" In the event, Karl did gallop to the threatened sector to rally his troops. French fire struck many of his nearby aides and killed his chief of staff, Count Colloredo. In battles past, the Austrian high command had taken a distant, and safe, view of combat. On this field, as in the earlier battles of the 1809 campaign, they led from the front.

Lannes's infantry had performed prodigies. What more they might have accomplished remains unknown, for at 8 A.M. a spurring courier brought orders to the marshal to halt in place.

Baron Lejeune, an imperial aide, had crossed the bridge to Lobau numerous times already while carrying orders. Shortly before 8 A.M. he rode across Lobau to the main channel and saw the bridge there virtually destroyed: "Here and there five or six boats still held together, and in one place there were as many as twelve, but there were wide gaps between with absolutely nothing to bridge them over." Even while Lejeune watched, the fast-moving current propelled a steady barrage of large trees and floating mills that hard-working Austrian pontonniers had pushed into the upstream current. They crashed into portions of the still-intact bridge, swamping some pontoons and sending others plunging downstream. Then came a large watermill straddling its two-boat base and burning with great black clouds from its tar-smeared planks. A handful of brave French pontonniers tried to grapple it with ropes and chains to guide it safely to shore. If the mill struck firm, the resultant fire would consume the remaining bridge sections. They managed to deflect the mill enough so that it burned only a short section of the remaining bridge. Lejeune was near enough to feel the heat from the furnace-like mill. To complete the amazing scene, along came a small herd of deer, driven off Lobau by the floodwaters. The deer tried to swim through the current, only to encounter French soldiers who, knowing a good thing when they saw it, temporarily ignored the bridge in pursuit of venison for their cook pots.[11]

Officers who came from the fighting regiments in search of ammunition to restore their men's dwindling supply found a scene of frightful chaos in the French rear. Austrian cannonballs periodically landed even behind the tête de pont, where they scattered the hundreds of milling wounded. More wounded kept arriving each minute. Worse, in too many instances the able-bodied availed themselves of the opportunity to escape the terrible fighting by carrying the injured to the rear. They saw that General Pernetty's engineers had built a shaky footbridge parallel to the pontoon bridge spanning the channel back to Lobau. Here was a route to safety, and they surged toward it, only to encounter stern gendarmes who forbade passage for any but the wounded. A surgeon examined the injured before they passed because many were shamming wounds in order to flee the field.[12] In this fashion a steady stream of walking wounded, many leading injured horses, snaked across the footbridge to Lobau. The more seriously injured collapsed in the mud and lay begging for water, for medical attention, for death.

After trying to arrange a ferry service using small boats, which did not work because of the current's force, and realizing that any sort of flying bridge was out of the question, Lejeune returned to the emperor to tell him the news. It was upon receipt of the "disastrous intelligence" that the bridges linking Lobau with the far bank had been shattered again that Napoleon had sent a courier to Lannes to order him to halt.[13] Meanwhile, the French engineers and pontonniers worked hard to rebuild the severed bridge, but by 9 A.M. Bertrand informed the emperor that the task would require a long time. Napoleon dispatched one of his aides to do whatever could be done to secure fresh ammunition. For the remainder of the day, his army had to rely on the few ammunition-laden boats and rafts that managed to cross to the French shore. As early as 10 A.M. many units ran out of ammunition.[14] The balance had to husband carefully what remained, firing only when pressed at close range by enemy soldiers.

Consequently, at this time Napoleon sent another order to Lannes instructing him to retreat in echelon formation. His decision to suspend the offensive left Lannes's leading units in a terrible plight. The momentum of their advance had obscured from their foe their palpable weakness. Once they halted, the Hapsburgs had time to rally and see a much thinned French line in considerable disorder. Their artillery faced about and resumed a horrific fire. Behind this shield the Austrian infantry and cavalry re-formed. Karl had been puzzled by the French hesitation. Then he received a message from his lookouts on the Bisamberg that the French bridge had broken. Suddenly he understood. Sending his reserve grenadiers and cavalry to drive Lannes back, Karl ordered the assaults against Aspern and Essling renewed. In particular, he urged his left wing to capture Essling in order to cut off Lannes's retreat.

The resultant frontal pressure against Lannes's infantry was terrible. They had no counter to the overwhelming Austrian cannon fire except a disciplined will-ingness to close ranks and hold their ground. When an Austrian cannonball took off the foot of Saint-Hilaire, Marshal Lannes personally intervened to lead this gallant division. Lannes rode among his front-rank fighters, always finding the right words to inspire. He joshed with his favorite battalion commander of the 10th Légère using loud, profane soldier talk to tell the battalion to be sure to see off the miserable Austrians.[15] The veterans responded. When he ordered them to form squares in checkerboard formation and then slowly retreat, they per-formed as if on the parade ground. The front rank of battalions passed through the interval of the second rank, and then the second, after presenting a bold front to the enemy, repeated this complicated passage of the lines. During this time Lannes's chief of artillery fell with a grievous wound. His replacement—Colonel Seruzier, the renowned "father of the cannon shot"—placed his guns in a wedge formation in front of one of the infantry intervals. This formation allowed the artillery to fire left and right across the division's front. When the Austrians approached to close range, Seruzier's cannons and howitzers sent them reeling with a barrage of canister and shell. Then the guns displaced through the interval to the rear and formed a new defensive wedge.[16] During this action Seruzier had two horses killed beneath him, and a musket ball struck his arm. The division's highly disciplined battlefield withdrawal managed to keep the Austrians at bay and helped cover the less supple retreat of Oudinot's conscripts.

Throughout this period mounted officers suffered catastrophic losses. In Oudinot's corps it proved impossible to maintain a headquarters group. Explosive shell, cannonballs, and musket fire killed or wounded Oudinot's entire staff. General Oudinot's horse was covered with wounds, and Oudinot himself took a musket ball in the arm. He mounted a fresh horse and told his grenadiers he would not leave a battlefield that had been soaked with his own blood.[17] Inspired by such leadership, Oudinot's young grenadiers vied to emulate the veterans' courage and managed to maintain a precarious front to the Austrians.

Between 10 and 11 A.M., Austrian infantry, flags flying at the front, assailed Aspern from three directions. No sooner had Legrand repulsed one attack than on came another. By now much of the village, including the church, was in flames. Displaying the kind of front-line leadership so lacking at Ebelsberg, Hiller personally led one assault against Aspern's western face. Ever willful, Hiller largely ignored Karl's recommendation to attack in battalion masses, preferring to use the traditional linear system. Relentlessly the Hapsburg infantry drove the French into a last redoubt in the southeast section of the village. Here a two-story stone building provided a strong point to which the French clung hard. Then howitzer fire set the roof alight, driving the defenders from this final bastion. By noon Aspern was in Austrian hands.

Meanwhile, on the opposite flank, the white-coated infantry assaulted Essling four times. Overnight, Boudet's men had transformed the village into a small fortress, with the cannon-proof granary serving as the central redoubt. The Austrian attacks failed. Just as the day before Aspern had mesmerized Karl's attention, so today Essling became his focal point. To capture the village, he committed his elite grenadiers. During the campaign to date, they had mostly remained in reserve. Now came their chance. Mounted officers, including Baron d'Aspré, vied with the standard-bearers to spearhead the assault. On came a "column of Austrian grenadiers, flags unfurled, with their officers on horseback riding at their front."[18] This fifth attack cleared much of the village except for the massive granary.

It was midday. The French position had shrunk to a line running from the tile works to Essling. The devastating Austrian artillery fire killed men in both the front ranks and in reserve. The nearly flat terrain offered no shelter. As had occurred the previous day, any shots fired high from Bellegarde's cannon flew over Aspern to hit the rear of the French right wing while Liechtenstein's long shots landed in the rear of the French left. One French artilleryman wrote, "All the ground behind the battleline was literally furrowed by the enemy's projectiles."[19] Total defeat appeared imminent.

THE COST OF GLORY[20]

Napoleon had foreseen the possibility that Essling would fall and retained in hand the foot soldiers of his Imperial Guard, the most renowned fighting men in Europe. The Imperial Guard infantry along with one foot battery had crossed over from Lobau around dawn. Their introduction to the battle had been hard. Ordered initially to march on Essling, they had been forced to countermarch to Aspern. This required a change of direction that exposed the Guard's right flank to enemy artillery fire. Although the Guard was not in the front line, in the time it took to march a mere 2,000 yards it suffered fearful losses. The accompanying foot battery briefly took position to provide covering fire and, in an unprecedented development, was driven to shelter by overwhelming Austrian fire, losing half its men and horses.[21] Unfazed, the Guard stood ready for whatever its beloved *le Tondu* (the shorn one) required.

Since becoming emperor, Napoleon had seldom required that the Imperial Guard actually engage in battle, a reluctance born from the twin recognition that they were irreplaceable and that they represented his last reserve. Even now he refused to unleash most of them. Instead, to meet the crisis at Essling he released a mere three battalions of his most expendable guardsmen. Known as the Young Guard, they were new additions to the vaunted ranks of the Imperial Guard and consisted of picked conscripts led by veteran non-commissioned and commissioned officers. To assist them in their first battle, Napoleon also committed one of his most reliable aides, General Georges Mouton.

A comrade in arms since his first Italian campaign, Napoleon once joked, "My Mouton [French for "sheep"] is a lion." The emperor had promoted the 39-year-old warrior to general and imperial aide. To be an imperial aide meant one was at the apex of courage in an army of brave men. It also meant that regardless of past feats, a fresh demonstration of devotion to the emperor might be required at any time. Already during the campaign Mouton had led a storming column across the Landshut bridge into the face of point-blank enemy fire.[22] Now he returned to the front ranks. Placing himself at the head of the attack column, Mouton led the onslaught of the Young Guard Tirailleurs against Essling. Although Mouton quickly received a wound, his counterattack stopped cold the advance of the Austrian grenadiers. Then the tirailleurs's impetus stalled. Again showing that his finger was on the battle's tactical pulse, Napoleon sent in two more Young Guard battalions along with another of his top aides, the Alsatianborn Jean Rapp. He told Rapp to relieve the pressure on Mouton and then concede Essling, withdraw, and form a line facing the village.

Rapp marched the Young Guard Fusiliers into Essling and halted them behind Mouton's men. He told Mouton about his orders and then said, "You have over-awed those masses by your resistance; let us charge them with the bayonet . . . if we succeed, the Emperor and the army will give us credit for our success; if we fail, the responsibility will rest with me." Mouton replied, "With both of us." The two imperial aides, exhibiting a fine disregard for orders, hurled their five battalions into a desperate, winner-take-all attack. Enemy fire wounded both General Gros, who commanded the Young Guard Fusiliers, and the commander of the division, Compte Curial. By the narrowest, French élan won out. The Young Guardsmen lost one-quarter of their effective strength but managed to evict the last group of defending Hungarian grenadiers from most of the village, bayoneting those who attempted to surrender. After this exploit, Rapp returned to the emperor who greeted him with the words: "If ever you did well by disregarding my orders, you have done so today; because the army's salvation depended upon the recapture of Essling."[23] Yet it was Mouton he honored the highest, raising him to the ranks of the imperial nobility with the title Count Lobau. Many years later, Napoleon reiterated that the personal bravery of Rapp and Mouton had decided the battle.

The Young Guard's counterattack against Essling closed out the maneuver portion of the battle. Karl had committed all of his reserves. Napoleon had only Demont's conscripts, whom he believed incapable of doing anything more than defending the earthworks at the tête de pont, and the Old Guard. The conflict degenerated into an artillery duel, with the Austrians doing most of the firing. Although directed aimlessly into the smoke, their bounding cannonballs continued to thin the French ranks. The French guns, nearly out of ammunition, made no response. At Napoleon's direction, artillerist Seruzier formed 24 guns in the belt of woods in front of the tête de pont. The gunners hastily took axes to the underbrush to clear fields of fire. Seruzier then addressed his weary men: "You know that the artillery is the soul of the army, and that the glory of this arm has never been tarnished since its origin: swear to be buried here, rather than fail to save the Grande Armée!" The gunners shouted a pledge to save the army or to die. Seruzier replied that with such fortitude the army would be saved.[24] Then the gunners resumed preparations for what they believed would be a last-ditch defense.

Napoleon recognized that he faced defeat and so undertook to limit its scale. At 12:30 P.M. he dictated a remarkable message showing that amid the din of battle he was thinking ahead. He ordered Davout to notify Marshal Bernadotte, who was defending the French line of communications all the way back in Bohemia, to suspend any offensive. The emperor did not want Bernadotte to become embroiled in fighting pending the outcome of the action at Aspern-Essling. Davout was also to inform Count Pierre Daru, the Intendant Général (Quartermaster General) to hasten the ambulances and food to Lobau, where they would surely be needed. Finally, once the bridge was rebuilt, Davout was to come to Lobau to meet with the emperor.

Davout received these instructions with an enormous sense of frustration. He appreciated that the balance of the Army of Germany was fighting for its life and that he could do little to assist it. Much of Vienna's population had taken to the rooftops to watch the battle, and the obvious signs of Hapsburg success had made them restive. The Iron Marshal ordered Doumerc's cuirassiers to parade through Vienna to cool their ardor, did what he could to send ammunition to the beleaguered army, and waited for the bridge to be rebuilt.

Back on the far shore, Napoleon's position had constricted to an area bounded by Aspern, Essling, and the Danube. For six hours, the French light horse could do little more than stand in line behind the artillery and suffer under a barrage of Austrian cannon fire. Although suffering from a chest wound, Marulaz remained with his troopers. Finally, at 5 P.M. they withdrew behind the thin shelter of the trees screening the tête de pont. The cuirassiers likewise could no longer endure the bombardment, and they too withdrew behind the infantry. Even close to the tête de pont they found no shelter. An imperial aide recalls that "the enemy cannon still hit them, and soon [the Austrian] shots were even reaching the banks of the Danube to our rear" where they struck the wounded waiting to cross to Lobau.[25]

It was the duty of the grognards of the Old Guard to offer a bold front to the Austrians by stretching out in line in front of the tête de point. Their mere presence served to strengthen French resolve. They never fired their muskets yet still absorbed significant losses as Austrian cannonballs skipped through their ranks. A 21-year-old guardsman who received three wounds during this phase of the battle compared the intensity of the bombardment to a thunderstorm.[26] The commander of the Old Guard, Lieutenant General Dorsenne, remained mounted and motionless in front of his men as if participating in a review. Two times cannonballs killed his horses, and two times he picked himself up and resumed his position. A third time a howitzer shell exploded, knocking him down and covering him with dust. This was too much. Dorsenne was a fussy dresser well known for his immaculate appearance regardless of conditions. Standing up and dusting himself off, Dorsenne spat out "Bunglers!" and returned to his position.[27] Finally, resentful of such enforced inactivity, he requested permission to lead an all-out charge and win the battle. The emperor responded no; the battle appeared to be petering out, and it was best that it should end thus.

By battle's end Napoleon was no longer on the right bank. Shortly after 2 P.M. he had summoned his marshals and instructed them how he intended to conduct his retreat. After ensuring that the Austrian army was a spent force, around 4 P.M. he retired to Lobau. The scene in the French rear was so chaotic that many soldiers no longer responded to the magic of being in the emperor's presence. Savary had to use the flat of his sword to clear a path so Napoleon could traverse the bridge.[28] So severe had the Danube's flooding become that the small stream in the middle of the island, a stream easily fordable to men and wagons the day before, had become an impassable barrier. Napoleon directed some of his over-worked engineers to build a trestle bridge across this stream.

At 7 P.M., Napoleon summoned his marshals to Lobau for a conference. Guarded by a four-man square of Imperial Guard Chasseurs à Cheval, the emperor asked what he should do. Berthier recommended a complete withdrawal, including the abandonment of Vienna. Amid talk of retreat, Massena said he preferred to cling to the bridgehead. Davout interjected that if his corps could cross the river, victory could still be earned. Napoleon applauded Massena's and Davout's ardor, but how, he asked, could the army continue to depend on the insubstantial lifeline of the Danube bridges. If it remained on the far shore and suffered a defeat, the army would have to leave behind its wounded and flee. The retreat might not stop until the army reached the Rhine. It was too much to risk. He would have to wait for another day to try conclusions with Karl, a day when the bridges could be properly secured and reinforcements from Italy, Styria, Bohemia, and France would be at hand. For the present, Napoleon instructed Massena to take command of the retreat. He ambitiously asked Massena to maintain a French bridgehead on the right bank while the bulk of the army retired to Lobau. As the conference ended and the generals began to return to their commands, the emperor saw some French carabiniers approaching with a cape slung between their hands and a body resting upon it. It was Lannes.

So lethal had been the Austrian cannonade that toward battle's end, Lannes had been forced to dismount and sit down to watch his men's final withdrawal.[29] While sitting with one leg atop the other, a ricocheting cannonball caught him just where his legs crossed. The ball smashed the top knee pan and tore the sinews of the other knee. Aides carried Lannes to the tête de pont, where surgeon Larrey had established a field hospital. Larrey had already experienced a far too busy day. The casualties among the guard fusiliers alone had been enough to fill his flying ambulances. When soldiers brought Lannes to his attention, he found a man with a pale face and gray skin caused by blood loss. Bloody, swollen tissue surrounded a gaping knee wound that exposed detached ligaments, fractured bones, and a severed artery. Larrey was certain that the marshal's left leg required amputation. Larrey had always believed that immediate amputation gave a patient the best chance of recovery. Yvan, Napoleon's personal physician, disagreed. He maintained that in the May heat, a fever would certainly follow radical surgery; instead they should dress the wound and then rely upon Lannes's renowned spirit to see him through. After some debate Larrey prevailed, and in a two minute operation he removed the marshal's leg.[30]

It was while he was being carried from the field hospital onto Lobau, that a shocked Napoleon recognized him. Napoleon hurried to Lannes's side and knelt. In a choking voice he asked: "Lannes, my friend, do you recognize me? . . . It is me. . . . It is the emperor . . . it is Bonaparte, your friend! . . . Lannes . . . Lannes, you must live for us!"

The ashen-faced marshal opened his eyes and weakly replied: "I want to

live . . . if I can serve you again . . . if I can serve France. . . . But I think that
before an hour is over . . . you will lose . . . he who has been your best friend."[31]

Then the Gascon lapsed into silence, and a distraught Napoleon, his waistcoat
smeared with his friend's blood, retired from the scene.

The experience so unnerved Napoleon that some hours later he abandoned
his entire army. He summoned a small group of men to row him back to the
safety of the Danube's left bank. The emperor undoubtedly believed that there
were compelling reasons for him to do so. From the Vienna side of the river, he
could facilitate the flow of supplies needed by his battered force on Lobau. He
would be in position to direct the defense should Karl try to cross anywhere along
the Danube. And until the bridges were rebuilt, only from the left bank could
he attend to the myriad demands of being head of state of a highly centralized
government. The image of Napoleon turning his back on his wounded army is
not a pretty one and is reminiscent of similar incidents. Back in 1799, when it
became clear that his grandiose schemes were doomed, he had abandoned his
army in Egypt. In 1812, during the retreat from Moscow, Napoleon would leave
his crippled army mired in a Russian winter and speed away to Paris. In 1815 he
would depart from the scene of his greatest defeat at Waterloo, leaving his men
to fend for themselves. In a word, his conduct on May 22, 1809, was typical, and
it suggests that the emperor was a poor loser indeed.

Before departing Lobau, Napoleon looked at his watch. It was 11 P.M. He told
Berthier, "The time has come; give the order for retreat." With difficulty, for the
night was very windy, a junior aide lit a torch. With the feeble illumination
provided by its flickering light, a senior aide wrote out the two-line order using
his sabretache as a desk. Berthier signed it, and Napoleon told an aide to take
the order to Marshals Massena and Bessières. Recalls an eyewitness, "The next
moment, showing no anxiety in spite of the pitchy darkness and of the rising
storm . . . he stepped into the boat . . . the moorings were cast loose, and the bark
shot forward like an arrow from a bow, and in an instant it had disappeared."[32]

Back on the right bank, a carefully orchestrated flow began crossing to Lobau.
First came the wounded, followed by the wagons and cannon, and then the
majority of the fighting formations. By 3:30 A.M. the retreat was complete, and
the pontoon bridge lifted. It was in a nick of time. Austrian skirmishers pressed
in against the tête de pont and exchanged fire with voltigeurs belonging to the
18th Ligne who remained to provide a rear guard. Massena had wisely chosen to
disregard Napoleon's desire to preserve the tête de pont and provided two fishing
barks to carry the last voltigeurs to safety. The marshal was among the last to
evacuate the right bank. At one point a nervous pontonnier captain asked if it
were not time to lift the bridge. Massena snapped, "No, it is not yet time! I will
spend the entire morning here if necessary, before leaving the Austrians a single
cuirass or a single horse."[33]

Indeed, Massena conducted a remarkably clean retreat. The only cannon left
behind had been dismounted by hostile fire during the battle. Very few wounded

and little equipment were abandoned. However, nothing could disguise the enormity of this, the first defeat Napoleon suffered since becoming emperor.

At 5 A.M. on May 23, Karl learned that the French had retreated to Lobau. He forgot entirely about his original plan to line the Danube with artillery and bombard Lobau. It was an amazing oversight compounded, during subsequent days, by his willingness to cancel various other offensive combinations because of poor weather. In Karl's defense it must be said that he keenly felt logistical constraints imposed by the prior loss of numerous supply depots and the abandonment of Vienna's well-stocked arsenal. In particular, his artillery had used up a prodigious amount of ammunition, and resupply was difficult. Four hours after learning of the French withdrawal, the Austrian generalissimus dictated a report to his brother, the kaiser. Karl began by praising the spirit and conduct of his army. The battle had been, he wrote, "a combat of giants."[34] It was also a magnificent Austrian feat of arms, a victory earned by the combination of Karl's iron determination and the willingness of his soldiers to stand and trade casualties with the French for 36 long hours. Precise Austrian staffers recorded the army's losses at 4,288 soldiers and officers killed; 16,326 wounded including 12 generals; 1,903 missing; and 837 prisoners.[35] The erzherzog concluded his report to his brother with the observation that the battle had removed Napoleon's aura of invincibility.

Kaiser Franz had watched the battle from the Bisamberg. Most of the action had been obscured by the dense smoke that engulfed the village fighting. When the combat extended into the more clearly visible Marchfeld on the second day, Franz had seen his army bend before Lannes's attack and had feared the worst. When he received Karl's after-action report, the kaiser responded ecstatically. Quickly he mounted and rode toward his brother's headquarters. He emptied his purse at the feet of the first Austrian soldiers he encountered and gleefully shouted out his praise. Seeing some French prisoners, he demanded that his aides "remove these horrible people from my eyes."[36] Relations between the brothers had never been easy, but in his joy, Franz forgot past resentments. Entering Karl's headquarters, he embraced his brother, telling him that he had saved the monarchy. The shy Karl was taken aback by this lavish display of emotion. Modestly, he attributed the victory to the leadership of Prince Jean Liechtenstein. Then the brothers reviewed the army. It proved a stirring tonic as the men cheered themselves hoarse in praise of their kaiser and their country.

In a letter written the next day, Franz again heaped fulsome praise on Karl. The victory had interrupted 15 years of French victories, a feat for which Franz vowed eternal thanks. Alluding to the emotional enthusiasm with which the army had greeted him, the kaiser concluded that it had been the happiest day of his life. In his joy he awarded the army a special ration of meat and wine. The army, in turn, had not been accustomed to victory, and they showed they could celebrate in style. Their camps resounded with laughter, cheers, and patriotic music played by regimental bands.[37] The next day the army held a Te Deum (a religious service of praise) and then continued with its joyous celebration.

News of the victory spread like wildfire. Karl's chief of staff ordered that church bells in all villages within 40 kilometers toll triumphantly. In Vienna an Austrian bulletin circulated that listed French losses as a staggering 22,000 killed and an additional 62,000 wounded or captured. The upper class nodded sagely and whispered that surely this must mark the end of the Corsican adventurer's reign. Within six days, a proud, much exaggerated announcement of Napoleon's defeat had been printed and circulated throughout the Hapsburg Empire. Some patriot nailed a copy to the wall of French-held Ratisbonne. Effective Austrian propaganda served to stimulate the spreading fire of German nationalism and to encourage the ongoing guerrilla insurrection in the Tyrol. Word of Napoleon's defeat rapidly reached Europe's distant capitals. On June 9 the *Times* of London carried Napoleon's Tenth Bulletin, containing his battle report, which had been smuggled across the channel by some enterprising watermen only sixteen days after it had been written at Napoleon's headquarters on the Danube. As the facts emerged, British papers gleefully trumpeted the news of Bonaparte's setback.

Meanwhile, Karl's soldiers proceeded with the unpleasant business of policing the battlefield. They recovered many abandoned French cuirasses and some 14,000 discarded muskets.[38] There were few other trophies of battle. Massena had left behind a mere three dismounted canon. The Danube continued to rise, forcing most of the Austrians to retire to higher ground. A thin infantry screen remained along the Danube shore where soldiers fortified themselves behind earthworks. The flooding and rain contributed to an onslaught of typhus that struck Karl's warriors. On May 27 a heavy rain exposed hundreds of hastily dug graves. The next day unfortunate peasants dug deep trenches to reinter the dead. The day after, they began to bury or burn the thousands of slaughtered horses whose lifeless bodies had begun to spread pestilence. Then, while the local inhabitants tried to resume their shattered lives, Karl's army waited to see what the terrible Corsican would do next.

The 48 hours following the battle were a time of great misery for the French soldiers isolated on Lobau Island. Napoleon had so rushed his offensive that there had been no time to make such fundamental logistical preparations as the establishment of medical facilities. Now the entire island seemed to be one great casualty clearing ground, a field hospital lacking medical supplies. Surgeons labored hour after hour in their makeshift, open-air operating rooms with nothing but branches and overcoats for a roof and leaves and a few blankets for beds. In the absence of the emperor, there was overwhelming confusion. Men who had been separated from their commands showed little inclination to rejoin the ranks. Most had not eaten since the predawn hours of May 22. When they retreated to the island, they found little food. Even generals had to beg for a drink or a morsel of biscuit.[38] So thoroughly had the connection with the far bank been severed that the badly wounded Lannes, a man who surely had priority over all save

Napoleon himself, could not be carried across the river until the early morning of the twenty-third. Thousands of wounded soldiers lay in the mud for up to 36 hours before receiving medical attention and being evacuated. Everywhere, recalls a survivor, one heard the "cries of despair and pain."[40]

Baron Larrey led by example. He ordered horses slaughtered to make a bouillon to feed the wounded. When General Boudet, in an effort to preserve his valuable headquarters mounts, vehemently resisted and threatened to take the matter to the emperor, Larrey replied that Boudet could do what he wanted, but the slaughter would take place regardless. The first horses killed belonged to Larrey. After the event Napoleon challenged Larrey, asking if it were true that he had ordered the soldiers to eat their general's horses. Larrey replied, "Yes, and he would do it again if need dictated." Furthermore, Larrey continued with some heat, Boudet had remained mounted on his precious horse while Larrey had slaughtered his own horses to feed Boudet's wounded! Napoleon affectionately pinched the surgeon's ear and told him he had done right.[41] The slaughter was hard on cavalrymen who had grown attached to their mounts. The day after the battle, one officer went looking for his wounded horse and found nothing left except the skin still attached to the bridle.[42]

When Napoleon had reached safety on the river's left bank, he had been so exhausted that he required assistance to walk from the landing into nearby Ebersdorf. Already once before during the campaign the emperor had exhibited what he called "the courage of 2:00 A.M." By this he understood the courage to respond to emergencies with "freedom of mind, judgment, and decision completely unaffected" by events.[43] Napoleon believed he possessed this courage to a higher extent than his contemporaries, and now again he demonstrated why. Overcoming his exhaustion, he rallied to dispatch orders to Davout and Quartermaster General Daru to forward supplies and food to the army on Lobau.[44] After a mere two-hour repose, Napoleon rose on May 23 to arrange the supply of his defeated army on Lobau. Next he inspected Davout's corps and then proceeded to put in a full day of work.

In spite of Napoleon's orders and his display of concerned energy, there was only so much anyone could do until the main bridge was fully restored. Davout organized a boat shuttle to bring bread to the island and to return with the wounded. Still, on the day after the battle, there was only enough to provide one loaf for each 12 men. Since there was so little to eat, the slaughter of the horses continued. Soldier diaries are replete with mention of how they were so famished that unseasoned, half-cooked horsemeat provided a meal of unsurpassed delight. The Austrian prisoners went unfed.

Meanwhile, Austrian efforts to break the bridge continued unabated. On the twenty-third, stone-laden Austrian boats again shattered the still-flimsy structure. Happily, back on March 9 Napoleon had asked Vice Admiral Decrès to provide him with a battalion of sailors who understood small boat operations (and who could swim). The day after the battle 1,200 sailors caught up with the army in time to relieve the exhausted pontonniers and rebuild the bridge by May 24.

Concurrently a dismal rain fell, soaking the already sodden encampment. While cursing the skies, the grognards did not know that this same rain had flooded the opposite bank and foiled Karl's plans to attack. Napoleon firmly believed that French soldiers exhibited fortitude only if they perceived they were participating in a winning campaign. In later life he would comment that a single lost battle negated a Frenchman's fortitude and courage, reduced his confidence in his superiors, and promoted insubordination. Yet this did not take place after Aspern-Essling in large part because the men in the ranks agreed with Napoleon that it had been the Danube that had defeated them, not the sausage-eating whitecoats.

Typically, French casualty accounting was indifferent, making it difficult to know how many men in the Army of Germany fell during the two-day battle. The French Tenth Bulletin tabulated losses at 4,100 men, an entirely fallacious figure underscoring the saying "to lie like a bulletin." Certain concrete figures are known. Molitor's division lost 79 officers and 2,107 men killed and wounded, a solid third of its strength.[45] Most of the losses occurred during its epic defense of Aspern on May 21. Boudet's three regiments that defended Essling entered the battle with 167 officers and lost 54 killed or wounded.[46] During Saint-Hilaires's 3-hour eruption onto the Marchfeld, 130 of 252 officers were hit, including 3 out of every 4 in the "Terrible 57th" Ligne.[47] The number of killed and wounded cavalry leaders underscored the fact that the French mounted arm had behaved with heroic self-sacrifice. All 4 colonels leading Marulaz's chasseurs regiments were wounded. Espagne's cuirassiers lost 61 of its 109 officers.[48] Half of Lasalle's division were casualties. Neither the artillery nor the Imperial Guard was spared. The IV Corps Artillery lost 74 men killed and 201 wounded.[49] French soldiers buried 243 guardsmen and retrieved 943 wounded from the field. These specific totals hint at the stupendous overall French losses that probably exceeded 22,000.[50] In time many of the wounded would return to the ranks, but the majority of those who did not were irreplaceable men who had once trained with the Grande Armée.

Austrian fire had subtracted a large toll from the army's high command as well. When Saint-Hilaire received his wound, field surgeons had recommended amputation. The general refused. In Larrey's opinion, the surgeons then botched the operation they did perform. Still, in the ensuing days it seemed Saint-Hilaire had chosen wisely, but then he contracted tetanus and succumbed. Napoleon noted Saint-Hilaire had been a comrade since Toulon and was called, in reference to Bayard, "the knight without fear and without reproach." Marked for higher command, Saint-Hilaire was one of those leaders whose abilities had permitted his soldiers to triumph against great odds. The able cuirassier General Espagne along with Lannes's good friend, General Pouzet, also died at Aspern-Essling. Seven divisional generals received wounds during the battle, with Legrand heading the list with one wound on each day. Nine brigadiers, four of whom served in the cavalry, had been hit. Cuirassier Brigadier General Lelièvre de Lagrange had his arm amputated. Included in the ranks of the wounded were two Württemberg generals.

At first the army's most famous casualty, Jean Lannes, seemed to be recovering nicely. The Gascon spoke optimistically of how he could be fitted with the latest in artificial limbs and manage to ride. Napoleon visited him twice daily. Berthier and many other high-ranking officers came often, and his devoted aides hovered around to attend closely to his every need. Then, on the fifth day, septic infection set in and slowly advanced toward its inevitable conclusion. Like another indomitable warrior 54 years later, Stonewall Jackson, as Lannes became delirious he called for his officers, dispatched aides to summon the artillery, ordered the cavalry to charge, demanded reinforcements. At daybreak on May 30, 1809, he died, the first of Napoleon's marshals to fall.

On numerous occasions Napoleon snapped that his marshals believed themselves "indispensable." He said that they failed to realize that there were "a hundred division commanders who can take their place."[51] Yet for the remainder of his days as head of the French state, Napoleon would grapple with the vexing problem of finding capable generals for independent army command. The emperor also said that at the time of his death, Lannes was without peer as a subordinate when commanding a force up to 25,000 on the field of battle. Lannes, only 40 years old when he died, had applied himself to his art and constantly improved his martial skills. Napoleon believed that had Lannes lived, he would have risen to the challenge of higher strategy. His death left a deep void in the empire's command structure.

Until his dying days, Napoleon denied that he had lost this battle. He would make the specious claim that the French had held the field until voluntarily retiring and blamed even this result on the river, not the Austrians. It was not his way to admit fault, but in fact the emperor had committed many fundamental errors. In 1806 Napoleon had said that everything about war required profound calculation and that the absence of thorough preparation leads to a "totally ineffectual" result.[52] During the Aspern-Essling campaign, the Great Captain violated his own dictate. His most important errors stemmed from the speed with which he pressed the offensive. He had waited for neither the arrival of the battalion of sailors (who might have staved off the small boats that pelted his bridge; remember that these sailors completed a bridge on the twenty-third amid conditions that defeated the regular engineers and pontonniers the two previous days) nor for the accumulation of bridging material. Instead, as soon as his pontonniers had completed a rudimentary bridge, he had sent his combat units across to Lobau. As soon as he had massed a striking force, he had crossed to the Austrian shore to engage. The bridge had been constantly packed with troops, leaving little opportunity for supply wagons to pass. Ammunition reserves, supply depots, and field hospitals were not built, and because they were not, the combat soldiers ran out of ammunition during the battle, the soldiers starved once they returned to Lobau, and the wounded went unattended. The frequent breakages demonstrated that the bridge was a poorly built, rickety structure, another consequence of surpassing haste. The careless French reconnaissance on battle's eve can also be attributed to a misguided mandate for speed. The battle proved that even a Great Captain overlooks the basics of his craft at peril of defeat. So eager was he to try conclusions with the enemy that a bold scheme became a rash gamble. Although Napoleon never acknowledged any of this, the way he prepared his next offensive showed he had absorbed some of the lessons of Aspern-Essling and that he could still learn from his mistakes.

On the other hand, he did recognize his overwhelming debt to André Massena. For two days Massena had exhibited the tenacity that had won him renown in 1799 at Zurich and in 1800 at Genoa. It was a rare blend of tactical acumen and personal bravery. The next year Napoleon would reward Massena with the title Prince of Essling. He never adequately acknowledged the efforts of his pontonniers and engineers. For all their difficulties, they had saved the army by preserving a path of retreat. Only in 1812 at the Beresina would they do more to serve Napoleon's army.

Why had Karl failed to accomplish more? First and foremost, he had set a limited goal for his army. His attack order specified that the objective was to drive the French back to Lobau and destroy their bridges, not to destroy the French army. By his own measure, Karl had done what he set out to do. Napoleon would never have been content with such an objective. One of his maxims applied to Karl's situation: "When two armies are in order of battle, and one has to retire over a bridge, while the other has the circumference of the circle open, all the advantages are in favour of the latter. It is then a general should show boldness. . . . The victory is in his hands."[53]

Part of Karl's inability to coordinate his attacks better stemmed from the battlefield's geography. He operated on long exterior lines against a foe drawn up in a compact semicircle. Napoleon, mounted near the middle of his position, could readily see tactical crises unfold and, by virtue of his interior lines, rush his reserves quickly to the threatened sector. Karl had to depend on couriers to carry his orders to distant commands. Unable himself to respond immediately to opportunity and peril, he had to rely on his subordinates. Unlike the French army, subordinate initiative had never been a hallmark of the Hapsburg military. Consequently Karl's attacks proceeded ponderously, featuring repeated assaults against the same sector. Since the front was narrow and both villages well lent themselves to defense, any assault was bound to degenerate into a frontal attrition battle. But there was a more fundamental flaw in Karl's battle management and it was something that seemed endemic to the Austrian war machine. Back in 1797, an astute British observer of the Italian campaign noted that "the Austrians persisted in dividing their forces and in making partial attacks."[54] This comment applied equally to 1809.

Karl's second important error had been the unwarranted attention he devoted to Aspern the first day and to Essling on the second. These strongholds attracted his energy and reserves like a magnet. If he had simultaneously advanced against the center, particularly on the first day, a greater victory would surely have been his. Moreover, according to Savary, Napoleon worried that during the days after the battle, if Karl maneuvered aggressively against the French line of communications, he would have had to abandon Vienna and retreat.[55] Karl's postbattle inertia was a great gift to the French cause.

Tactically, the battle witnessed two developments. It had been the first field test of the Austrian battalion mass, and the formation had proved nearly as solid as a square when confronting cavalry while providing more firepower and capability of maneuver. Karl particularly praised this formation in his postbattle report. The French infantry, on the other hand, had been forced to employ more massive formations than had been the Grande Armée's habit. Too many confident, well-trained veterans were either absent in Spain, maimed, or dead, their ranks replaced by less skilled conscripts. As Savary observed, French colonels and generals showed less confidence in them and thus kept them in close formation because of the nearby enemy cavalry. The employment by both sides of heavy formations had much to do with the battle's fearful carnage. Coupled with the billiard table–like flatness of the Marchfeld, Aspern-Essling had been a nearly perfect killing ground for the artillery.

The weeks following Aspern-Essling were an anxious time for French and French-allied governors in occupied Europe. With the Army of Germany penned up on Lobau and along the Danube, French agents reported numerous conspiracies and predicted outright revolt. Let us now take leave of the wounded armies outside of Vienna and see how French and Austrian diplomatic and strategic initiatives fared in the wake of Napoleon's first defeat and then how operations in adjacent theaters affected the next great battle.

Chapter 5

TOUR DE HORIZON

At home as abroad, I reign only through the fear I inspire. If I renounced this system, I would be dethroned before long. This is my position, and these are the motives that guide me.[1]

BUDA

The kaiser's daughter, 18-year-old Marie-Louise, has been taught since early childhood that Napoleon Bonaparte is a monster. Back in April she greeted news that Napoleon had joined battle against her uncle Karl's army with the fervent wish that the Corsican ogre "lose his head." When the fugitive Austrian court in Buda hears the news of Aspern-Essling, she confides her feelings to a friend: "It's the first time that Napoleon himself has been defeated, and we must thank God for it . . . but we mustn't be too puffed up with pride because of this victory, and I must confess that I'm so accustomed to disappointments, that I daren't hope for too much."[2] In five months this young, ignorant woman will emerge on the world stage in a leading role.

LONDON

Since 1793 Britain has repeatedly bankrolled opposition to France. The loss of trade revenue caused by Napoleon's Continental System—a series of measures designed to force an economic blockade on the British isles—inhibits the munificence of the past. But memories of British money and gunpowder are fresh among those who plot opposition to French rule. Consequently, the late winter and early spring of 1809 witnessed a stream of visitors to London, with everyone promising great things if only they received money and perhaps help from a few British troops.

Prussian patriot Ludwig von Kleist met with Foreign Secretary George Canning and claimed to represent Berlin's central insurrectionary committee. Kleist wanted Britain to establish an arms depot off the Danish coast and requested at least 50,000 pounds sterling in specie for immediate expenses. Hapsburg agents initially asked for the stupendous sum of 7.5 million pounds sterling. When Canning objected, they reduced it to 2 million along with a 400,000-pound monthly subsidy. They also requested a British descent somewhere along the north German coast. In addition, the Austrian envoy to the Papal states urged a British landing on the Italian coast to support a popular uprising against the French.

The problem of Canning and fellow British strategists was to assess the many schemes and to allocate scarce resources months in advance of the proposed action's taking place. They asked, What assurances can all these foreign agents provide that they will actually implement their plans?

Canning and his government decide to proceed cautiously. Unaware that the war was just weeks away, early in April, the Royal Navy had delivered 250,000 pounds in silver to an Austrian port in Illyria and established a military chest in excess of 750,000 pounds on Malta for Austrian use in the event of war. They assured the Prussian Kleist that an arms depot would be established on the island of Heligoland and that Kleist, accompanied by a British agent, would receive a letter of credit for 20,000 pounds once he returned to Hamburg.

Finally, in lieu of other plans, the cabinet resolves to capture the great French naval base at Antwerp. The first step is an amphibious invasion of the island of Walcheren in the Scheldt estuary. A massive fleet and a good-sized infantry force begins to assemble for the first substantial strike across the channel in a decade.

HAMBURG

The Continental System continues to fail, its blockade of the British Isles porous and ineffective. Trade through Oldenburg takes place as if in peacetime, with English goods, letters, and newspapers arriving in regular fashion. The return trip takes French goods and papers to England. In one skirmish on the coast, the locals attack French customs house officials, and recapture 18 wagon loads of English contraband goods. Hamburg prefers subtlety. When word circulates that certain Hamburg streets are to be repaired, smugglers fill the sand wagons with brown sugar brought through the blockade and carry the scarce commodity into the city to sell at huge profit. Finally the lack of progress at road repair alerts French officials, and they put an end to this operation.

Customs agents observe that a certain small coastal village seems to have an extraordinary mortality rate. Regular funeral convoys travel from the village to Hamburg where the dead are buried. When an officer insists on searching a hearse, he finds sugar, coffee, vanilla, and indigo—scarce commodities smuggled by British traders onto the Continent. So it goes along the entire coast of the French Empire, a debilitating corruption that reaches high into the ranks of French leadership—all the way up to the government, marshalate, and Napoleon's immediate family.

BERLIN

Major von Schill had gained renown at the siege of Kolberg during the 1806–1807 war. For his conduct he received the command of a splendid regiment of Brandenburg hussars. On April 28 he leads them from the depot near Berlin on a madcap dash across Pomerania in an effort to ignite a popular insurrection against the French.

Initially Schill enjoys some success, particularly since the man charged with stopping him—Napoleon's younger brother and the King of Westphalia, Jerome Bonaparte—exhibits far more interest in a pretty actress featured in the Kassel theater than in chasing Schill. So inattentive is Jerome that one of his aides-de-camp manages to create a small mutiny within the ranks of his bodyguard. Meanwhile, Schill invades Mecklenburg, levies contributions on both banks of the Elbe, and inspires terror among the French garrison commanders. Schill's exploits create a conundrum for Prussian authorities.

For some time, Austrian diplomats have been meeting secretly with the Prussians in an effort to enlist Prussia in the war. Simultaneously, army officers have begun a comprehensive reform of the military. Then comes news of Aspern-Essling. The Prussian king is tempted mightily, but his fear of the French is strong. Keeping an eye on the main chance, he writes to Kaiser Franz to urge one more victory and to promise that after that victory he will declare war against France. Then the king attends to the disobedient Schill by disavowing his conduct. The timid Prussian leader does not know that all along Napoleon had denigrated the likelihood of Prussian intervention: "The idea of Prussia declaring war with us is folly."[3] He instructs his Minister of War to ignore the Prussian threat.

Isolated in the heart of enemy territory, refused assistance by his own army, Schill leads his men on a desperate ride to the coast, where he hopes to find succor from the Royal Navy. As he approaches Hamburg, the nervous garrison sends the customs house chest under strong escort to Holstein. Pursued by Dutch and Danish troops, Schill is finally cornered in the north German port of Straslund. Operating under orders to take no prisoners, the French allies engage Schill and his men in a desperate battle in the streets of the port. A French officer relates what transpired: "All the troop of Schill was then massacred—a half-hour of combat sufficed."[4]

ROME

At the opposite end of Europe, Pope Pius VII learns of Napoleon's decree that annexes the Roman states into the French Empire. Pius responds with a bull of excommunication that says in part, "Let monarchs once more learn that by the law of Jesus Christ that they are subjected to our throne."[5] It does not quite work out that way. Napoleon responds to the Papal Bull by writing to his brother-in-law, Joachim Murat, the King of Naples: "This instant I have received the news that the pope has excommunicated all of us. By this he has excommunicated himself. No more regard for him! He is a raving madman and must be locked up."[6]

The impact of the dispute is to give devout Catholics, particularly in Italy, Tyrolia, and Spain, another motive to resist French hegemony. Sensing opportunity, Austrian strategists send clear orders to its minister to the Papal States. His task is to "organize an Italian uprising" against the French.[7]

MOSCOW

While the British hover off the French-held coast and various factions work to spark guerrilla warfare against Napoleon, no other piece on the strategic chessboard exceeds the importance of imperial Russia and its impressionable Czar, Alexander. Napoleon understands that he possesses an alliance with Russia that requires Alexander to join the French against Austria. To cement the alliance Napoleon has granted free rein for Czar Alexander to add Finland, Moldavia, Walachia, and a part of Galicia to his empire. He appreciates neither that his Minister of Foreign Affairs, Karl Talleyrand-Périgord has betrayed his cause to the Russians nor that skillful Austrian and British diplomacy has been at work to foil him. Although Russia dutifully declares war against Austria, its armies do not engage. Each week brings another courier from St. Petersburg to assure Napoleon that an offensive is imminent, but they mislead. Slowly Napoleon realizes that Alexander is playing him false, conduct that infuriates him. The emperor can do nothing about it until he defeats the Austrians, so on the surface he maintains amicable relations with Alexander. Inside he simmers and plots revenge.[8]

WARSAW

The Polish people see Napoleon as the great opportunity to restore their nation. Patriotism is what inspired Count Walewska to send his superb young wife to the French emperor's bed in 1807. Hopes for a new nation motivate Josef Poniatowski and his army to fight heroically against an overwhelming Austrian army in 1809.

Yet Polish aspirations are tragically at odds with Napoleon's plans. In 1807 Napoleon instructed his aides to omit any mention of Polish independence from his annual message on the state of the empire because he had yet to explain himself on that subject. In 1810 he will explain, in private, his position: "Poland exists only in the imagination of those who want to use it as a pretext for spinning dreams."[9]

ISTANBUL

The Napoleonic Wars also have an impact on places as far away as Persia—where authorities await the muskets promised by French diplomats, muskets that must be used instead to arm the conscripts to fight the Austrians—and Turkey. In Istanbul, violent change featuring mutinous janissaries hunting Ottoman leaders through subterranean tunnels linking palace and seraglio characterizes recent Turkish politics. It makes for difficult diplomacy among the nations seeking to control the Dardanelles. This strategic waterway is much desired by the czar, who wants his navy to have access to the Mediterranean; by Napoleon, who wishes both to limit Russian expansion and to impose his Continental system on Levantine ports; and by Britain, which takes a proprietary interest in anything having to do with saltwater. As a consequence of the 1808 Treaty of Erfurt, Napoleon has departed from his alliance with the Ottoman Empire in favor of Russian claims to Ottoman territory in Moldavia and Wallachia. This has opened the way for British diplomats to reestablish relations with the Turks.

As international attention focuses on the battles around Vienna, the desultory conflict downstream between Russia and Turkey begins anew and will continue into the next year. The continuing dissolution of the Ottoman Empire provides challenge and opportunity. In August, Serbian rebels will contact Napoleon offering key forts in return for French recognition. Briefly Napoleon flirts with a resumption of his efforts to strike at England via Egypt and even Persia. But these are passing fancies. While the French consolidate newly acquired territory in Illyria, British trade and the Royal Navy hold sway in the Levant. The Ottoman Empire is left to muddle on until the beginning of 1812, when Napoleon will again seek military alliance.

STOCKHOLM

A palace revolution sweeps the erratic (some say crazed) King Gustavus Adolphus from power. The new king must make peace with Russia before more territory is lost. Henceforth, Sweden also must adhere to Napoleon's Continental System, and thus the Royal Navy can no longer depend on Swedish timber for its ships. But this does not overly interfere with friendly relations between Britain and Sweden. Although the British subsidy payments end, British goods continue to arrive in Swedish ports, from where they are transshipped across the Baltic to circumvent the Continental System.

Sweden's new king is elderly, infirm, and childless. Members of the Swedish court consider who will succeed him and recall that Jean-Baptiste Bernadotte, one of Napoleon's marshals, had been exceptionally courteous toward captured

Swedish officers back in 1806. The idea has merit, they decide. Bernadotte bears watching.

WASHINGTON

As was the case before the United States became a nation, rivalry between London and Paris has immense impact on the former British colonies. Both nations are so consumed by their death struggle that they throw international law to the winds and wage war on American commerce. In addition, the Royal Navy's desperate need for manpower to maintain the blockade of Europe prompts British officers to board American ships and impress sailors. When the American frigate *Chesapeake* declined to submit, a British man of war opened fire (although the *Chesapeake* had not even cleared for action) and killed or wounded 21 sailors. In spite of such provocation, American leaders refrain from entering the conflict.

The *Chesapeake* affair changes American public opinion from anti-French to anti-British. Napoleon declines to avail himself of this opportunity. To him, the United States is a nation of "mere merchants" who "put all their glory into making money."[10] Having renounced all territorial ambitions in the Western Hemisphere with the sale of the Louisiana Territory back in 1804, the emperor retains scant interest in American affairs. The fact that the American ambassador in Paris does not even speak French adds to Napoleon's contempt.

American proposals to France to lift decrees aimed at American trade are forwarded to Napoleon in Vienna. The French Minister of Foreign Affairs tells the American ambassador that Napoleon intends to modify his decrees in a manner favorable to U.S. interests. Then comes Aspern-Essling and the realization that nothing regarding the trade issue will be determined until the campaign against Austria is concluded. During his time in Vienna, Napoleon never recognizes the consequences of his American policy. When he does attend, it is only to complain that letters received from President James Madison are addressed "to our great and good friend" and that this salutation (a legacy of the Franco-American alliance that helped give the U.S. its independence) lacks the correct protocol due his position as emperor. Meanwhile, a French warship burns another American merchantman at sea, and British warships continue to impress sailors from American vessels.

President James Madison has a tremendous stake in Napoleon's affairs. The cry of "Free Trade and Sailors' Rights"—two items in short supply because of the Napoleonic Wars—will lead to war with Britain in three years. It is the same year that Napoleon, in an effort to tighten his economic blockade of Britain and because of his desire to punish Alexander for his conduct in 1809, will invade Russia. Napoleon's catastrophic defeat will fatally weaken him, permitting Britain and its allies to drive him from his throne in 1814. British success allows it to spare soldiers to deal with the Americans. They will thrash the defenders of the capital and burn Washington, D.C., before being recalled to Europe to confront a returned exile.

PARIS

France is a police state, and among the many things the state controls are the newspapers. Since becoming emperor, Napoleon has made his position clear, telling editors that he would never tolerate the newspapers acting against his interests. He allowed that they might publish a few little articles with a hint of poison in them, but warned ominously that "one fine morning somebody will shut their mouths."[11] The public keenly follows the army's exploits as reported through the bulletins printed in the pages of Le Moniteur. Years of battlefield success have taught them to expect victory. Blinded by victory, they have not yet learned to read the bulletins with a cynical eye; the phrase "to lie like a bulletin" will soon enter popular usage. Generally they accept constant war as the price to pay for stability and prosperity. Nonetheless, the enormous losses at Aspern-Essling disturb. It is an anxiety fed by the appearance of the Austrian account of the battle that some anti-Bonapartist smuggles to Paris, prints, and circulates. Speaking for many, the Duchess of Abrantes observes, "This campaign, however, was not like that of Austerlitz, crowned with laurels interspersed with flowers: mourning followed in the train of triumph, and every bulletin plunged a thousand families in tears."[12]

Prices fall on the Paris bourse, a sure sign of lack of public confidence. In Brittany, Bourbon sympathizers among the peasants, the chouans, again take up arms. In spite of the police state's control, signs of decay abound. Armed brigands, often composed of deserters and men avoiding conscription, haunt the countryside.[13] Napoleon's apparently insatiable appetite for manpower has triggered enormous opposition. Relentless conscription saps at the people's will. One of Napoleon's astute observers reports that the public's "frightened mind created, each day, new and terrible nightmares."[14] War weariness is manifest by the growing numbers who shrug at news from the front and attend exclusively to their own interests. An active minority seize upon the defeat at Aspern-Essling to plot the downfall of the hated Corsican tyrant.

Although Napoleon's genius is now clouded by self-deception, he understands much of this. It reinforces his conviction that only one thing can set matters right: decisive victory in his next battle.

1. The sieges of Saragossa exemplified Spanish resolve to resist Napoleon's veteran legions. The manpower drain forced Napoleon to fight Austria with numerous conscripts. (Anne S. K. Brown Military Collection, Brown University)

2. Veterans, such as this grenadier corporal, composed about half the French infantry that fought at Aspern-Essling. (Anne S. K. Brown Military Collection, Brown University)

3. The Emperor Napoleon Bonaparte, 40 years old in 1809. (Anne S. K. Brown Military Collection, Brown University)

4. The 38-year-old Generalissimus Erzherzog Karl at Aspern-Essling. (Anne S. K. Brown Military Collection, Brown University)

5. French infantry begin the assault crossing of the swollen Danube. (Anne S. K. Brown Military Collection, Brown University)

6. Aspern church, the tactical key to Napoleon's left flank. (Anne S. K. Brown Military Collection, Brown University)

7. The granary at Essling, the tactical key to Napoleon's right flank. (Author photo)

8. Cavalry combat in the center, Espagne's death, May 21, 1809. (Anne S. K. Brown Military Collection, Brown University)

9. The descendant of the armored knight, a French cuirassier in 1809. (Anne S. K. Brown Military Collection, Brown University)

10. Spearheading French cavalry break against an Austrian square on May 22, 1809. (Anne S. K. Brown Military Collection, Brown University)

11. Napoleon at Aspern-Essling. (Anne S. K. Brown Military Collection, Brown University)

12. Austrian landwehr counterattack the Kis-Megyer farm, Battle of Raab, June 14, 1809. (Anne S. K. Brown Military Collection, Brown University)

13. The Russbach at Baumersdorf where the Army of Italy tried to penetrate Karl's center on July 5, 1809. (Author photo)

14. Having remained saddled overnight, the Austrian cavalry, including these dragoons, was in poor shape for prolonged combat. (Anne S. K. Brown Military Collection, Brown University)

15. View from the tower at Neusiedel. On the plain below, Karl's surprise counteroffensive began on July 6, 1809. (Author photo)

16. At Wagram, only the open French right flank permitted extensive cavalry versus cavalry combats. (Anne S. K. Brown Military Collection, Brown University)

17. The flat Marchfeld, the killing ground ravaged by Austrian artillery firing from the gentle rise in the background behind the Russbach. (Author photo)

18. After Wagram, vicious combat continued in the Tyrol. (Anne S. K. Brown Military Collection, Brown University)

19. Bavarian cavalry confront Tyrolese guerrillas who set fire to a bridge to delay pursuit. (Anne S. K. Brown Military Collection, Brown University)

Chapter 6

IN FLANK AND REAR

The conduct of a general in a conquered country is full of difficulties. If severe, he irritates and increases the number of his enemies. If lenient, he gives birth to expectations which only render the abuses and vexations inseparable from war the more intolerable. A victorious general must know how to employ severity, justice, and mildness by turns, if he would allay sedition, or prevent it.[1]

"THE MUSIC OF THE BRAVE"

In 1796, an unknown French general named Bonaparte had emerged on the world stage during his Italian campaign against the Austrians. In 1800, when Hapsburg strategists concentrated their major forces on the Rhine, Bonaparte had surprised them by crossing the Alps into Italy to seek and win the decisive battle of Marengo. Five years later, Hapsburg planners sent their best army to Italy in a campaign that pitted Erzherzog Karl against Marshal Massena. To the consternation of the Austrian strategists, Napoleon chose this time to make his major thrust across the Rhine. Against this background, in 1809 Karl had again to allocate resources to the central theater along the Danube Valley and to northern Italy.[2] Napoleon counted on the Austrian generalissimus's making a characteristic major dispersion of force. Instead, showing fine strategic ability, Karl created an unprecedented concentration of strength in the Danube valley. He gave his brother, Erzherzog Johann, command in Italy with the triple mission of reconquering as much territory as possible, containing French forces occupying Dalmatia, and raising the Tyrol in revolt. Johann's army numbered almost 100,000 men, of whom only half were regulars. The balance composed landwehr,

Hungarian Insurrection forces, and other reserve units. On April 9, the day the war began, Johann led his field army across the border to invade French territory.

The French commander in Italy was Eugène Beauharnais, Napoleon's stepson. The 28-year-old Eugène had served as Napoleon's aide-de-camp in campaigns past. Napoleon promoted him to general in 1804 and named him Viceroy of Italy the next year. Happily wed that same year to the King of Bavaria's ravishing daughter (Napoleon conceded nothing to the matchmaking machinations of the old European royal houses), Eugène settled into administering his Kingdom of Italy. By all accounts he was one of the most admirable figures in the Napoleonic entourage—kind, generous, and loyal. But he thirsted for military glory. The Austrian invasion provided him with opportunity.

The emperor's strategy relegated Italy to secondary importance. He had ordered the establishment of a fortified line based on the fortress cities between the Mincio and Adige rivers. In the event of an Austrian attack, he wanted Eugène to withdraw to this line until he could muster sufficient force to deliver a counteroffensive. Recognizing his stepson's inexperience, Napoleon drafted a series of notes explaining what Eugène should do under a variety of circumstances.[3] Seldom, until his forced retirement, did Napoleon comprehensively elaborate upon his strategic notions. His "Notes" to Eugène are an exception. They contain explications of many of the emperor's favorite principles: concentration of force prior to battle, use of natural barriers to mask rapid movement and use of interior lines to mass against and defeat enemy detachments. In addition, he surrounded his stepson with experienced officers. They included General Charpentier—an officer who had campaigned in northern Italy with Massena—to act as chief of staff; the veteran General Etienne Macdonald to serve as military adviser; and General Paul Grénier, a distinguished veteran who had served with the Army of the Sambre and Meuse, to command an infantry division.

Eugène worked hard to become a respected military man. He had a keen interest in the military life and had taken to signing himself "Eugène Napoleon."[4] Napoleon, in turn, invested high hopes in him. He had tried to provide the distillation of his own vast experience by issuing comprehensive strategic guidelines and staffing his army with veteran leadership. The problem was that Eugène disregarded the lot and advanced to seek glory by attacking the invading forces.

Erzherzog Johann commanded a two-corps field army; the VIII Corps with 23 battalions and 16 squadrons and the IX Corps with 30 battalions and 28 squadrons. He had detached from this latter corps GM Andreas von Stoichewich with six battalions, a squadron, and two batteries to watch Marmont in Dalmatia.[5] Early on the morning of April 14, Johann learned that one of Eugène's detachments was in the village of Pordenone, east of Sacile. Johann resolved to pounce on this isolated force and marched his army at daybreak. In Pordenone were two French light cavalry regiments and the 35th Ligne Regiment. Converging Austrian columns overwhelmed them. The Hapsburg horse drove their counterparts from the field, leaving the hapless French infantry to fend for themselves. The Austrians quickly surrounded the 35th Ligne. The Hohenzollern Chevaulegers crossed a ravine and found themselves at close quarters with the French infantry in the village. A Captain Martyn led an impetuous charge up the street and captured 300 prisoners. His charge broke the French spirit, and soon the entire regiment surrendered. At small cost the Austrians inflicted 2,100 casualties, destroying half the 6th Hussars and the entire 35th Ligne while bagging 1,800 prisoners and 4 cannon. It was a disastrous introduction to independent command for Eugène.

Although he expected the imminent arrival of reinforcements, the viceroy resolved to restore his fortunes the next day by launching a dawn attack against one Austrian flank while he defended against the opposite Austrian flank. For this operation he commanded about 34,000 infantry and 1,950 cavalry. To oppose him, Johann had an equal infantry force but a far superior cavalry that outnumbered the French 36 squadrons to 8. During the first stages of the ensuing Battle of Sacile, Eugène's offensive wing encountered resistance at the village of Palse, an outpost protecting the Hapsburg left flank. This flank featured rugged terrain well suited to the defense. When the sounds of fighting interrupted Johann at his breakfast around 9 A.M., he could not believe that the main French blow was directed against his left flank. He judged it to be a feint. This misconception gave Eugène his best chance for victory because the Austrian IX Corps, fully half of the Austrian force, remained on the defensive while its sister corps fought alone against the majority of the Viceroy's army.

Having overrun Palse, Eugène's men pressed on to encounter the Austrian main line of resistance based on the village of Porzia. As skirmishing and cannonading announced the beginning of a serious assault against Porzia, the erzherzog finally realized that it was here the fight centered. He sent GM Colloredo with part of his brigade to reinforce the village. In Porzia, FML Johann Frimont commanded six battalions of jagers and grenzers. These troops, well suited for defending a village surrounded by broken terrain, held off the French until Colloredo arrived. Frimont saw that a creek divided the French axis of advance and channeled it into two unsupported division-sized forces. The Austrian general decided to defend against one—it was General Jean-Mathieu Seras's division—and attack the other. While the St. Julian Infantry repulsed Seras's repeated attacks against the village, Frimont pounced on Severoli's Italian division. Hit in front and flank, the Italians broke badly. Their flight carried one of Seras's brigades with them. Seras committed his reserve, and Eugène also sent in more units against Porzia.

The fresh French forces drove Frimont's tired men from the village, but Austrian reserves from the VIII Corps' second line counterattacked. Although twice wounded, GM Colloredo provided gallant front-line leadership and with the aid of the reserves, along with Frimont's rallied grenzers, managed to stabilize the front. Porzia exchanged hands repeatedly during a protracted battle of attrition. Finally alive to the battle's possibilities, Erzherzog Johann decided to march his

Battle of Sacile
(April 16, 1809)

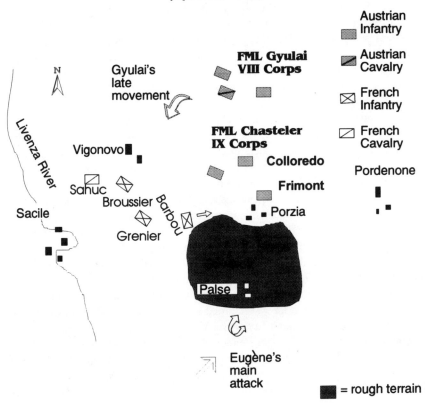

IX Corps by the plains of Vigonovo for a decisive strike against Eugène's left flank. If successful, this maneuver would cut his opponent's route of retreat across the Livenza River. But the well-conceived movement progressed too slowly. In the absence of the IX Corps, GM Gajoly took his VIII Corps brigade to Vigonovo. As Gajoly approached, he saw the French abandon the village. Instead of redoubling his effort, he exhibited a characteristic Austrian hesitation upon spying a French mounted outpost line near Fontana. Worried about his own flank, he waited for the IX Corps to arrive.

Meanwhile, Eugène had kept pounding against the Porzia front, summoning reserves from all available formations. Although the 1st Ligne (the historic old Picardy regiment) finally managed to capture the village for good, it was too late. The Austrian IX Corps had reached the battle at last. Its appearance, at 4 P.M., first forced the nearest French division to suspend its offensive and then caused Eugène to march troops from the Porzia sector to buttress his imperiled left flank. The French troops holding the viceroy's left wing tried a limited, four-battalion counterattack supported by Sahuc's cavalry to slow the Austrian advance. But now the Hapsburg cavalry superiority took effect. While the Hohenlohe Dragoons engaged the advancing French from the front, a sister regiment, the Savoy Dragoons, hit Sahuc in flank.

The failure of the counterattack convinced Eugène that the battle was lost. By 5 P.M. he began to retreat. He was very fortunate that the Croatian commander of the IX Corps, FML Ignaz Gyulai, maneuvered ponderously and failed to press his advantage. The veteran French leaders coolly conducted the withdrawal. Broussier's division formed two ranks of squares in checkerboard formation and held steady against furious charges. The Austrian Colonel Fulda died while leading his Ott Hussars against these squares. Whenever there was a lull between Hapsburg cavalry charges, the first line of squares would file back through the interval and re-form. At the next lull the process would be repeated. In this manner the French army retired across the Livenza. Eugène was in the ranks of the last regiment to leave the field.

The Battle of Sacile was the first Austrian victory of the war of 1809, earned at a cost of 3,600 men. Eugène lost some 3,000 men killed and wounded. During the battle and the ensuing retreat, the Austrians captured 4,666 prisoners along with 16 cannons and 19 caissons. With French losses from the previous day, this totaled about 9,000 men. It could have been far worse if FML Gyulai had shown more dash. Throughout the battle both sides had exhibited good front-line leadership, with FML Frimont particularly distinguishing himself. Eugène, on the other hand, had fought poorly the first battle of his career, an unnecessary engagement at odds with Napoleon's directives. He wrote candidly to his wife: "Yesterday my dear Auguste, I was in despair when I wrote you because I had witnessed the complete rout of our army. Today I am more tranquil and have recovered my courage; the enemy has not profited from his advantages, while I will gain from his mistakes which will allow me to rally my army."[6] The coming weeks would test the accuracy of Eugène's postbattle evaluation.

Although Eugène had displayed battlefield courage, he lacked the moral courage to write to his stepfather about Sacile. He sent Napoleon a deliberately vague report that acknowledged setback but gave no particulars. An angry Napoleon replied, "I am ignorant about the last battle, the number of men and guns that I have lost, and what caused the defeat. . . . Not having the slightest idea of what took place on the 16th . . . upsets all the calculations for my campaign."[7] Indeed, Napoleon now had to consider the possibility that Johann would turn his army against the flank of the Army of Germany as it advanced toward Vienna. To keep Johann from thwarting his campaign, he needed assurance that Eugène could at least occupy the opposing army. His confidence in his stepson shaken, Napoleon deliberated relieving him from command. He finally decided to replace him with Marshal Joachim Murat. What helped Eugène enormously was the slow communications between Italy and Austria. The rebellion in the Tyrol cut direct communications, necessitating a roundabout courier route that required nine days to carry a message. By the time Napoleon fully comprehended what had taken place at Sacile and the order to relieve Eugène arrived in Italy, the strategic situation had been entirely reversed.

Following Sacile, Eugène adhered to Napoleon's guidelines. He left a garrison in Venice and retreated west. As he withdrew, his army gained strength. By April 27 all of the major elements of the Army of Italy were together. The viceroy had finally achieved the concentration that the emperor had urged him to accomplish before offering battle. Erzherzog Johann, on the other hand, suffered from strategic consumption. Just as Eugène had hoped, Johann told off 10,000 men to mask Venice and advanced slowly west. Eugène appreciated that the strategic initiative had swung in his favor. His ensuing counteroffensive chased Johann back east and led to another battle.

This time the viceroy commanded more than 45,000 men, including three cavalry divisions. He had also made some organizational changes that increased his force's effectiveness. Foremost among these was the establishment of an artillery reserve formed by drawing artillery from the different divisions and adding them to the guns of the Royal Italian Guard. To command this force Eugène selected General Jean Sorbier, an officer whose experience extended back to the pre-Revolutionary Royal Corps of Artillery. Unwittingly taking a page from the Austrian practice of using advance guard divisions, Eugène also organized a special unit composed of six infantry battalions made of voltigeurs taken from the line units, a light cavalry regiment, and four guns. The viceroy intended to use it as a spearheading task force and assigned it to a promising brigadier general named Joseph-Marie Dessaix.

General Macdonald also arrived to join the army. According to one French officer, his presence helped restore confidence among the common soldier. Certainly Macdonald created a highly visible display. He wore his old uniform dating back to the days of the Republic, a uniform "that gave pleasure to the old soldiers, but was ridiculed by the young ones and some presumptuous officers."[8]

To get at the enemy, Eugène had to cross the Piave River. The Piave generally rose to uncrossable dimensions during the day, so any crossing had to take place in the morning.[9] The frightening prospect of fighting a battle with an unfordable river to the rear did not daunt Eugène. He selected two crossing points and began his attack at dawn on May 8. Under a covering barrage from Sorbier's guns, Dessaix's voltigeurs stripped naked and forded the river carrying their weapons and equipment with arms extended high. Once across, they easily drove off the lone Austrian battalion guarding the ford. While Seras's division feinted opposite the Austrian camp upstream, Eugène's cavalry began to cross downstream. Even at relatively low water, fording the river was difficult. One of Sahuc's officers saw his 16-year-old trumpeter drown in the swirling current. By the time Johann realized an assault was underway, he was already in a vulnerable position. If he chose to retreat, he would have to contend with the superior French cavalry advancing against his supply trains. Rather than take this risk, the erzherzog decided to attack the French.

Johann, fooled by the upstream diversion, sent some of his men to confront it. Not realizing the size of the French column crossing at the downstream site, he merely sent one cavalry regiment and an infantry brigade to block it. He made his main effort with his remaining five cavalry regiments, some 3,000 troopers, against Dessaix's bridgehead supported by a massed battery of 24 guns. Seeing the enemy advance, Dessaix formed his units into square, arrayed them in checkerboard formation, placed his own artillery at the corners, and shot the first Hapsburg charge into tatters. But his units in square presented superb targets for the Austrian artillery. As some squares began to waver, alarmed French staff officers galloped downstream to seek reinforcements. Meanwhile, the French cavalry advanced upstream from their crossing point and encountered the Austrian blocking force defending a defile. The commander of the leading brigade of French light cavalry asked General Pully "to dismount two or three of his squadrons, to try to dislodge the infantry . . . a duty these dragoons might possibly have succeeded in performing, as they were armed with fusees, and drilled to fight on foot."[10] Pully refused, explaining that his orders were to support the light cavalry, not to open the way for them.

Because of this lack of cooperation, the cavalry contented itself with covering the crossing to allow the infantry passage. Then a staff officer arrived with the order to hurry to assist Dessaix. A trooper recalls:

We went off at a trot in column of sections, ascending the course of the Piave. It did not take us long . . . we saw a cloud of dust thrown up by a mass of fugitives running towards the river. This sight made an impression on General d'Avenay [one of Sahuc's brigadiers] and he said to me:

"This is beginning badly, we shall very likely be thrown into the water."[11]

It was 10:30 A.M. Eugène had secured one downstream crossing site, but his main crossing on Dessaix's sector had stalled under an intense bombardment from the Austrian massed battery. The voltigeurs' squares shrank from casualties. An eyewitness reports that the dead piled up around the squares while the fearfully mangled wounded sheltered in the center. "General Desaix [sic] came out to speak to us, and was very nearly carried off by a shot that passed an inch from his shoulder. They literally hailed upon the spot where we were; some could be seen to ricochet, the wind of others could be felt, and there was a continuous hissing that caused very grave reflections."[12] The Piave's waters were rising, and already the passage of reinforcements had slowed to a trickle. There was no bridge but rather two parallel ropes stretched from bank to bank to help the men as they waded across.

Eugène realized that the Hapsburg battery firing against Dessaix was the tactical key. At the moment, only the re-formed Austrian cavalry supported this battery. However, seeing Austrian infantry approaching rapidly, he knew he must hurry. Quickly he summoned 20 more artillery pieces from the opposite shore and had them join Dessaix's four guns in a ferocious counterbattery bombardment. It was nip and tuck. Sahuc had deployed his cavalry division poorly so that the "overs," the Austrian balls aimed too high, crashed into his troopers, causing unnecessary losses.[13] One ball mortally wounded General d'Avenay. Captain Noël's battery had two of its four guns dismounted by Hapsburg fire. Moreover, in their effort to cross the Piave rapidly, the French gunners had left behind their reserve ammunition. Soon many of their guns fell silent for lack of ammunition.

While the rival gun lines still filled the intervening ground with a dense smoke, Eugène sent his cavalry in a pincers attack against the Austrian artillery. Pully's dragoons trotted unseen to the flank of the artillery. Trumpeter Chevillet describes receiving the command: "Dress on the first dragoon squadron, deploy the column, on the right in line!" Then, "Forward, guide left, charge the artillery!"[14] Pully's troopers crashed into the unsuspecting artillery and struck the Hapsburg horse as well. A brief, hard-fought melee ensued.[15] The opposing cavalry leader, FML Wolfskehl, struggled to extricate his men, only to fall dead from a saber blow delivered by a French dragoon. Meanwhile Sahuc attacked the opposite flank. When the demoralized Austrian cavalry fled, the French turned their blades against the brown-coated gunners. They mortally wounded the battery's commander and captured 14 guns.

Still General Sahuc continued to have trouble. He failed to re-form his men in time to receive a counterattack from a rallied regiment of Hungarian cavalry. Thus the Army of Italy saw the amusing spectacle of the 8th Chasseurs à Cheval—a swaggering regiment that had bragged about its exploits and worn on this day their full dress uniform so as to stand out during the battle—routing toward the river. Fortunately for Sahuc, his other regiments charged to drive off the pursuing hussars. Then Pully's troopers tried several unsupported charges against the approaching Austrian infantry. They calmly formed square and drove off the dragoons. However, the capture of the battery allowed the French buildup to proceed until rising water put an end to crossing operations in midafternoon. During this time the French cavalry continued to be plagued by Austrian artillery fire. When one regiment wavered, a veteran major rode to their front and even while men and horses fell around him said, "This is nothing! Chasseurs! Steady in the ranks. This [the cannonfire] is the music of the brave!"[16]

While Eugène completed the concentration of his army on the enemy-held bank of the Piave, Erzherzog Johann deployed his infantry along a formidable position behind an earthen dike that blocked egress from the French bridgehead. However, the position was thinly manned. To avoid being outflanked, Johann had to stretch his line, retaining only one brigade in reserve. Although at this point Eugène appreciated that the rival forces were roughly equal, he knew that his force had a substantial morale edge and he opted to attack. He ordered his right wing force commanded by Grénier to turn the Austrian flank. His left wing would perform a pinning attack. When Johann weakened his center to fend off Grénier, the French artillery would deliver a shock bombardment, and Macdonald's corps would charge against the center. This is about what took place.

During the battle Eugène showed inspirational leadership, at one point riding up to the very front of the action to address a cavalry regiment with fiery words: "Now then, hussars! Let me see you charge those blackguards!"[17] If he made any significant tactical errors, it was his decision to rein in his pursuit prematurely. Still, in its results, the Battle of the Piave was almost a mirror image of Sacile. Both sides lost perhaps 2,000 battle casualties, but the French captured 3,000 men on the field, 2,000 more during the ensuing days, and 14 guns and 30 caissons. More important, the battle broke the offensive capability of Johann's army and relieved Napoleon of any immediate concern that a hostile force would attack his strategic right flank and impede his drive on Vienna. In contrast to his poor planning for Sacile, Eugène at the Piave had exhibited a fine sense of grand tactics coupled with good battle management skills.

RAIDS IN THE REAR

Belgian-born FML Johann Marquis de Chasteler had first encountered war during the 1789 campaigns against the Turks. At age 46 he was young compared to the typical venerable veterans whose ranks populated the Hapsburg high command. His theater of operations—the alpine region bordered by Switzerland, Bavaria, upper Austria, and northern Italy— required youth and a good deal of dash. His mission was to serve as a link for Austrian operations on either side of the mountains and to promote the Tyrolese insurrection. Aided by detailed knowledge of Franco-Bavarian movements provided by the loyal citizens, Chasteler began the campaign by overrunning the Tyrol and hounding the enemy toward Innsbruck. Here the Tyrolean leader, Major Teimer, launched repeated day-and-night attacks for 48 hours until forcing the Bavarian lieutenant general commanding the garrison to capitulate. A total of 3,860 Bavarians and 2,050 French surrendered along with five cannon, two mortars, and considerable supplies. This success was key to the prolonged guerrilla campaign in the Tyrol because henceforth there were enough weapons to arm sizable numbers of insurgents.

An emboldened Teimer spread the rebellion to the Inn Valley and the Vorarlberg. Joining the fight was Andreas Hofer, a 43-year-old innkeeper who was to become a national hero. In fact, Hofer apparently did most of his leading well to the rear from the comforts of the neighborhood drinking establishment, but during the first blush of insurrectionary fever no one seemed to mind. At least 12,000 Tyrolese guerrillas turned out to participate in the rebellion. News of the victory at Sacile further encouraged them. Much like what would occur a century and a half later when the U.S. military confronted a mix of regular army forces and guerrillas in Vietnam, Chasteler's handful of Austrian regulars provided a nucleus to shield and rally the local guerrillas. Typical were the exploits of a column commanded by an Austrian major general named Fenner. Its regular forces composed two companies of the 9th Jagers, one regular infantry battalion, a platoon of the Hohenzollern Chevaulegers, one 6-pound cannon, and one howitzer. The militia of Nons and Sulzberg provided the bulk of its manpower.

This column displayed a fine combination of audacity and mobility by attacking Eugène's lines of communication in northern Italy. It managed to penetrate down the shores of Lake Garda to threaten the bridges over the Adige, thereby tying down a disproportionate number of adversaries. Meanwhile, operating out of the hills bordering the Danube valley well to the north, the Tyrolese jubilantly launched raids into Bavarian territory to capture towns and cities briefly, levy contributions, and then depart before any counterattack.

By mid-June, when Napoleon was ordering all available manpower to Vienna, such thrusts were annoyingly compelling the emperor to allocate many soldiers to guard the rear. Napoleon badly needed the six regiments of dragoons who were en route to Vienna in order to fill his depleted ranks. Instead they were drawn off to garrison the Tyrol. Too frequently Hapsburg strategists had committed too much strength to secondary theaters. An exception was the Tyrol, where the Austrians enjoyed a fine economy of force. Each French soldier engaged in antiguerrilla operations was one fewer man to fight against the main Austrian army. There were many factors that impaired effective French resistance to the guerrillas. Morale—Aspern-Essling elated the Tyrolese and depressed Napoleon's soldiers—terrain—the mountains provided sanctuary for the guerrillas—and rivalry between the king of Bavaria and the king of Württemberg all worked in favor of the guerrillas. Finally Napoleon decided to pull most of his men back into enclaves located at important towns and concede the countryside to the Tyrolese. It was the time of triumph for Teimer, Hofer, and their people.

While the Tyrolese fought hard to interdict Napoleon's line of communications from the south, multiple threats also emerged from the north. On May 21, the first day of battle at Aspern-Essling, the 38-year-old Duke of Brunswick issued a proclamation to the people of Germany: "Now or never, the time has come when we Germans can fight for our lawful freedom." He alluded to Austria's fight and how it should inspire everyone to throw off the yoke of French tyranny. Past failures, he said, had stemmed from the German people's inability to act in concert. Anticipating Otto von Bismarck by a half-decade, he said, "We are now joining together, whether we be North or South Germans," to fight for the Fatherland.[18] The duke's father had fought under Frederick the Great and had led an army against Napoleon in 1806, when he had been killed on the field of battle. The ensuing peace terms dispossessed the son of his estates. Now the duke proposed revenge by engaging in what he styled a "Little War" against Napoleon's line of communications. He had a small force, popularly known as the Black Brunswickers because of their black uniforms, with which he set out to attack French depots, wagon trains, and couriers. He believed he could kindle the fire of German nationalism through action and word.

But Saxony was not yet ready to join in a greater German confederation. The day the duke circulated his proclamation around the city of Zittau, only two men answered his call to join the ranks of the Black Brunswickers. Over time, a mere 300 Saxon recruits "of doubtful aspect" enlisted.[19] The duke tried to reassure civilians that unlike the French, his men would not unjustly take their property.

But guerrilla war can easily descend to pure banditry. The duke punished his thieving officers and men alike with lash and stick, but the Saxons continued to view his force as brigands rather than liberators.

At the end of May, a scratch 6,000-man Austrian force commanded by General Carl am Ende joined the duke. Am Ende had orders "to exploit the sensation caused by the victory" at Aspern-Essling by invading Saxony.[20] Like the Duke of Brunswick, am Ende tried to pave the way with propaganda. His proclamation reminded the Saxons of their historic ties with Austria, urged them "to fight for Germany's freedom," and warned that if they remained loyal to Napoleon, "you can expect no other fate than to bleed in Spain or another distant land."[21] Time would prove the general's prophecy extraordinarily accurate, but it swayed the Saxons not one bit.

During June, the allied Austrian-Brunswick force, joined by patriotic (or rebellious, depending on one's viewpoint) Hessians, maneuvered between Dresden and Leipzig. Because the best Saxon units were operating with Napoleon near Vienna, the King of Saxony had to turn to a fellow monarch, the King of Westphalia, for assistance in defending his kingdom. Westphalia was hardly a state, having been created by Napoleon in 1807 from bits and pieces of several German territories, including the Duchy of Brunswick, and its ruler was not of royal lineage. But King Jerome was Napoleon's younger brother, so the King of Saxony had every expectation that Jerome would come marching to his aid. Indeed, the Emperor Napoleon shared this expectation, although had Napoleon been more open-eyed, he might not have had such confidence.

Although not devoid of ability, Jerome Bonaparte was unlike his older brother in most aspects. Jerome had often shown a preference for personal pleasure over duty to his older brother. In the past the emperor had dealt with him with a stern hand, even going so far as to recall him from his posting in America and then forbidding entry into France of his new wife, the lovely Baltimore-born Elizabeth Patterson. Napoleon's Corsican sense of family impelled him to install Jerome as ruler somewhere, so he chose Westphalia, and to make everything tidy, he directed Jerome to marry a Württemberg princess. In 1809 he gave Jerome command of the X Corps with the duty of defending the upper Danube and resisting raids out of Bohemia. When Jerome failed to support promptly the King of Saxony, the latter had to evacuate his capital on June 16. His brother's behavior dismayed Napoleon: "You are making war like a satrap. Is it from me, good God! that you have learned this?"[22]

Finally stirred into action, Jerome entered Saxony, joined up with Saxon forces commanded by a Colonel Thielmann (six years later the two would meet again on opposite sides during the Waterloo campaign), and regained Leipzig on June 26. This proved a mixed blessing for the local inhabitants. Jerome's Westphalians exhibited an equal, if not superior, capacity as looters compared to Brunswick's men. There ensued much purposeless march and countermarch as Jerome sought to corner am Ende's force, the Austrian general sought to evade contact, and the Duke of Brunswick tried to levy contributions on as many Saxon towns as possible. The armistice at Znaim ended am Ende's participation in the campaign and placed the Black Brunswickers in a serious bind. Pursued by a superior force, the duke courageously led them on a two-week march to the North Sea port of Brake where ships of the Royal Navy rescued them. Ahead for the duke and his men lay a difficult campaign with Wellington's army in Spain and confrontation with Napoleon's army during the Waterloo campaign.

Except to the men involved, operations in Poland were of decidedly secondary importance. Austrian war planners had assigned the entire VII Corps with 25,000 infantry to this front. In view of expected resistance by the famed Polish light cavalry, the VII Corps also had close to 5,000 cavalry. Against them the Polish General Prince Josef Poniatowski could muster only a 14,000-man field army. Led by Erzherzog Ferdinand, whose qualifications for command largely rested on the fact that he was the kaiserin's brother, the Austrians advanced on Warsaw during the first weeks of April. Poniatowski bravely but foolishly tried to defend his capital near the village of Raszyn on April 18. It was a well-chosen position along a wooded height that overlooked a marshy stream. Swamp and forest protected both flanks. Poniatowski and his officers inspired their men to brave resistance by exhibiting reckless disregard for enemy fire. At one point, following a failed counterattack led by his chief of staff, Poniatowski placed himself at the head of his 1st Infantry Regiment to lead a triumphant bayonet charge across the same ground. For hours the Poles and some 2,000 Saxon allies fended off all attacks. But a final frontal attack pierced Poniatowski's center and forced him to retreat after losing about 1,400 men.

Poniatowski signed a convention that peaceably yielded Warsaw to Ferdinand's men. Then, in a daring surprise turnabout, while Ferdinand marched north against the Polish fortress of Thorn, Poniatowski marched south to Galicia, where he provoked a rebellion among the many Poles who had been unhappily living under Austrian rule. This *guerre de partisan* ("partisan war") succeeded famously.[23] Ferdinand countermarched, gave up Warsaw, and spent the balance of June and July fruitlessly chasing Polish partisans. Meanwhile, Poniatowski expanded his control over the countryside, becoming a national hero in the process, only to be foiled from complete success by the adversarial behavior of his erstwhile Russian allies. The Russians had appeared on the scene overtly in response to their treaty commitments to France. They contributed not at all to Poniatowski's campaign and displayed a ravenous appetite for all things Polish.

Thus much of Poland witnessed the same sad scenes that were happening in Saxony and the Tyrol, as first one army and then the other passed through, leaving behind a wasteland of burned villages and a throng of deserter bandits to prey on the population. Strategically, affairs in Poland well served Napoleon by tying down substantial Austrian forces. In appreciation for Poniatowski's conduct, the emperor sent him a saber of honor. For the Austrians, the Polish campaign was a strategic dead end. There was nothing to be gained here with an offensive that could not have been captured later after defeating Napoleon's main army. The commitment of such a large force for defending Austrian territory was also unnecessary because Metternich, through dint of superb intelligence work, had informed the kaiser that Russia would not fight against Austria. Austrian strategists should have deduced that the Russians would adequately occupy Poniatowski's forces, leaving him with little strength to bother Hapsburg territory. The Polish campaign was another example of the difficulty Austrian war planners experienced when trying to concentrate all available resources on the decisive front.

PREPARATION FOR BATTLE

The outbreak of the 1809 war had caught Napoleon by surprise. So rapid had been the campaign to date that he had not had time to organize his army in the desired manner. In the weeks following Aspern-Essling, he summoned reinforcements from every quarter and restructured his army. In the normal scheme of things, conscripts entered the depot battalions that each fighting regiment left behind in France. Here they learned about soldier life from a cadre of veterans. The increasingly heavy losses that were now typifying Napoleonic battles meant that untrained men served as replacements. So long columns of raw troops departed from the depots and hurried toward Vienna, their experienced non-commissioned officers ever vigilant for deserters. They followed the route taken by the Army of Germany, and the Danube corridor was now a scene of ruin and desolation. Sapper Jean-Lambert Saive relates, "we have had to forage on the countryside from thirty lieues distant all the way to Vienna. We rationalized this because the inhabitants had abandoned their homes and many had been burnt, while the small towns and villages" were completely destroyed.[24] The excesses committed during the earlier passage through the region provided an excuse for additional depredations. Typical of the men who followed this route was a batch of 500 conscripts from the Department of the Ardennes who arrived in Vienna on June 1. Aged 24 to 28 years old, they had escaped previous calls. They entered the ranks of the 18th Ligne, where they were much welcomed by the regiment's colonel. He was eager to have these older soldiers since he believed them more capable than the teenagers to "sustain the fatigues and privations of war."[25]

Another source of replacements was the return of previously wounded soldiers. About half of the 943 Imperial Guardsmen who had been wounded at Aspern-Essling rejoined the ranks in time for the next battle. Soldiers of the line had a lower recovery rate. Still, among many there was Jean-Joseph Jeunechamps, one of Oudinot's grenadiers who had been grievously wounded on May 22. After three weeks in the hospital, he rejoined his unit in time to fight at Wagram and receive another wound. The French blitzkrieg to Vienna had managed to liberate prisoners who had surrendered at Ratisbonne back in the third week of April. These men made up a reconstituted 65th Ligne, a regiment that contributed one feeble 236-man battalion that served in Davout's corps. Raw conscripts, recovered wounded, and returned prisoners of war were not the equal of the men they replaced. Clearly the army's quality was on the wane.

Whereas replacement manpower could still be found, replacing the fallen senior officers was far more difficult. Some of the new troops marching to Vienna passed a small, somber convoy that traveled in the opposite direction. Six horses bedecked in black pulled a wagon carrying the corpse of Marshal Jean Lannes; four pulled another wagon with the body of General Saint-Hilaire. Each night after crossing the Rhine into France, the convoy halted, and the coffins were displayed in the village church. A female eyewitness wrote that it was "a very sad and melancholy spectacle."[26] The deaths of Lannes and Saint-Hilaire left a command void. Napoleon appointed General Oudinot to lead the II Corps, announcing to his army that Oudinot was "a general tested in a hundred combats, where his intrepidity has equalled his knowledge."[27] If this rather overstated Oudinot's intellectual prowess, there was no doubt he possessed fiery tactical aggressiveness. Whether this attribute was appropriate to high command remained to be tested. The emperor elevated General Grandjean to succeed the irreplaceable Saint-Hilaire and Arrighi de Casanova to lead Espagne's cuirassiers. The fact that both were only average officers underscored the fact that the talent pool of senior leadership had become shallow by mid–1809.

Because of the infantry's decline, Napoleon took dramatic steps to increase his artillery. On June 9 he created three oversized companies of Imperial Guard conscript artillery. Along with the arrival of the Guard formations from Spain, this gave him a 72-gun artillery reserve crewed by the world's finest artillerists. In the line artillery, wherever possible he authorized the substitution of Austrian 6-pounders for the French 4- and 8-pounders.[28] This exchange increased the artillery's hitting power and mobility. The emperor also made a decision, two days after the Battle of Aspern-Essling, to reinstitute the practice of assigning two cannons to each infantry regiment.[29] Earlier in his career he had dispensed with the so-called regimental guns because regimental officers tended to utilize their cannon inefficiently, and more important, their presence slowed down the foot soldiers. He had seen in the recent battle that his troops no longer had the battlefield maneuverability of the Grande Armée. He decided to compensate by increasing their firepower.

Baron de Seruzier received the assignment of organizing the regimental cannon in the II Corps. He culled the ranks of the infantry for veterans from the camp at Boulogne because most soldiers who had attended that camp had received rudimentary artillery instruction. Each two-gun section composed either 4- or 6-pound weapons with a crew of 24 cannoneers, 2 sergeants, 2 corporals, 1 drummer, and 1 lieutenant. Seruzier set them to exercising immediately and by July found they could perform adequately. French officers had a mixed reaction to the return of the regimental cannon. General Louis Friant reported that in his division they maneuvered in step with the infantry and "vied to mimic the zeal and ardor" of the divisional artillery.[30] Other officers were not so sure. The very able General Berthezène of the 10th Légère observed that in all the actions in which he participated, the extra cannon offered no advantage. Worse, fear of losing them caused the regiments to be "more timid and much slower in the maneuvers."[31] Napoleon had been outgunned at Aspern-Essling, and, by virtue of these decisions, this master artillerist did not intend to allow it to happen again. On the eve of battle he had concentrated some 550 artillery pieces served by 12,000 gunners.

Infantry replacements could be found. The Vienna arsenal could provide numerous artillery. It was far less easy to replace the thousands of dead horses. Between the attrition on the battlefield and repeated dinners of horseflesh on Lobau Island, the cavalry required many remounts. Napoleon ordered his agents to purchase or seize as many horses as possible but ruefully noted "that whatever is done I always have many unmounted men."[32] Consequently, his heavy shock cavalry units would fight with depleted strength in the next engagement.

Napoleon counted heavily on the arrival of Eugène's Army of Italy to give him the strength necessary to try conclusions again with Erzherzog Karl. After the Battle of the Piave, Eugène had pursued Erzherzog Johann through the Styrian Alps into Hungary. When Johann returned to Austrian territory, he had only about half his strength remaining in his two battle corps. However, he fell back upon reinforcements, whereas Eugène suffered the effects of strategic consumption. By the time the rival forces confronted each other for a third field battle near the Hungarian village of Raab, 65 miles southeast of Vienna, Johann enjoyed approximate numerical equality. Most of his added strength were raw troops: landwehr, Hungarian Insurrection forces, and the like. He did receive some additional regular artillery to replace his losses from the Piave, and it was in this arm, plus his choice of terrain, that he placed his trust.

The center of his position occupied a large plateau, the Szabadhegy Heights. Running in front of the plateau was a small stream, the Pansza brook, which flowed into a marsh that protected Johann's left flank. Two formidable outworks guarded a direct attack against the heights: the Kis-Megyer farmhouse, a stout structure enclosed by a thick, cannon-proof stone wall, and, 300 yards to the east, a steep earthen mound topped by a solid stone chapel. The position's weakness lay in its 1 1/2-mile gap between the plateau and the town of Raab. Johann deployed his 43 infantry battalions, about 27,000 men, on the heights, the mound, and in the farmyard. Between the mound and the marsh was GM Meczery's 40-cavalry squadrons, a formidable sounding force largely made up of Hungarian troopers of unknown fighting quality. Between the plateau and Raab were another 26 squadrons, half Hungarian and half regular cavalry, commanded by FML Frimont. These two forces numbered almost 8,000 men. He distributed his 30 artillery pieces across his front and waited for Eugène to attack.

The Army of Italy comprised 27,982 infantry, 10,229 cavalry, and 42 guns, Eugène's largest command to date. He drew up another Frederick the Great–style battle plan (the same as he had done at Sacile) involving a passive left wing and an oblique assault by his right. Just before the battle began at noon, Eugène reminded his men that they would fight on a day made famous by prior French

Battle of Raab
(June 14, 1809)

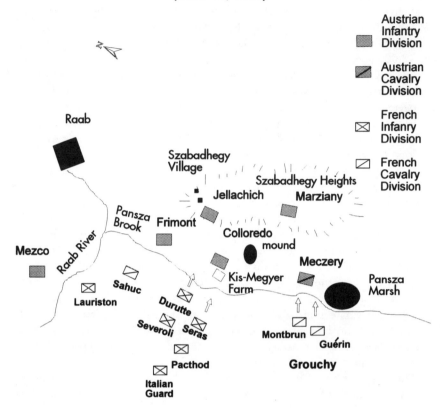

feats of arms. June 14 was the anniversary of Marengo and Friedland. Eugène told his men he expected nothing less on this field. Then there was a stupendous army-wide beating of the drums to signal the beginning of the assault.

Advancing in echelon from the right, the French infantry divisions deployed in two lines of battalion columns with a thick skirmish line in front. Timing is crucial in an oblique attack, since each unit keys its advance upon the advance of its neighbor. As had occurred at Sacile, difficult terrain—on this field the Pansza brook and its marshy banks—disrupted the plan. Instead of Grouchy's right flank cavalry striking first, followed by Seras and Pierre Durutte with their infantry, Durutte's division made initial contact near the center of the Austrian position. Unsupported, he made no progress. Seras finally struggled across the brook to encounter the key to the Hapsburg position, the Kis-Megyer, the enclosed farmhouse reminiscent of Hougoumont on the Waterloo field. Three times Seras led his division against the Kis-Megyer and three times failed. Meanwhile, Grouchy's cavalry on the right found the paths leading over the brook very narrow, marshy, and easily defended. In such terrain even the raw troops of the Hungarian insurrection could hold off a superior force.

At this point Eugène wisely discarded his battle plan. He sent in Severoli's division on Durutte's left and resolved to fight a battle of attrition against the center of the Austrian position until Grouchy could extricate himself and turn its flank. The viceroy anticipated that these maneuvers would have the same effect as a similar set of maneuvers on the Piave field: stretch the defender to the breaking point. Then he intended to commit his reserve to pierce the Austrian center.

Eventually Grouchy managed to cross his troopers over the Pansza and charge GM Meczery's Hungarians. The Hungarians had proved themselves loyal to the Hapsburg monarchy and utterly resistant to Napoleon's propaganda urging them to create their own separate state. They proved less resistant to French cannon fire and cavalry charges. Although they fought bravely for a time, when Captain Forgeot aggressively led his horse artillery well to the front to deliver close-range canister fire, it was too much, and they broke badly. Grouchy sent one brigade in pursuit and turned against the Austrian infantry's flank. So far this infantry had managed to repel the frontal pressure from the opposing French infantry. However, with their flank turned, FML Colloredo, who commanded here, ordered his infantry to abandon the mound and establish a new line facing Grouchy.

In spite of having the French occupying a commanding position 300 yards distant, the defenders of the Kis-Megyer continued to hold. By stalling the advance of Eugène's entire right wing, they gave Johann a chance for victory. Revealing unsuspected tactical skill, the erzherzog counterattacked against Durutte's division with troops drawn from his second line and three battalions taken from his reserve. Down the slopes came the bayonet-tipped Austrian line. Their impetuosity overwhelmed Durutte's men, who broke and ran toward the rear, carrying with them many of the Italians in Severoli's adjacent division. Here was the battle's crisis. If Johann committed his final ten-battalion reserve to exploit this success, he might drive the French from the field. But such was not the Austrian way of war.

Severoli's second line of battalion columns held firm against the unsupported Austrians, thus limiting the size of their breakthrough. Their resistance gave time for Eugène to rally Durutte's people and send Pacthod's fresh division storming back up the crest. Simultaneously, ax-wielding sappers managed to batter down the gates of the Kis-Megyer, permitting Seras's division finally to capture the farm from Colloredo's gallant but exhausted warriors. Montbrun led the 1st Chasseurs à Cheval in a spirited charge that routed the few remaining Austrian cavalry defending the Hapsburg left flank. Spearheaded by the fierce charge of the 30th Dragoons, Grouchy then penetrated the heights on the Austrian left. The erzherzog could see French reinforcements approaching and knew that Grouchy had turned his left. With the French also breaching his position on the heights, he decided to use his reserve to cover a retreat and concede the field.

Sahuc's division had spent the day observing Frimont's cavalry across the Pan-sza. Unleashed at battle's end, it advanced to encounter hastily formed squares of Hungarian insurrection infantry. A French participant describes what took place:

Our charge was received by a poorly sustained fire, their confusion was evident . . . but our regiment lost its chance, because instead of attacking a single side [of the square], we advanced overhastily without order to envelope the square from all sides . . . our chasseurs dispersed in the midst of this mass of infantry lacked the strength to force the squares.[33]

Repulsed with loss, the chasseurs à cheval re-formed and charged again. This time they concentrated on one face of the square and broke through. Angered by the losses they had just suffered, they slaughtered the virtually defenseless Hungarians. Trumpeter Chevillet describes calling out in German to surrender, seeing an infantryman drop his musket, and running him through regardless. Next he encountered a wounded grenzer, who managed to defend himself with his bayonet against the trooper's lunges as they circled one another warily. The unfortunate foot soldier eventually left an opening that allowed Chevillet to fell him with a blow to the head. In a letter the next day, Chevillet wrote that it was difficult to paint an adequate picture of the slaughter of "all these poor Kaiserlites."

Generally, however, the French cavalry mounted an ill-coordinated pursuit. Grouchy complained that several thousand Austrians laid down their arms when charged by his regiments and then picked them back up after the French swept by. He attributed this to the lack of adequate support and cooperation among the French cavalry.[34] Such bungling helped the Austrian army withdraw intact.

After his initial defeat at Sacile, Eugène had won his second battle in a row. At a cost of about 2,500 casualties, his Army of Italy had inflicted 6,000 losses and driven the enemy from the field. But it was a tactical victory devoid of strategic significance. Johann was able to retreat with an intact force, and his presence south of Vienna would cause Napoleon much anxiety all the way through the Battle of Wagram.

After May's setback, when the emperor cast his eyes about for fresh men, his gaze alighted upon General Auguste Marmont's two small divisions garrisoning the Adriatic coast. Thirty-five-year old Marmont was one of Napoleon's com-rades dating back to the siege of Toulon. For nearly three productive and satis-fying years, Marmont had been serving as governor-general of Dalmatia, the Balkan region ceded to France after Austria's defeat in 1805. When the 1809 war began, Napoleon intended Marmont's small army corps merely to tie down enemy forces in the region. Marmont's units had trained at the camps of Bou-logne and composed battalions undiluted by conscripts and unharmed by cam-paign attrition. Napoleon described them as "the finest corps in my army."[35]

What transpired in Dalmatia was mountain warfare combined with counter-insurgency operations. Terrain dictated the former; the historic warlike nature of the inhabitants caused the latter. To campaign in the rugged terrain, Marmont stripped his corps of most baggage. This was hard on his soldiers who had grown soft after three years of garrison duty. Captain Marc Desboeufs, a voltigeur in the 81st Ligne, describes the load he carried: "Three munition breads attached to my haversack, which was full of cartridge packets, rice and biscuit. A large gourd full of wine was suspended on one shoulder and the other was garnished with twenty small tortes attached to a cord. The weight of these provisions, combined with my weapons, ten cartridge packets and my clothes, approached fifty kilos [110 pounds]."[36] Undoubtedly, after the campaign's initial march, the captain found himself quite exhausted.

In the campaign's opening engagement, fought in a driving rainstorm atop a mountain on April 30, the French fared poorly. Some of GM Stoichewich's skilled grenzers dominated the action and drove the French from the heights. During the ensuing retreat, the civilian population turned out to snipe at the retiring French. Revenge came on May 16 when Marmont feinted against an artillery-studded mountaintop position with his own artillery and some skirmishers and launched a decisive flank attack with a column composed of the 23d Ligne. Marmont's men captured 600 prisoners including the elderly GM Stoichewich himself.

Marmont drove the Austrians north and next encountered them defending a river line near the town of Gospich. During the subsequent battle, which took place on May 21, the first day of Aspern-Essling, the soldiers who had trained with the Grande Armée again showed what they could do. Voltigeur companies crossed a difficult ford while under fire, scaled the adjacent cliffs, and clung to their rocky aeries against a succession of counterattacks. Marmont reinforced this bridgehead, and a hard fight in extremely rugged terrain took place. A 12-gun Austrian battery dominated the field. To confront it, the French infantry formed "in a single line with three pace intervals supported at some distance by ten-man platoons commanded by an officer."[37] Few units in Europe could emulate such modern, open-order tactics. Mountain howitzers carried on mules provided mobile fire support. Marmont allowed one of his divisions to fight unaided in order to expose Austrian intentions. When he saw the enemy advance in three unsupported columns—the rugged terrain compartmentalized the different tactical sectors—he resolved to crush the opposing center. The 18th Légère delivered an audacious charge that sent the whitecoats reeling and captured five cannon. Marmont then turned to deal with each of the flanking enemy columns in succession. It was not done without cost. A battalion of the 81st Ligne lost one-quarter of its strength in a mere two minutes from Hapsburg canister fire. But by day's end, the flexible French tactics triumphed and drove the Austrians from the field.[38]

Entering Hungary, Marmont made contact with Broussier's division assigned to Macdonald's Corps of the Army of Italy. But cooperation was not what it should have been. Macdonald had left behind Broussier's division to invest the citadel of Graz. When FML Ignaz Gyulai marched with some 20,000 men to relieve the citadel, Broussier panicked and retired. Marmont did not know this, which set the stage for one of the celebrated epics in Napoleonic history, the 84th Ligne's fight at Graz. On the evening of June 25, 1,200 soldiers belonging to two battalions of the 84th Ligne approached Graz. Around 10 P.M. they encountered surprise fire from a stable. Colonel Gambin massed his elite companies, seized the outpost, and continued into the town. His battalions methodically cleared the streets, capturing some 450 prisoners. Around midnight, they encountered a formidable strongpoint based on the Church of Saint-Leonhard and its adjacent cemetery. A stiff musketry fire repulsed the first attack.

Gambin sent his adjutant with one company to work around to the cemetery rear. Sheltered by a very dark night, this company silently scaled the cemetery's crenellated walls and took the defenders by surprise. The balance of the regiment charged to capture another 125 prisoners. Sending out pickets, Gambin began to realize that he had encountered a much larger force than expected. In fact, he had merely defeated Gyulai's advance guard. The colonel considered a retreat, only to find that enemy forces had surrounded his position. Filling the nearby streets with his two voltigeurs companies, Gambin positioned his two cannon and the balance of his force behind the walls of the cemetery, herded his prisoners into the church, and resolved to hold hard. Dawn brought the first of a succession of Austrian attacks. Although fully half of Gyulai's men were poorly trained Croatian and Slavic militia, they still outnumbered the defenders by at least ten to one.

Throughout the morning, as soon as the 84th Ligne repelled one column, on came another. The attacking waves lapped all around the cemetery and at one point penetrated the church to liberate the prisoners. During another assault, a Graz citizen guided a column via a covered approach, while the Simbschen Infantry Regiment attacked from the opposite direction. The column erupted in the midst of the French position and managed to drag off one of the cannon before being evicted by a desperate counterattack. By 1 P.M. the defenders were running out of ammunition. They searched through the pockets of the dead and dying and resumed the battle with what they could find. Losses had so stretched the defenders that when another assault came, only two men, Colonel Gambin and a Corporal Humblot, remained standing to defend the sector where stood the solitary cannon. Humblot told his colonel that the Austrians would have to tear the cannon from his dying hands before they could have it. A ball shattered the arm of another soldier, and his sergeant ordered him to leave the ranks. The soldier refused, saying, "The arm can wait."[39] During yet another assault, the Austrians scaled the walls and captured one of the regiment's eagles. Sergeant Legouge, a Chevalier of the Légion d'honneur, single-handedly entered the melee to save the eagle.

With the situation growing increasingly desperate, Gambin took advantage of a lull to send a small detachment to carry off the two eagles before they fell to the enemy. After 16 hours of combat, reduced to defending his position with the bayonet, Gambin decided to risk all and cut his way to safety. Drum major Maisonneuve beat the pas de charge, and the survivors managed to overthrow all opposition—the tired Austrians had suffered heavily, losing more than 500 men, and offered feeble resistance to the breakout—and escape carrying their one artillery piece with them. When they met up with a relieving column sent by a concerned Marmont who had heard the sounds of the fight, the men of the 84th Ligne embraced their liberators. The action at Graz ended on an ugly note. The French reinforcements stormed back into the town "like a torrent overflowing its banks" to drive the Austrians at point of bayonet. A veteran officer wrote that he had never before witnessed such a spirited assault. But battle spirit gave way to savagery as the French refused to grant quarter, bayoneting wounded and prisoners alike.

The 84th Ligne lost 3 officers and 31 men killed, 12 officers and 192 men wounded, and 40 prisoners. Its magnificent defense of the Saint-Leonhard cemetery against all comers earned the admiration of the entire French army. When Napoleon inspected the regiment on Lobau, he handed out 84 crosses, including one to Corporal Humblot, and he made Colonel Gambin a count. To honor further the regiment, he authorized it to inscribe in gold lettering the words *un contre dix* ("one against ten") on its standards.

Marmont's Corps reached Lobau on July 4. An eyewitness remembers them arriving bronzed by exposure to the Adriatic sun with a mule train carrying their mountain howitzers.[40] They were only one component among several important additions to the Army of Germany. Marshal Jean-Baptiste Bernadotte brought his 14,650-man Saxon IX Corps to Vienna. Bernadotte was a gifted but troublesome subordinate. His Saxon generals had neither training nor experience in the command of brigade and division-sized formations. Although Saxon cavalry were fine troops, the artillery had only recently been mobilized for field service and lacked realistic training and firing practice. The infantry included willing soldiers, but they employed outdated tactics emphasizing perfect alignment and formal movements. There were two excellent light (*schutzen*) battalions drawn from select sharpshooters of the line regiments, the pride of the Saxon infantry. Their commander wrote to the King of Saxony, "I cannot describe to your Majesty the excellent spirit reigning in the two Rifle Battalions. It can be seen how enthusiastic a troop of carefully chosen men with selected officers can be."[41] Overall, however, the Saxons were well behind the French in military experience, tactical training, and maneuverability.[42] The French would only suspiciously cooperate with them. On July 5, when some Saxon cavalry retired before an Austrian onslaught and fouled the ranks of the supporting French infantry, one of Marmont's veterans described their behavior as "typically German."[43]

General Karl Wrede also joined the Army of Germany with his 5,544-man Bavarian division. They had fought well during the Eckmuhl phase of the 1809 war and, if not quite up to French standards, still could be relied on for steady service. Lastly, Napoleon summoned Eugène and his Army of Italy to join his host. By the time all was done, Napoleon commanded an impressive 180,000-man force divided into four French corps: two allied corps, the Army of Italy, and the reserve cavalry corps. As he perfected his arrangements, he set his soldiers to drilling incessantly. Among many, the Young Guard fired at targets three times per week.

When Marmont marched his men onto Lobau, he found a well-organized fortress base. He observed that after Aspern-Essling, "The lesson Napoleon had learned was that of probity," by which he understood integrity to his art.[44] Since that battle Napoleon had worked hard to ensure that there would be adequate logistical support for his next crossing.

Immediately after the defeat at Aspern-Essling, Napoleon gave General Bertrand carte blanche to procure bridging material. Bertrand boasted to a fellow engineer that he commanded "all the engineer and sapper companies, all the marines, the naval artificers, the pontoons," along with civilian workers and the bridge-building and maintenance machines from Vienna. Bertrand concluded, "I will build solid bridges."[45] And that was what he did. He put a veteran engineer major, renowned as the "grand Pontife," in charge of the great bridge. By the time he and Bertrand were done, an 800-yard-long, iron-reinforced, 60-arch trestle bridge wide enough to permit the simultaneous passage of three carriages had been built. This stout structure was reserved for the artillery and great trains. Next to it was smaller structure, also built on pilings, that would be reserved for the wounded when the battle began. Pontonniers built a third floating bridge as well. Workers established a line of upstream stakes to break the flow of the current and deflect floating missiles, and they even strung a great iron chain they had discovered in the Vienna arsenal that had been used by the Turks in 1684. Napoleon frequently visited to encourage and critique. "He would sit on a block of wood, and exchange ideas and chat familiarly with each of us," recalls an engineer officer.[46] It was hard work for all involved, but the officers at least ended each day with a fine feast because Bertrand set a distinguished table featuring boar cutlets and roast venison. The only problem, remembers an aide, was that the friendly engineer invited too many guests, and the resultant portions were too small!

Workers transformed Lobau into an arsenal complete with workshops, hospitals, and powder magazines—everything that had been so painfully lacking during the earlier attempt to cross the Danube. Sappers widened the paths while workers dredged the small canal that bisected the island. Soon the pontoons and other small craft necessary for an assault crossing filled the canal, ready to emerge into the Danube yet concealed from prying eyes. Behind the island pontonniers secreted a special one-piece, flexible bridge 80 meters long.[47] When the time came, they intended to launch this structure into the current, where it would unfold to touch the Austrian-held shore. Napoleon was everywhere: inspecting the troops, poking into the kitchens, supervising the siting of batteries. Often during the days following Aspern-Essling, he also circulated among the quarters of the

Imperial Guard to visit the injured. Preceded by a secretary who called out the names, he chatted with each man about his service, his wound, and his future and about glory. Then he gave them the cross, a pension, and, gesturing to trailing soldiers who lugged baskets full of 3-franc pieces, immediate cash gifts. It all went down very well.

Napoleon also spent time examining the Hapsburg positions. During one of these reconnaissances he and Marshal Massena dressed in sergeants' greatcoats, walked to the river bank, and while an aide stripped and bathed, stood posed as if about to enter the water but instead closely studied the opposite shore. At other times the emperor would dress in simple soldier's attire, take a musket, and walk to the front line to serve as sentinel in order to see the enemy positions close up.[48] Once he strayed to within 150 feet of the Austrian outpost line. An Austrian officer admonished him: "Retire, Sire, You have no business here!"[49] During the following days Napoleon persisted and almost lost his life. While he gazed at the Austrian lines, a bullet whizzed by close to his head. He turned to Roustam, his Mameluke, and complained that it was Roustam's white turban that attracted the hostile fire and ordered him to wear something else. Seeing the Austrian sentinel reload, he concluded, "It's hot here, let's leave!"[50]

These observations showed Napoleon that his foe had built a formidable line of earthworks from Aspern through Essling to Enzersdorf. If he were to repeat his May crossing, his soldiers would squarely confront these works. Accordingly, the emperor resolved to do two things. Within a week of the defeat of his first crossing attempt, he began hounding the Army of Germany's chief artillerist to concentrate all available heavy artillery on Lobau. He planned to begin his next offensive as if it were a siege, and a siege required battering weapons. Using the siege mortars, heavy howitzers, and cannons so providentially abandoned in the Vienna arsenal, French gunners converted Lobau into an artillery-studded fortress with the weapons sited to pound the Austrian earthworks. Using bridges as if they were saps, he advanced his artillery toward the enemy shore by seizing the many small islets located along the right bank. On these islands his engineers dug fortified battery sites, thereby giving the French the opportunity to deliver converging fire with 109 artillery pieces against selected enemy targets. Napoleon demanded his heavy artillery have a ready reserve of 300 shots and shells.[51] When the day came, he would employ this force to deliver a furious bombardment.

The second thing Napoleon did came about from mature reflection based on his personal scouting missions. Instead of repeating his prior crossing, he would cross downstream from the southern tip of Lobau and thereby outflank the Austrian works. The beauty of this scheme, he explained to Bertrand, was that most of the preparations for battle—the construction of secure bridges to Lobau, the massing of the troops—were the same ones needed to duplicate the May crossing.[52] They could not be kept concealed from Austrian observers on the Bisamberg. Seeing the French preparations would naturally make Karl wonder if Napoleon intended another effort in the same place. Napoleon would turn this to his advantage. For example, the bombardment from Lobau would both secure the left flank of the actual crossing site—its vulnerable flank since any counterattack would come from Karl's camps to the northeast—and serve as a feint to persuade the Austrians that the main crossing would take place at the old crossing site.

All of these preparations somewhat perplexed the isolated men of Massena's Corps who spent 43 days on Lobau. Not knowing when they might be ordered elsewhere and not wishing to waste their energy, most camped in the open for the entire time, although a handful built huts. None of these structures surpassed that built by musician Philippe René-Girault, and therein lay his downfall. His comrades had laughed when Girault began his labors and then looked on with envy. Even the Mameluke Roustam visited to remark that these were fine quarters. Inevitably it attracted the attention of more senior officers. A marshal joked that he must be at the Royal Palace because here was the Café du Caveau![53] Of course, *les grosse épaulettes* could not leave it at that. Once Napoleon established his headquarters on Lobau on July 3, his grand marshal of the palace, General Duroc, shifted lowly Girault from his quarters and made them his own.

While Napoleon's fighting army prepared for battle, the service troops in the rear grew rich by creating a thriving black market. It was all too easy for them to levy their requisitions on the Viennese and keep a little on the side. The challenge was to convert their illicit gains into hard currency and return to France with the money. They could send only a small amount through the post because a large sum would attract attention from the authorities. They dared not leave their hoard in their lodgings because of the risk of theft. Consequently, the black marketeers walked around laden with full money belts and looked for ways to launder it. They made deals with convalescing soldiers who had earned a leave and employed them to return to France with their money. Apparently there were too few such soldiers because the racketeers began making arrangements with perfectly healthy officers, particularly ones who had relatives in the banking world, to carry money back to France once the campaign ended. Captain Elzear Blaze recalls that many officers of his acquaintance received a commission of 50 percent for this service. All of this was not entirely risk free. On the eve of the Battle of Wagram, 12 commissary troops were caught in the act of selling rations intended for the Imperial Guard. A few hours later they were executed by firing squad.

One week before all was ready, Napoleon received a serious alarm when his scouts and spies warned that something was astir in Karl's camps. It appeared that Karl intended to march elsewhere, perhaps to join with Erzherzog Johann or perhaps upstream to threaten the French lines of communication. After laboring so hard for a set-piece battle on the Marchfeld, either possibility was intolerable. Accordingly, on the last day of June he ordered a crossing to the enemy shore in the same place where the May attempt had been made. His men drove off the Austrian pickets and rebuilt the old tête de pont. The totally passive enemy response worried Napoleon. Perhaps Karl had already begun his march. After an exceptionally anxious night, Napoleon awoke to the agreeable news that enemy infantry was now in force behind their fortifications facing the tête de pont. If Karl had intended to maneuver, Napoleon's ploy had convinced him to stay put. The remanning of the tête de pont was a brilliant stroke: it convinced Karl that the French intended to repeat their May maneuver and thus give battle on terms Karl wanted. Instead the ruse gave Napoleon the battle he desperately needed on the terms that he himself dictated.

Cut off from the resources of his capital, the Austrian generalissimus could not match Napoleon's supply of men and war materials. In Karl's mind, this made retention of his remaining resources, particularly the arsenals at Brunn and Olmutz—some 75 and 100 miles northeast of Vienna, respectively—vital. Although he considered various offensive options against the French lines of communication, he could not bring himself to uncover his own sources of supply. This constraint effectively pinned his army to the east bank of the Danube opposite Vienna. Instead of maneuvering, Karl spent the weeks after Aspern-Essling carrying out an extensive reorganization.

For the erzherzog, the best aspect of this effort was the loss of the detested Hiller. Four days after Aspern-Essling, Hiller requested sick leave to journey to the hot baths to seek a cure. Karl happily obliged. Difficult to the end, Hiller would return at the end of June only to ask for leave again on the eve of battle. Karl selected FML Johann Klenau to replace Hiller and assume command of the III Corps. Karl also partially dispensed with the advance guard divisions that previously had been assigned to each corps. Instead, he assembled one powerful advance guard division under the command of the émigré officer Armand Nordmann. Nordmann's division featured light troops, regular regiments including the famous Deutchmeister Infantry—a unit associated with the Teutonic Order—landwehr, cavalry, and 24 artillery pieces equally divided between foot and cavalry batteries. Karl intended the division to operate as the screen for his entire army. Lastly, his army absorbed thousands of landwehr into its ranks. Some served as replacements in line formations, while most remained in autonomous units ranging in strength from the 252-man 3d battalion of Mahrische landwehr to the 690-man 3d Lower Austria landwehr. In the coming battle Karl's field army would engage with 158 infantry battalions. Of these, 34 derived exclusively from the landwehr.[54] Here was the manifest spirit of German nationalism, a willingness to risk all in open battle against the world's most formidable war machine. For these dedicated men the Battle of Wagram would be an overwhelming introduction to combat.

One year before, the Austrian general staff had conducted an exercise based on the idea of an enemy assault crossing from Lobau onto the Marchfeld. Karl utilized this document while preparing for battle. It posited a direct strike much as Napoleon had done in May. To block this blow, the army built the line of fieldworks running from Aspern to Enzersdorf. The staff study never conceived of the idea of a flanking thrust through Enzersdorf, and in 1809 neither did Karl nor his staff.[55] In fact, although Napoleon did not know this, Karl did not seriously consider contesting a French crossing at the water's edge. The fieldworks were merely to serve as an outpost line. The erzherzog intended to fight his battle well back from the river with the aim of not merely repulsing an enemy crossing but annihilating a major French force.

Controversy about how best to contend with another French crossing divided the Hapsburg general staff. One faction wanted to pack the fieldworks and fight to the last on the river line. The other faction, favored by Karl, wanted a mobile battle away from the French artillery on Lobau, in a position offering the possibility of decisive victory. The erzherzog failed to do his duty by resolving this debate. Because he wanted to please both factions and because he was doubtful that Napoleon really intended another maneuver based on Lobau anyway, Karl took half measures. He issued orders to his soldiers manning the works to defend them tenaciously. This made no sense. Either it was an outpost line or it was a main line of resistance. It could not be both. Karl's indecision would condemn thousands of his men to useless sacrifice.

Chapter 7

IN SEARCH OF BATTLE

To sum it up, a battle is my plan of campaign, and success is my whole policy.[1]

RIVER ASSAULT

The stakes this time would be even greater than in May. With Russian animosity confirmed, Germany and the Tyrol aflame, and a British invasion force looming off the North Sea coast, there could be no misstep. Marmont spoke with the emperor on battle's eve. He heard him pass lightly over his May defeat, instead paying homage to his men's heroic courage under difficult circumstances. The tremendous force he had assembled on Lobau inspired him. Marmont saw his old friend's face glowing with excitement and anticipation. Napoleon issued his customary proclamation designed to inspire his troops. After again blaming the earlier setback on the fickle Danube, he said: "March against the enemy; annihilate this power that for fifteen years has menaced our nation and our children; march for victory, a victory that I have the right to expect from your will, your courage and your love for your country and for myself."[2]

As recently as four years ago, on the eve of Austerlitz, Napoleon's prebattle proclamation had inspired his men to prodigies of valor. Before Wagram, they greeted it with indifference. Along with the proclamation there were specific orders that the soldiers took more seriously. Among them was the directive that no one could leave the ranks to succor the wounded. This behavior had weakened the fighting ranks back in May. Now it would be left to the ambulance train to evacuate the wounded. The directive displeased many in the rank and file. The ambulance train had earned an ugly reputation for rifling the wounded's pockets as they transported them to the field hospitals.[3] Although adherence to the directive cut off one avenue of escape for the shirker, for the dedicated soldier it raised the prospect of rough treatment from uncaring hands.

In addition to the emperor's oratory were the words of the combat leaders. Eugène's Army of Italy had marched hard and fast through sweltering summer heat to arrive at the crossing sites on July 4. As they moved toward the bridges, soldiers were acutely aware that they now marched shoulder to shoulder with the Army of Germany. Cavalry Brigadier Sahuc galloped before his troopers and demonstrated that he could speechify better than he could fight battles. Sahuc said, "Chasseurs, victory beckons us to the far side of the Danube. . . . We are going to prove to the Emperor that his expectations for the Army of Italy are well founded. Remember, there is no hope of retreat for the French army, it is necessary to defeat our enemy."[4] It was difficult for soldiers to take seriously such words spoken by an officer who had displayed cowardice and ineptitude in the face of the enemy.

Amid bombastic oratory there were also some truthful utterances. Napoleon told his men that "the Danube no longer exists for the French army." This statement was surprisingly accurate because of the mighty labor of Bertrand's engineers. In addition, Captain Baste of the Imperial Guard Marines had organized a small riverine fleet to patrol the Danube and ward off the waterborne missiles that had destroyed the bridges back in May. Lookouts stationed on the upstream tip of Lobau watched for these missiles, and their warning would send the pontonniers swarming into boats to fend them off. Indeed, when Austrian pontonniers did cast off 18 great fire rafts into the upstream current, they caused no damage. The proof of the adequacy of French preparations came in the ominous early hours of the operation. A hard rain fell, and the river rose. A trooper relates, "We passed the river's first branch on a superb bridge, artfully built on a solid wooden framework."[5] Although the second bridge was more precarious— the horses hooves pressed its decking down into the fast-flowing water—it too held firm. There would be no broken bridges this time.

So Napoleon's infantry tramped over the bridges to Lobau in endless columns. The cavalry crossed, their mounts laden with fresh hay, for there would be no opportunity to graze once the battle began. An enormous train of ammunition and bread wagons followed. It was an unprecedented buildup of force and a fine logistical feat. By July 4 some 180,000 men had assembled on Lobau or on the shore opposite. Marshal Davout took control of the military police on the island and ran things with his customary "fierce severity."[6] There were many happy renewals of friendship as French soldiers who had been scattered in garrisons throughout Europe met one another for the first time since departing the camps along the Atlantic coast back in 1805. And there were some surprising meetings between old foes, as when officers of the 11th Chasseurs à Cheval spoke with officers belonging to the Saxon cavalry. The last time they had encountered one another had been three years ago on the battlefield of Jena when their regiments, fighting on opposite sides, had engaged in a furious melee. Now the survivors boasted about what they would accomplish fighting side by side.

Napoleon carefully reviewed his plans with Chief of Staff Berthier and Marshal Massena. Just now Massena was in an awkward situation. A few weeks earlier Napoleon had heard that Massena's chief of staff, General Becker, had taken to criticizing the emperor's strategy. In spite of Massena's protests—the marshal depended heavily on Becker for the day-to-day running of his corps—Napoleon summarily relieved him. This was a serious blow to the corps' intellectual resources. Then came a crippling physical blow when Massena suffered a bad fall from his horse that rendered him unable to ride. Napoleon excused his old comrade from the coming battle, saying that one of his senior aides could replace him. Massena replied, "No sire, I will not abandon my post. I will command from a coach."[7] Massena being the man he was was not content with any coach. He procured a splendid calèche—a light, open carriage—drawn by a matched team of four white horses and crewed by a tophat-bedecked coachman and postilion. If this guaranteed being highly visible to his men, it also meant that he would be easily spotted by enemy gunners.

By the evening of July 4 Oudinot had massed his corps on the southwest side of Lobau. Henceforth, and in great contrast to the improvisational efforts back in May, events proceeded with clockwork precision according to Napoleon's detailed orders.[8] The weather also helped: a terrific thunderstorm raged, and its fury made the Austrian sentinels less vigilant. At 9 P.M. some 1,500 veterans assembled around the well-known gunner Colonel Seruzier, who explained what had to be done: "Comrades, we have a glorious mission to accomplish; it is difficult, but success is certain if you have confidence in me; obey your officers and don't say a word, because success depends upon our silence." The veterans replied, "Commanded by the 'father of cannon shot,' we would attack the devil without saying a word. . . . Let's go!"[9] They donned white armbands so as to be able to identify one another during the night combat. Protected by Captain Baste's gunboats, Seruzier and his men crossed in boats and rafts to storm the Hansel-Grund. They had orders to advance with the bayonet and avoid firing. The wind drove the boats ashore on the Hansel-Grund while the swaying limbs of the riverside trees made enough noise to prevent the Austrians from hearing the French movement. The troops assembled and attacked the Austrian camp, taking it by surprise and capturing scores of prisoners and their general to boot.

Five large flatboats carried across another 1,500 men and were then employed as pontoons to carry a bridge.[10] Napoleon had allocated two hours for the construction of this bridge, and his pontonniers, toiling heroically, complied with his demand. As soon as the bridge was secure, the balance of Oudinot's Corps crossed to the Hansel-Grund. However, whatever glory lay ahead would be exclusively claimed by Oudinot's French soldiers. While they continued on through the woods to capture a fortified Hapsburg outpost, Oudinot assigned his Portuguese contingent the uncomfortable task of digging trenches in the rain-sodden earth to protect the bridge. The first crossing had been crowned with success. So far the Austrian command had no idea that a major assault was underway.

At 11 P.M. the 109 guns on Lobau and on adjacent isles opened a furious bombardment of the Austrian fortifications between Aspern and Essling. Gunboats sailed up and down the river to create further diversions. On schedule, fifteen minutes later Sainte-Croix and 1,500 men pushed off from Lobau to land a half-mile upstream of Oudinot's bridge. With a small bridgehead established, now was the moment for the one-piece, flexible bridge to be swung out into the current. Napoleon personally supervised the operation. Addressing the officer in charge, he asked: "How long do you require for the swinging?"

"A quarter of an hour, Sire."

"I give you five minutes. Bertrand, your watch!"[11]

The operation went off without a hitch and before the far end had been completely secured, Napoleon sent Massena's men swarming across. Pontonniers had also built several raft bridges and prepositioned them upstream of the crossing site. By 2 A.M., in the middle of a driving rainstorm, they completed four more bridges to allow the rest of Massena's Corps passage to the far shore.

By now the Austrians understood that something was afoot and their guns also began to fire. General Lejeune, an imperial aide, related:

The sullen roar of the enemy's cannon and the flashes of fire from their guns now began to mingle with the thunder and lightning from the sky. A flash suddenly revealed to me when I least suspected it that I was standing side by side with the Emperor, whose profile with the little cap and the grey cloak stood out distinctly for a moment.[12]

The rain ended at 5 A.M., and the sky brightened to produce a warm and muggy July day. Sappers immediately went to work fortifying the bridgeheads, while Davout's Corps joined Massena and Oudinot on the right bank. Behind them additional troops filed toward the bridgehead. Legrand's men, having fulfilled their role to feint from the old tête de pont (and undergone an intense nocturnal bombardment in the process), withdrew to Lobau, their places taken by General Jean Renyier's command. They had 30 minutes to eat a bit of bread and receive extra cartridges, and then they too crossed the river to join the main army.

Around 8 A.M. Napoleon ordered the grand left wheel begun. Enzersdorf was the southern anchor of the Austrian line and was well protected by a crenellated town wall fronted by a tall dike. Austrian engineers had strengthened the position with fieldworks. Massena sent Sainte-Croix and Pelet with the 46th Ligne to storm the position. Three hundred soldiers of the Bellegarde infantry clung to the chateau. French sappers shouldered to the fore, battered down the doors, and opened the way for a winning assault by the grenadiers. As soon as they captured the chateau, pontonniers built another bridge to connect with Lobau. Joined now by Bernadotte's Saxons, the French advanced as if on parade on a four-corps front, the individual battalions massed in serried columns at deployment distance with artillery in the intervals. By noon the Army of Italy, Dupas's division, Marmont's Corps, and the Guard—the last in full dress uniform—had filed over the bridges to provide a second line while Bessières's cavalry reserve formed a third rank. For the remainder of the day, a steady stream of artillery, wagons, and reserves flowed over the bridges.

Napoleon's objective had been to interpose his army between Karl and Erzherzog Johann and to outflank the line of works facing Lobau. By noon he had accomplished this. Equally important, he showed that he had learned well the logistical lessons of Aspern-Essling. He waited until his supply train had crossed the Danube before pressing on. This time his men would not run short of ammunition. Now he had to locate Karl's army and defeat it. Toward this end he continued his advance onto the Marchfeld. While Massena proceeded parallel to the Danube, his veterans gleefully clearing first Essling and then Aspern against negligible resistance, the balance of the army wheeled to the right toward the Russbach. Officers from Napoleon on down speculated whether here the Austrians would offer battle.

On the evening of July 4, Austrian observers on the Bisamberg had witnessed the massing of the French troops on the bridges leading to Lobau. Although the field telegraph quickly transmitted a report to Karl's headquarters, somehow the soldiers manning the forward defenses never received an alert. To escape from the mud caused by the thunderstorm, many Austrian troopers remained mounted overnight. This poor equestrian care weakened the horses for the coming ordeal. The infantry pickets also sought shelter. It was this lack of vigilance that helped the French crossing.

When Erzherzog Karl received his lookouts' reports on July 4, he immediately sent a courier off to Erzherzog Johann requesting that he march upstream to join the army. Johann's army was about 30 miles away, manning a bridgehead over the Danube at Pressburg. It would require swift marching to link up with Karl by July 6, but Karl did not expect that there would be a battle until July 7. The Austrian generalissimus anticipated that Napoleon would require one day to cross the Danube and most of a second to close up on his inland defensive position behind the Russbach. He calculated that Johann should have ample time to reach the battlefield. He did not know that Johann would find reasons to delay his march and thus fail to arrive in time. Moreover, the velocity of the French advance on July 5 totally surprised Karl. From the Bisamberg he and his brother the kaiser watched the French expand from their crossing sites. Franz asked what he intended to do. Karl replied that he planned to allow the French to cross and then attack and throw them back into the river. A trifle alarmed at the French masses maneuvering quickly across the Marchfeld, the kaiser responded, "So be it. Just don't let too many cross."[13]

Karl left FML Nordmann, with his 24 battalions, 20 squadrons, and 48 cannon, to contest alone the weight of Napoleon's entire army. The French soldiers marched against Nordmann through waist-high wheat. During this advance, the much-strengthened French artillery proved its worth. The divisional and horse batteries were well forward. Whenever the leading infantry encountered any opposition, a few artillery blasts, eagerly seconded by regimental guns, proved able to force back Nordmann's vedettes. Outflanked, FML Nordmann could do little to slow the French juggernaut. When one of his battalions tried to defend Raasdorf, a small village in the middle of the Marchfeld, Marshal Bernadotte sent in the 5th Légère to clear them out. A brief combat ensued and the white-coats fled, leaving behind 100 prisoners.

In midafternoon Napoleon's army surged through Raasdorf toward Wagram, led by sixteen squadrons of Saxon cavalry. Commanded by officers who retained "the old knightly spirit of the Seven Years War," these troopers represented a proud lineage.[14] However, they had fared poorly when fighting with Prussia against Napoleon in 1806 and been forced to hand their superb horses to the French as part of the peace terms. Mounted on young and indifferently trained mounts, they now opposed an Austrian cuirassier brigade commanded by a French émigré officer, GM Vicomte Roussel d'Hurbal. A French staff officer arrived with instructions for the Saxon cavalry to drive off the cuirassiers. The order caught the Saxon cavalry leaders unready. To cover their deployment, the 250-man-strong Prince Clement Chevaulégers charged. The Austrian heavy cav-alry easily repulsed this effort, but it had served its purpose by permitting the remaining ten Saxon squadrons to deploy.

Saxon Generals von Gutschmidt and Feilitzsch placed themselves at the head of their troopers. Saxon cavalry doctrine taught that a charge begin at a sharp trot, then accelerated to a short gallop, and finally to a headlong charge. The two cavalry leaders followed this doctrine precisely. Instead of countercharging the galloping Saxon cavalry, Vicomte d'Hurbal ordered his cuirassiers to fire one carbine volley and receive the enemy on the points of their swords. Already outnumbered three to one, this tactical blunder sealed the fate of the Hapsburg horse as the Saxons shook off the effect of the carbine fire and closed in. Included in the ranks of the attackers was one squadron of the Prince Albert Chevaulégers. Among the defenders was the Erzherzog Albert Cuirassiers. Such was the con-fused state of central European politics that both units were nominally com-manded by the same man, Albert of Saxe-Teschen. Those troopers fighting under the French émigré officer fared less well than those fighting on Napoleon's side. In a brief melee, the Saxon cavalry drove the Austrian cuirassiers from the field.

During the charge, an unobserved Austrian infantry battalion fired into the right flank of the Saxon cavalry. A Saxon major commanding the 1st Hussar squadron wheeled his unit to face this fire and charged, a commendable display of tactical initiative that dispersed the infantry and led to the capture of nearly 500 men and a standard. The next day the four hussars who seized the flag presented it to Napoleon. Well pleased, the emperor proclaimed the Saxon Hus-sars as "one of the bravest in his Army."[15] Bernadotte was even more effusive in his praise. He told the officers of the Leib Cuirassiers that "I have always counted on you, but today you have surpassed my expectations."[16]

In spite of this satisfying progress, something unintended had taken place, the consequences of which were shortly to be revealed. Napoleon had sent Massena to operate on his left wing and Davout to maneuver on his right. The Army of

Italy advanced to fill the void in the middle. This meant that Bernadotte's Saxons and Eugène's men, Napoleon's least trustworthy units—suspect because of their foreign component, and more important, their officers' inexperience—held the center of his position.

EVENING DEFEAT

The two-day Battle of Wagram was a military rarity: a decisive combat between the rivals' main field armies that featured the initiative swinging back and forth as both generals committed their armies to the offensive. Some 5 miles across the Marchfeld from the bridgehead that the French army had used back in May lies the village of Wagram. A small brook, the Russbach, curves around the village and meanders parallel to the Danube for 3 miles until reaching the hamlet of Neusiedel.[17] Along this sector the Russbach's depth did not exceed 3 feet, but its steep banks prevented the passage of cavalry and artillery and impaired the movement of infantry. Behind the Russbach and between Wagram and Neusiedel the ground rises gently. Here were the famous "heights" of Wagram. *Heights* misleadingly conveys hills and ridges, an impression strengthened by the battle paintings made long after the event. Moreover, French participants invariably used the word *heights* to describe this portion of the field even though it seldom rose more than 10 feet above the plain. Postbattle recollections reveal the point that in battle a slight rise that has important tactical significance becomes a daunting obstacle to those who must surmount it. Indeed, artillery sited on the elevated ground behind the Russbach dominated the flat Marchfeld. A 50- to 100-yard-wide vale between the stream and the higher ground provided defenders with a natural glacis, a perfect shooting range for infantry and gunners to deliver point-blank fire against a foe already distressed after wading the stream and climbing the muddy bank.

Karl recognized the strength of the Russbach position and based his strategy on it. He divided his army into two wings. One wing occupied the ground between Wagram and Neusiedel facing southwest toward the Danube. At Wagram his line turned due west and continued toward the river. This southward-facing wing occupied the foothills around the Bisamberg. Wagram was the hinge linking the two wings of the Austrian army.

Around 5 P.M. Sahuc's cavalry deployed in the Army of Italy's front line facing the Russbach. For the first time they could see their foe. A line of white-coated skirmishers blazed away and caused some losses. Then several batteries appeared and deployed to begin a lethal short-range bombardment. In the 8th Chasseurs à Cheval, the trumpeters, mounted on white horses, massed in the regiment's center. Ruefully a trumpeter commented, "This time, my friends, look out for the white horses! They are about to be fricasseed along with some of us."[18] The French artillery arrived to return the fire while behind them the infantry deployed. Men in reserve could not see past the thick cloud of smoke enveloping the front line; the battle's roar numbed their senses. All they could do was close ranks to fill the gaps caused by bounding ball and plunging shell.

By 6 P.M. Napoleon's army had overrun the entire plain while the curiously inert Austrians watched from the heights to the north and from behind the Russbach. Three Austrian corps defended the Russbach, a force easily able to hold this position during the remaining hours of light. Two corps and the grenadiers held the high ground on the northern border of the Marchfeld, secure against any evening attack. Inexplicably Karl had failed to link these two forces with anything more solid than a handful of regiments from his reserve cavalry. Only a few battalions of Bellegarde's Corps were in Wagram itself, yet this village was the absolute key to his entire position. Although Karl possessed an army of more than 135,000 men and had had the entire day to watch the French maneuvers unfold, he had left himself hugely vulnerable should the French be bold enough to try an assault during the remaining hours of daylight. Even as Karl began to appreciate all of this, he saw to his horror that Napoleon apparently intended to seek decisive advantage before the sun went down.

Napoleon had ridden to the forefront of his army to scout the Austrian dispositions. He did not know the strength and disposition of his opponent. Some of his aides argued that the Hapsburg cannonade was merely a screen to cover a retreat. The emperor disagreed. Furthermore, his experienced eye saw that Karl had presented him with a priceless opportunity. Emboldened by the heretofore feeble Austrian resistance, he immediately improvised an assault. Davout, on his right flank, would attack along both sides of the Russbach to roll up the Austrian line. Massena, on his left flank, would defend against any enemy advance onto the Marchfeld. The main effort would be conducted by Oudinot and Bernadotte against Wagram. He sent a senior aide to Oudinot to tell that general "to push a little further forward" to "make some music before dark."[19] The Army of Italy would support this attack. To ensure that Eugène made no serious mistakes, Napoleon sent one of his experienced aides, General Reille, to advise his stepson. Because the different formations involved had not uniformly closed up to the Russbach, most had to make approach marches of varying distances before being in position to attack. To accommodate them, Napoleon did not specify a time for the attack to commence. A more serious omission was his failure to delineate clear objectives for his assault leaders. When his artillery began its bombardment at 7 P.M. the consequences of his overly hasty preparation became evident.

FML Hohenzollern, an officer Karl considered among his best, had deployed his II Corps along the Russbach with great care. In spite of persistent deficiencies, the Hapsburg light infantry had made important strides, which showed during the evening of July 5. Hohenzollern guarded his front with a solid chain of skirmishers who took advantage of the folds in the ground to conceal themselves until contact. Behind them, farther up the slope, he arranged his infantry in a double line strengthened by 68 artillery pieces. The first line manned a set of fieldworks. The village of Baumersdorf, the center of the Hapsburg defense of the Russbach, served as an outwork. Hohenzollern sent General Hardegg with

Evening Battle
(July 5, 1809)

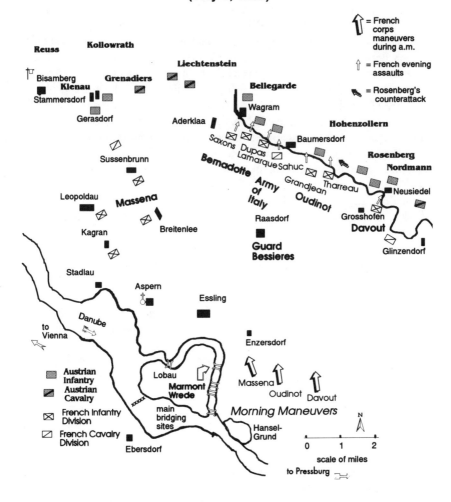

1,500 men of the 8th Jager Battalion and the 2d Battalion of the Erzherzog Karl Legion to defend it.

Baumersdorf should have been a first objective for the French attack. Capture of its two bridges would permit the passage of cavalry and artillery over the stream so that they could support an infantry attack against the higher ground. However, Baumersdorf lay athwart the corps boundary between Eugène and Oudinot, and both commanders overlooked it. Instead of concentrating on this village, Eugène bypassed it to the west while the balance of Oudinot's Corps bypassed it on the east. The unit that did attack the village, the 57th Ligne, was the most renowned regular infantry formation in the army. The "Terrible 57th" assailed Baumersdorf with customary élan but was quickly repulsed by Hardegg's defenders. Such things did not happen. Joined by the majority of Grandjean's division (formerly Saint-Hilaire's unit), the regiment attacked again. Baumersdorf was a mere hamlet of some 30 buildings, yet the 7,300 French veterans could not capture it. The Austrians clung to the buildings and gardens with desperate tenacity and FML Hohenzollern fed in more troops as the situation warranted.

Meanwhile, the 10th Légère bypassed the hamlet, outfought most of an entire Austrian brigade that manned the stream bank, climbed the slope, and deployed into line. The gallant 10th Légère had made a serious penetration of Hohenzollern's position. Briefly it seemed that the wavering defenders could be overmatched if only fresh troops arrived to support the regiment. But no help came. Instead, while subjected to a merciless artillery crossfire, the regiment had to stand and face a determined counterattack by units from Hohenzollern's second line. Then, boring in against its right flank, came 2,000 men of the Hiller Infantry Regiment released by FML Rosenberg when he saw the neighboring corps in trouble. Isolated and overwhelmed, the 10th Légère yielded its position and retreated.

The fact that the regiment had received no help from the rear was due to Grandjean's failure against Baumersdorf. The fact that it also had no flank support stemmed from the failure of the adjacent division on its right. Here Tharreau's division of Oudinot's Corps had driven in the Austrian skirmishers, crossed the stream, and encountered a terrible artillery fire. Among many, a cannonball tore the backpack off a grenadier who had recently rejoined his unit after surviving a grievous wound received at Aspern-Essling. This time Jean-Joseph Jeunechamps escaped with a slight wound. Tharreau's men battered away against the steady Zach and Joseph Colloredo Infantry Regiments without success. Seeing Tharreau's men waver, FML Hohenzollern placed himself at the head of the Vincent Chevaulégers (a much depleted regiment that had dwindled to a mere 517 troopers) and led a charge that drove Tharreau's soldiers back over the Russbach. By 8 P.M. Oudinot's Corps was in retreat, having lost close to 5,000 men even while Eugène and Bernadotte were launching their assaults.

The next division to engage in this disjointed succession of attacks was the Dupas Division in Bernadotte's Corps. The division was a scratch force of five French battalions numbering slightly over 3,700 men. Two Saxon battalions, Metzsch's light infantry and von Radelof's grenadiers, added some 1,000 muskets to Dupas's strength. Dupas attacked Bellegarde's center between Baumersdorf and Wagram. Austrian light infantry, firing from concealed positions among a collection of farming hovels and soldiers' huts, took a heavy toll, but the soldiers waded across the waist-deep Russbach and hurled themselves against the Austrian gun line. After delivering several blasts of canister, some of the brown-coated gunners abandoned their weapons and sought shelter in the nearby battalion masses. Dupas's soldiers overran the silent cannon and sent the Austrian first line reeling. The routing soldiers of GM Wacquant's brigade threatened to carry away the second Hapsburg line until Erzherzog Karl appeared to rally them. Dupas had seized a small bridge over the stream, only to find it unable to carry the weight of horses or guns. Thus it was particularly fortunate that, as the division fought against mounting odds, it heard the welcome sound of support on its right. It was Generals Macdonald and Lamarque leading seven Army of Italy battalions in column over the Russbach.

After crossing the stream, these battalions deployed into line and charged up the slope. Bellegarde's defenders stood in battalion masses. Given that they confronted no French cavalry, this was a poor choice since they could hardly trade volleys with the French on an equal basis. The Vogelsang Infantry Regiment broke first, and as its men fled, they spread disorder among the supporting second line. The combination of Dupas's assault and the success enjoyed by the seven Army of Italy battalions left Bellegarde's Corps in parlous straits. But there remained a powerful Hapsburg artillery that vomited canister into the French lines and brought them to a halt. Because their own artillery could not cross the Russbach, the French had no answer to this punishment. Four of Eugène's generals received wounds during this phase of the fighting, and Austrian fire killed the colonel of the 13th Ligne.

Displaying surpassing valor, the divisions of Dupas and Lamarque managed to shake off the effects of the Hapsburg canister fire and press forward. Lamarque's men captured hundreds of prisoners and seized five standards. It appeared as if these two divisions alone were about to pierce the Austrian center, but Karl and his lieutenants were alive to the threat. Karl ordered reserves from both flanks and hurled them into the breach while he rode among Bellegarde's wavering soldiers to steady them. With their generals leading the way, the Austrian counterattack gained momentum. The Erbach Regiment covered itself with glory when its 2,000 men made a successful frontal charge attack against Lamarque. At this time, having driven Oudinot off and cleared his own front, Hohenzollern rallied his chevaulégers and saw that he was on Lamarque's flank. He wheeled his light horse and bore in against this vulnerable target, a charge that sent Lamarque's men tumbling back over the stream. General Macdonald related: "The great effort to rally the soldiers was useless; a panic had seized the men."[20] The Hapsburg light horse chased the fleeing French and forced them to abandon their prisoners. They killed four of the five French grenadiers who were trying to carry off the captured standards.

In addition, the failure to capture Baumersdorf allowed the Austrian infantry to pour a withering fire against the Army of Italy's right flank. Macdonald continued: "General Grénier's troops, amazed at this unexpected onslaught, threw themselves in disorder among my men, breaking their lines and scattering them. All my efforts to restrain them were vain. . . . The rout commenced, and we were carried away, crossing the stream in the utmost confusion."[21] Macdonald lost around 2,000 men killed, wounded, or taken prisoner. It had been an inauspicious debut for the Army of Italy, and Eugène worried what his stepfather would think. Macdonald reassured him, "Nothing detrimental to you or me. He will realize, now that it is too late, that his orders were ill-considered."[22]

With the collapse of the Army of Italy, Dupas's battalions could do little more. Around 8 P.M. they too broke in rout. During the evening battle, the French elements of the division lost nearly two-thirds of their strength. Fortunately, Sahuc's light cavalry division had finally managed to find a crossing point. It was so narrow that the unit could advance on only a four-man front. As the sun set behind the Bohemian mountains, Sahuc's men charged the pursuing Vincent chevaulégers and Hesse-Hombourg Hussars. A French trooper describes the scene: "The shouts of the victors and vanquished, the smoke, the fire, the noise, the blast of the guns, the explosion of the caissons . . . and worst of all the screams of the wounded who were consumed in the burning fields."[23]

Ten yards before contact, the chasseurs discharged their carbines and pistols. The two sides closed and fought hand to hand, and soon both of Sahuc's colonels went down with wounds. In the murky twilight, the white uniforms of the Austrian chevaulegers provided unmistakable targets. Trumpeter Chevillet describes how he forced "my horse between two enemy horses and ran the point of my saber into the belly of the nearest dragoon [sic]. At the same moment, I received a furious blow on my head, that stunned me a bit." Chevillet's leather colbak cushioned the shock, and he recovered to find himself behind the Austrian line, separated from his unit, and beset by three or four enemy troopers: "Two saber blows hit me, one on the back, which was parried by my equipment, and the other [from the front] I parried with my saber."[24] Breaking free, Chevillet encountered a fifth foe, ran his saber through him, and rejoined his comrades.

Fortunately for the French, the growing darkness put an end to the day's close combat. One officer was totally dissatisfied with what had taken place. Determined that if the French could not hold it he would be damned if the enemy was going to possess it, Seruzier massed his howitzers and opened a destructive bombardment against Baumersdorf. Peasants had already made their first cutting of hay and straw and stored it in the village. This made a dry, combustible load easily ignited by howitzer shells. After an hour's firing, Seruzier had the gratification of seeing the burning forage spread flames to the timber-built village. The fire burned most of the night.

The entire assault had been a most disjointed affair. The salient failure to capture Baumersdorf meant that the attacking infantry did-not receive support from their cavalry and artillery. Infantry alone, confronting a stout enemy force of all arms, could not win. That night the soldiers muttered to one another, "Ah! If Saint-Hilaire had been present . . . things would have been different."[25] The senior officers reflected that in the absence of Lannes's tactical direction, Oudinot had displayed impetuosity and little else. Three days later Oudinot would also show an ability to write an official report. All he said of this action was that "the night having arrived, we could not continue our attacks with success."[26]

There remained one more series of assaults. Although French historians would long deny it—in fact, Napoleon's bulletin explained away the action on July 5 by saying that in the growing darkness the Saxons had mistakenly fired into the

French thus forcing both to retreat—Bernadotte's Saxons now entered the fray in a most gallant style.

Around 7 P.M., Bernadotte's IX Corps received orders to attack Wagram. Besides Dupas's division, Bernadotte had in hand some 9,000 Saxons and 14 guns. The Marshal perfected his dispositions and had his artillery open a preliminary bombardment. By the time he ordered the advance, about one hour later, Dupas's and Eugène's men had already been defeated. A battalion of light infantry screened the march of the six battalions of Le Coq's Brigade. The Saxon battalion columns drove in a thick line of Austrian skirmishers belonging to the 2d Jager Battalion who lined the Russbach. Passing over the 20-pace-wide bridge, the Saxons entered Wagram proper, where they received heavy fire from the tall buildings lining both sides of the street. General Le Coq, his horse shot out from under him, continued to lead the charge on foot. His men could make no impression against a dominating church on the town square. From its confines a battalion of the Reuss-Plauen Regiment repelled repeated charges and managed to wound the brave Le Coq.

In fighting reminiscent of Ebelsberg (even the town caught fire) the balance of the Saxon infantry entered into house-to-house fighting in Wagram but could make little headway. At 10:30 P.M., Marshal Bernadotte ordered his remaining two battalions—the Leib Guard and von Bose's Grenadiers—to capture "the burning town."[27] All these elite troops managed to do was to run up the butcher's bill. In the confused night action, white-coated Saxons mistook one another for the enemy and fired into each other. In spite of inspired front-line leadership—here Brigadier General Hartitzsch received a mortal wound—the Saxons made scant progress. At an hour before midnight, GdK Bellegarde fed in the Mittrowsky Regiment from reserve. These fresh troops drove the Saxons from Wagram. They had fought a hard fight, losing numerous senior officers. But they had entered the combat piecemeal, and for this tactical sin they had paid a high price: the von Low and Konig Regiments lost close to half their men; most of the other Saxon units suffered 33 percent losses. The next day would demonstrate the consequences of their sacrifice.

Thus the first day of battle ended. While the French soldiers ate whatever meager rations were available, and in truth there was very little with even the preferred guard light cavalry going hungry, the emperor summoned his senior commanders. Marshals Berthier, Davout, and Bessières; Generals Fririon (the injured Massena's chief of staff) and Oudinot; and the army's senior artillerist, General La Riboisière, attended. Notably absent was Marshal Bernadotte, presumably still sorting out his command after the debacle in Wagram. Napoleon explained to his lieutenants that Karl had three choices: to stay put; to attack the French right flank and thus preserve communications with Johann's army; or to attack the French left, cutting the connection with the bridges. His counter was to order Davout to conduct an assault against Karl's left flank while massing the balance of his force in the center. Thus, if Karl fought a defensive battle, he would be defeated by Davout. If Karl attacked either French flank, his center would have to be weakened. Then it would be another Austerlitz, because Napoleon would respond with a mighty frontal attack to pierce Karl's center followed by a turning movement to defeat the Austrian wings. Pointing to his map, he indicated the position he wished to find his corps occupying when the sun rose. In order to create the concentration he desired, Davout would incline toward the French center while Massena would march 5 miles from the Danube toward Wagram.

One of the axioms Napoleon had developed and practiced in his earlier campaigns demanded that "a general should say to himself many times a day: If the hostile army were to make its appearance to my front, on my right, or on my left, what should I do? And if he is embarrassed, his arrangements are bad; there is something wrong; he must rectify his mistake."[28] Having accounted for all alternatives, the emperor dozed briefly in a tent stretched over a stack of drums, confident that the morrow would bring victory.

The morning would show that Napoleon went astray by failing to comprehend the changing nature of warfare. Aspern-Essling had provided a hint, but the powerful role of the Danube obscured the lesson. Artillery, concentrated in unprecedented numbers, could dominate a field. He also underestimated his opponent's audacity. Lastly, then and thereafter, he entirely ignored the significance of the evening's tactical setbacks. Napoleon merely referred to the combat of July 5 as "this brush." In fact, it was more than that. The drubbing set the stage for Karl's surprise counteroffensive.

Chapter 8

THE KILLING GROUND

A battle is a dramatic action which has its beginning, its middle, and its end. The battle order of the opposing armies and their preliminary maneuvers until they come to grips form the exposition. The countermaneuvers of the army which has been attacked constitute the dramatic complication. They lead in turn to new measures and bring about the crisis, and from this results the outcome or denouement.[1]

SPOILING ATTACK

The emperor's servants shook awake his imperial aides in time for them to enjoy a splendid predawn breakfast. As the sun emerged from behind the Carpathian Mountains, it reflected off the bayonets, helmets, and breastplates of 320,000 men and illuminated the dull bronze of over 1,100 artillery pieces. At 4 A.M. the sounds of firing from the south end of the line around Neusiedel disturbed this scene of martial splendor and sent the aides hastening to their mounts.[2] The Hapsburg artillery positioned behind the Russbach joined in to announce the beginning of the world's largest battle since the invention of gunpowder.[3]

One aide in particular found himself in a most awkward situation. Since Napoleon remained uncertain of Karl's intentions, at 2 A.M. Chief of Staff Berthier had dispatched one of his trusted aides, an officer named Lejeune, to scout the Austrian position and ascertain whether Karl planned to offer battle or to retreat. Lejeune stealthily crossed the Russbach, approached the enemy camps, and found the Austrians resting. He moved south toward Neusiedel to discover soldiers massing in preparation for an attack. Lejeune appreciated that this blow would take Napoleon by surprise. Although he understood that he was now the bearer of priceless intelligence, he found the line of Austrian vedettes too thick to risk a dash to headquarters. Forced to take a wide detour, Lejeune did not return until nearly an hour after the battle began. Lejeune's failure contributed to a chain of events that allowed Erzherzog Karl to achieve a profound tactical surprise.

Overnight the Austrian generalissimus had resolved to risk all by seizing the initiative. The perimeter of his picket line extended from Neusiedel on his left flank to the Bisamberg overlooking the Danube on his right flank. This line was nearly three times as extensive as the French line. For an outnumbered army to occupy such an extensive position along exterior lines and use it to launch an offensive was a military rarity. This too contributed to Napoleon's surprise. During the handful of hours following the end of the fighting in Wagram until dawn on July 6, Karl made few adjustments to his position. He sent a cavalry division from his mounted reserve to FML Rosenberg who held his left flank, dispatched a regiment of cuirassiers to buttress Hohenzollern's II Corps position behind the Russbach, and ordered GM Frelich to take his two hussar regiments east to reach out toward Erzherzog Johann. Otherwise Karl left his dispositions intact. Between 11:30 P.M. and midnight, he issued battle instructions.

His major attack would be delivered by fresh troops who had spent the previous day holding the high ground northwest of the Marchfeld. Just before nightfall Karl had seen the French mass for an apparent renewal of the attack against Wagram. Accordingly, he instructed the VI and III Corps to descend from the heights and attack the exposed French left flank between Breitenlee and the river. They would begin their approach march at 1 A.M. The grenadiers of the Reserve Corps would advance through Sussenbrunn to support this effort and similarly take the French in flank. Liechtenstein's cavalry, minus detached elements, had the mission of linking the attacking right wing with Bellegarde's I Corps. The I Corps, in turn, accompanied by Karl himself, would advance against Aderklaa. The II Corps would hold its position behind the Russbach at all costs until the attacking wing gained momentum, at which time it was to cross the stream and join the advance. On Karl's left flank, the IV Corps also received orders to attack. All attacks would begin at 4 A.M.

As he had done back in May, Karl provided specific tactical guidance. He stipulated that his infantry would fight in battalion mass or battalion square with skirmishers in front. Whether in attack or defense, his corps were to form in two lines. He strictly enjoined his infantry to refrain from useless long-range fire. Recalling the success of his fire ships, the erzherzog ordered that the 18 great fire rafts already built by his pontonniers be launched into the Danube's current laden with stones and barrels of gunpowder. Karl hoped that they would ram and burn their way through the French bridges to create havoc similar to that which had occurred in May.

Altogether this was a boldly conceived stroke. Yet in characteristic Hapsburg style, Karl was unwilling to summon every available bayonet and sword for the decisive toss of the die. He left the 8,000-man V Corps and an 1,800-man brigade of the III Corps back on the high ground facing Vienna. Although outnumbered,

The Battle of Wagram
(July 6, 1809, 4:00 A.M. Positions)

he had evenly spread his strength along his entire line. Not only had he ignored the virtues of mass, he had no reserves. There was no doubt that an effort to attack simultaneously on two far-flung flanks would be difficult to coordinate. Whatever possibility existed for coordination went sour from the beginning. Karl wanted his units farthest from the field to begin marching at 1 A.M. in order to reach their assault positions 3 hours later. Yet by issuing his orders only 60 to 90 minutes before his troops had to march, he much reduced the likelihood that this would occur. It would take time for his couriers to find the relevant commands, for those commands to assemble, and even longer for them to make a nocturnal approach march of some 6 to 8 miles. Then they would have to deploy within cannonshot of a formidable foe, something that would require even a well-led, veteran corps 1 to 2 hours to perform. Karl's timetable was too tight and made no allowances for the inevitable friction of war. Nonetheless, it almost worked.

Napoleon's plan hinged on the power of Marshal Davout's attack against the Austrian left flank. Napoleon ordered Davout to begin at first light. Davout believed that the previous evening's probe had demonstrated the strength of the Neusiedel position. Rather than directly assault the village, this time Davout planned to use two divisions to fix its defenders while his other two maneuvered to outflank it. The problems with Davout's scheme were two: it would leave the bulk of Napoleon's army subjected to punishing Hapsburg crossfire until his flank attack took effect, and it would take time to implement. As matters turned out, time was at a premium this morning. To Davout's (and Napoleon's) considerable surprise, while the French maneuvered to strike Rosenberg, Rosenberg attacked Davout.

FML Franz Rosenberg was one of Karl's best tactical commanders. He commanded his own IV Corps, Nordmann's battered task force, and FML Nostitz's cavalry division.[4] Around 4 A.M., three Hapsburg columns (these were the men Lejeune had seen) descended from the Russbach plateau. One aimed at Glinzerdorf, one marched against Grosshofen, and the third—composed of cavalry—screened the open eastern flank. The Austrian infantry advanced with great enthusiasm, bands playing, officers riding at the front, the men in well-closed ranks with muskets resting on their shoulders.

Acting on the emperor's instructions to concentrate toward the center, Davout had been prepared to abandon Glinzendorf and Grosshofen. Fortunately some of Friant's men still had a toehold in Glinzerdorf. Aspern-Essling had been a recent demonstration of a Napoleonic verity: continental infantry attacking veteran French infantry who defended a village were in for a very tough struggle. As had occurred in May, the French managed to repulse initial Austrian attacks. Friant was a time-proved tactician. He fed in reinforcements who lined the dike between the two villages while using his 31 artillery pieces to pelt the attackers with shot and canister. Meanwhile, Rosenberg's attack against Grosshofen enjoyed initial success, but here too French tactical leadership, this time provided by another of Davout's triumvirate of superb generals, Charles Etienne Gudin, rose to the occasion to take neatly the Hapsburg column in flank and drive it off. Rosenberg's offensive had not lasted long, but it had large consequences, not the least of which was the way it occupied Napoleon's attention.

The emperor had been inspecting his center when he heard the sounds of Rosenberg's attack. Fearing that it marked the arrival of Erzherzog Johann, he ordered Eugène and Oudinot to suspend their attacks, ordered the Guard and two divisions of cuirassiers to march toward his right flank, and galloped toward the sound of the guns. He arrived to see that Davout had matters well in hand. The only assistance needed had been provided by Oudinot's artillery, which Seruzier, acting with characteristic vigor and initiative, had turned to fire into Rosenberg's flank. However, Rosenberg's eruption had disordered Davout's arrangements. His infantry and cannon had fired a prodigious amount of ammunition. Davout told Napoleon that it would take about two hours to replenish stocks and reach the position to deliver the flank attack. Satisfied, Napoleon left

Davout to fight his battle and returned to Raasdorf to draft instructions for his center to attack once they saw Davout's line pass the battle's major landmark, a prominent square stone tower in Neusiedel.

During the day of July 6, Napoleon would confront three heavy shocks. Rosenberg's attack against Davout was the first. He had delivered a very effective spoiling attack, disrupting French preparations and deflecting attention from the pending main blow along the Danube. In sum, it had set Napoleon up for defeat, as became apparent when the emperor learned that a second Austrian blow had nearly shattered his center.

The second attack came from GdK Bellegarde's I Corps, 20,000 infantry whose ranks included some of the finest regiments in Hapsburg service. At 3:30 A.M. they had begun their approach march toward Aderklaa, a village with enormous tactical importance. In Austrian hands it permitted enfilade fire against any French offensive over the Russbach while simultaneously covering Wagram, the hinge for Karl's entire position. In French hands it was a dagger pointed at the place of greatest vulnerability. Leading the I Corps was General Stutterheim with three infantry battalions and eight squadrons of the Klenau Chevaulégers. In accordance with Karl's tactical instructions, behind the advance guard came a first line of eight and a supporting line of four battalions. At 4 A.M. Stutterheim's men reached the outskirts of Aderklaa and girded for a stiff fight. To their amazement, they occupied the village with ease, capturing several score of wounded Saxons in the process.

Had Bellegarde pressed on at this point, the result might have been stupendous. Rosenberg was in full cry, Napoleon had shifted his reserves toward that flank, and only a collection of very shaky Saxon infantry stood before him. But Karl's plan did not call for Bellegarde to deliver the main blow. The Austrian generalissimus watched with full approbation as Bellegarde halted his corps, stretched it to join with the grenadiers on his right and Wagram on his left, deployed his 68 artillery pieces, and awaited developments. Only Stutterheim exhibited any energy as he set his infantry to making Aderklaa a miniature fortress.

Aderklaa had been undefended because of a curious blunder made by Marshal Bernadotte. Bernadotte appreciated that after their bloody street fight in Wagram, his Saxons required rest and reorganization. To accommodate them, he unwisely abandoned Aderklaa, leaving behind a mere detachment. They spent the night happily looting, doing nothing to prepare a defense, and running at first contact with Stutterheim. Because of Bellegarde's hesitation, Bernadotte had time to prepare a counterattack, a task that consumed the next 45 minutes. Not knowing that the Austrians were content with holding the village, Bernadotte ordered his artillery to defend the ground northeast of Aderklaa until his infantry was ready. It was an extremely difficult position for the Saxon gunners. A lethal crossfire from Bellegarde's gunline between Aderklaa and Wagram and from the Hapsburg batteries on the slope behind the Russbach dismounted 15 of their 26 guns. The Saxon gunners frequently had to change position simply to survive. Worse, the fields around them caught fire.

Around 7 A.M. Bernadotte committed both his cavalry and infantry in an attack against Aderklaa. The Saxon infantry had not recovered from the battering received in Wagram 6 hours earlier—Le Coq's Brigade had suffered 891 casualties, a solid 50 percent—and they fought poorly.[5] The Austrian artillery overwhelmed the Saxons, causing the infantry to break badly and rout toward Raasdorf. Bernadotte's intact formations withdrew to a position 1,500 yards east of Aderklaa. Dupas's depleted division, now merely capable of forming two small battalions, stood in a supporting position. Two of Bellegarde's batteries aggressively sought a position on Bernadotte's flank and poured in a destructive enfilade fire, pressure that forced Bernadotte to refuse his right flank. Meanwhile, the Saxons who were fleeing realized they were not alone; a substantial number of French were on the run as well.

According to orders, before dawn Marshal Massena left Boudet's division in Aspern and began a flank march with the balance of his corps in the direction of Wagram. Karl's unexpected offensive interrupted this march. The Austrians swarming down from the heights northwest of the Marchfeld were squarely on Massena's flank. The marshal's trailing division, Legrand, saw FML Klenau's people debouching from Breitenlee and stopped to face them. Carra Saint-Cyr, in the middle of the march column, saw the Austrian grenadiers emerging from Sussenbrunn, brushed past them, and hurried on toward Aderklaa. Nearing the village at about 7:30 A.M., Saint-Cyr grew cautious and sent his voltigeurs groping warily forward through the tall grain. Massena's carriage appeared and the marshal spoke to Saint-Cyr: "Go, my friend, into that village and slaughter those rogues!"[6]

Forward went the columns of the 4th Ligne and 24th Légère while the Hessians advanced on their right and the 46th Ligne remained in reserve. From a drainage ditch 100 paces in front of the village, a battalion of Austrian jagers rose up to deliver a heavy fire. The French infantry closed ranks and pressed forward. Stutterheim's 2,700 men, sheltered behind the earthen dike surrounding the village, put up a stout defense. Fighting quickly degenerated into the type of bloody melee already seen at Ebelsberg and Aspern-Essling. Garden walls, farmyards, and individual buildings were captured and recaptured. When Saint-Cyr committed the 46th Ligne and his Hessians, French weight of numbers told. Stutterheim's men broke and ran back through Bellegarde's first line commanded by FML Graf Fresnel. Fresnel's men had already suffered from Saxon artillery fire. The sight of their fleeing comrades was too much, and they joined the general rout toward Wagram. The 4th and 24th emerged on the far side of the village to see substantial numbers of Austrians flying in panic. However, in gaining their victory, Saint-Cyr's division had lost all order. While struggling to compose themselves they saw Fresnel's intact second line looming through the wreckage.[7] What they did not see was a force of grenadiers closing rapidly on the exposed left flank.

The wisdom of Karl's tactical instructions requiring his corps to deploy in two lines now manifested itself. As had occurred back in May, after a first line yielded there remained a strong second line to hold the front and provide the first line time to re-form. This is what took place outside Aderklaa. When Karl saw Saint-Cyr carry the village, he rode behind Fresnel's second line to rally his soldiers. Embarrassed by their conduct, they quickly re-formed and were joined by Stutterheim's men. Then Karl continued on to his grenadiers—GM Merville's men in the reserve corps—gave them a short speech, a liberal distribution of brandy, and handed three battalions to Stutterheim. He ordered his eager lieutenant to recapture the village.[8] Inspired by Karl's presence, the Austrians charged against the open left flank of the 4th Ligne. The regiment had already suffered fearfully, with all three battalion commanders dead or wounded. Hit in flank it routed, its colonel wounded and captured. To its great disgrace it managed to repeat its performance at Austerlitz by losing an eagle.[9] At the same time Bellegarde's second line surged forward. The double attack proved too much for the 24th Légère. Some of its men had ill-advisedly pursued Stutterheim's soldiers and had not yet returned to the ranks.[10] During the regiment's collapse, a lieutenant in the Argenteau Infantry Regiment captured the 24th Légère's eagle.

Saint-Cyr committed the 46th Ligne to stop the Austrian counterattack. The ensuing collision was bloody. Among many, Stutterheim and the grenadier commander GM Merville went down with wounds; on the French side Brigadier General Cosson and two of Saint-Cyr's three French colonels were also hit. Karl fed in additional troops, including the recovered regiments who had originally been in Fresnel's first line. The 46th Ligne yielded, but during their withdrawal a voltigeur officer spotted an attractive target, a senior enemy officer riding at the front of his men. The Frenchman ordered his voltigeurs to shoot him down. Only the fact that the range was rather long spared Erzherzog Karl, who survived with a painful shoulder wound. The Austrians carried on to encounter Saint-Cyr's Hessians, who fought hard to hold the village. The Hessian Regiment du Corps suffered horrific losses, but they too failed. This Hessian unit lost one of its flags and would have lost the other except that a quick-witted soldier tore it from its staff and hid in a barn until a new French attack relieved him. Some of Bernadotte's Saxons delivered another charge into the deadly vortex between Aderklaa and Wagram. Again artillery fire from front and flank ravaged their ranks, and they withdrew. Once more the Austrians possessed Aderklaa. With the gifted Stutterheim down, Karl assigned his brother, the young erzherzog Ludwig, the special mission of holding the village.

Ludwig had not long to wait before he faced a new attack. Massena also had reserves in hand belonging to Molitor's division. This unit had managed to bypass the Austrian eruption from the heights and reached the village's outskirts in good order. Molitor formed his 2d, 16th, and 67th Ligne into column while two batteries of 12-pounders punched holes in the garden walls that sheltered the waiting Austrian infantry. Then Molitor hurled his columns against the village. Even while these columns were storming the village, a new threat emerged on

Molitor's left flank. They belonged to GdK Liechtenstein's Reserve Corps. As the Hapsburg horse advanced at the trot, Molitor rapidly formed four reserve battalions into square and shot apart the charging cavalry. With their flank secure, Molitor's tough veterans systematically drove the Austrians from Aderklaa. Although losing more than one man in three, they then repeated their May performance at Aspern by clinging to the ruined village against all odds for the next two hours.

Around 9 A.M. a courier arrived at imperial headquarters to tell Napoleon that the Austrians were assaulting Aderklaa. Staring disaster in the face, Napoleon galloped to the front, passing Marmont's reserve position "like the wind, with Berthier and his escort riding hard in his wake."[11] Napoleon arrived to occupy a position on a slight rise east of Aderklaa. His eyes took in a scene unlike any other in his experience with his Grande Armée: "Our soldiers ran pell-mell across the plain, carrying away with them the officers and generals who were trying vainly to rally them."[12] He saw Marshal Massena's carriage driving among French and Saxons alike, with Massena futilely trying to make them stop. Thousands ran all the way back to Raasdorf. By midafternoon there would be more than 12,000 stragglers milling about the village. Riding Euphrates, his snow-white Persian horse, Napoleon coursed the field to rally the Saxons. He said to the Saxon chief of staff, "Hold on for awhile, Saxons—soon everything will change."[13] The French soldiers facing the Russbach needed encouragement as well because they were beginning to waver under the Austrian bombardment. One of Berthier's aides recounts, "It is really no exaggeration to say that I saw balls rush through the air and ricochet from the ground much as hail rebounds in violent storms."[14] To steady his men Napoleon rode "from one extremity of the line to the other, and returned at a slow pace." So many shots were flying past him that Savary kept his "eyes rivetted upon him, expecting at every moment to see him drop from his horse."[15]

Under a barrage of canister Napoleon met Marshal Massena in his carriage. Dismounting, he climbed aboard and asked, "Well, what about this brawl here?" Massena replied, "As you see, sire, it is not my fault." "Oh! I well know, it's that braggart Bernadotte."[16] In fact, neither Napoleon nor Massena was blameless, but they found it mutually convenient to blame someone else. The choice was easy; they would blame the Saxons. Here, in the midst of a firestorm of Austrian shot, shell, and canister (and, in truth, a fleeing horde of Saxons, although there were just as many running French nearby), began an agreed-upon fiction that was to explain this phase of the battle. It was used in postbattle reports and repeated then and thereafter when participants wrote their memoirs: it was the Saxon's fault. Having distributed blame, Napoleon set about the more productive task of explaining to Massena how he was going to win the battle.

In the emperor's mind, the fact that Massena had recaptured Aderklaa was critical. Possession of that village secured the left flank of the forces facing the Russbach. All that remained was to endure the bombardment until Davout began his assault on the Austrian flank. From the plain, Napoleon and his lieutenants could judge Davout's progress as the wall of smoke marking his front line slowly approached Neusiedel. Davout's progress mesmerized the French high command. Meanwhile, a third crisis was brewing along the Danube plain.

DISASTER ALONG THE DANUBE

Erzherzog Karl intended that the assault against the French left rear take place simultaneously with Rosenberg's and Bellegarde's attacks. For FML Klenau and his VI Corps, this meant that they would have to begin their approach march at 1 A.M. But Klenau did not receive his orders until 2 A.M., and so, through no fault of his own, he was already an hour behind Karl's schedule before he started. Few Hapsburg leaders had ever displayed an ability to make up for lost time, and Klenau was no exception. He marched his corps down from the heights and deployed them carefully according to Karl's instructions. There was the usual advance guard—four battalions and a cavalry regiment commanded by FML Vincent—and a main body of 21 battalions drawn up in a triple rank of battalion masses. Veczay's brigade, detached from Reuss's V Corps, guarded the rear while a hussar regiment extended out into the plain to link with Kollowrath's III Corps, which was also advancing south. Klenau's and Kollowrath's corps combined numbered about 30,000 men.

In Aspern, General Boudet saw this impressive move upon his position. He believed it his duty to delay the Austrians for as long as possible. Accordingly, he stationed his 93th Ligne in the burned ruins behind the cemetery along Aspern's northwestern face (the same position occupied by Molitor back on May 21) with the 3d Ligne coiled around the village's northern edge. Thinking to impose upon the Hapsburg deployment, Boudet boldly placed the 56th Ligne 400 yards north of Aspern (closer to the enemy) in support of his two batteries. Beyond the 56th's right flank there was a wide void extending north for more than 4 miles across the Marchfeld. At first Boudet's strategy seemed to be working. Klenau advanced slowly, in part because of Boudet and in part because the battalion masses were an ill-chosen formation for an approach march. Seeking to exploit the Austrian's caution, one of Boudet's overly zealous battery commanders permitted a two-gun section to move even farther out into the plain in order to deliver enfilade fire against the approaching masses. The French cannon fire cut furrows in the packed Hapsburg ranks.

Between 6 and 7 A.M., Klenau's Corps arrived within cannon shot of Aspern, Where he deployed his 64 artillery pieces and opened fire. The bombardment lasted 50 minutes and inflicted great damage on the French artillery. Although the fire was thus not wasted, time was important to the Hapsburg cause this morning, and using it up for an extended softening-up bombardment was not wise. Although slow to begin, the corps proved irresistible once in motion. At 7 A.M. some of Veczay's grenzers chased the French voltigeurs from the Gemeinde Au, thus turning Aspern from the south, while a battalion of Saint-Georges grenz made a false attack against the village's northeastern face. The main attack came from the north. Austrian cavalry poured in from beyond the 56th Ligne's flank and quickly snapped up the two French guns, which until now had been too focused on the infantry target. General Walmoden then led a charge of the Liechtenstein Hussars against the ten remaining French guns. As Boudet later ruefully noted, the charge came from the direction of Raasdorf, where the emperor had had his headquarters the previous evening and thus was entirely unexpected. The hussars sabered the French gunners and overran their guns. Boudet galloped to the scene and led a counterattack with the 56th Ligne. Blasted by an overwhelming fire, the 56th struggled forward to the abandoned guns. Here Walmoden's cavalry forced them into square. In the absence of any horses to pull off the guns, Boudet led the 56th in sullen retreat and then ordered his entire division back to the safety of the old tête de pont. Their retreat became a near rout as Austrian cavalry pressed hard. Marbot, who had to deliver a message to Boudet at this juncture, relates that the "sabres and lances were working terrible execution among this rabble of terrified men, who were flying in disorder."[17]

Klenau had some difficulty extracting his victorious soldiers from Aspern before continuing his drive along the river. A portion carried on toward Essling, while another group turned toward the tête de pont. The 93d Ligne made a brief stand at the tile works—Napoleon's headquarters during the May 21 fight—but the audacious Austrian infantry carried the place with a spirited attack. However, once the 93d retired behind the earthworks of the tête de pont and the balance of the division ran back to Essling, many of the 109 heavy French guns and mortars on Lobau became unmasked, and these weapons opened a destructive fire. Their first shots erased nearly three white-coated companies who had been in close pursuit. Meanwhile, Boudet managed to rally four battalions in Essling, but they proved unable to hold the place against Klenau's advance. By 10 A.M. the Austrians had captured Essling and established two large batteries to open fire against the French bridges south of Enzersdorf. Klenau's advance spread panic in the French rear. Crying, "Retreat! Retreat! The cantoniers, the musicians, the sick, the non-combatants, the beef herd, the supply column, the ambulances, all were plunged in disorder" around the bridges leading to Lobau.[18]

While Klenau conducted his methodical advance, out in the Marchfeld FZM Kollowrath had also enjoyed an important success. Kollowrath had experienced even more difficulty than Klenau in extricating his III Corps from the Bisamberg and thus began his attack late. His first target was Sussenbrunn, where he encountered Legrand's division of Massena's Corps on its way toward Wagram. Legrand's division consisted of veteran regiments who had distinguished themselves at Ebelsberg and Aspern-Essling. On July 6 fewer than 3,000 remained, and they confronted odds of worse than five to one. Kollowrath's attack sent them flying, some in rout toward Raasdorf while the balance retained their order and retired toward Aderklaa. Kollowrath's Corps pressed on to capture Breitenlee. This success released the Liechtenstein Hussars to conduct their previously described successful charge against Boudet's artillery.

Kollowrath's orders were to strike the French left flank south of Wagram. Having penetrated into the void between the Danube and the French around Aderklaa, he was now in position to deliver a telling blow. Napoleon did not yet appreciate the extent of the disaster along the Danube. His uncommitted reserves faced north toward the Russbach. Kollowrath could turn his corps toward Massena's exposed flank outside Aderklaa and achieve an important tactical triumph, or he could continue to advance east toward an undefended Raasdorf. He did neither. In typical Austrian fashion he had already left an entire brigade on the Bisamberg facing Vienna and told off a sizable detachment to garrison Gerasdorf back in the foothills along his line of march. Now he created a task force of three battalions, a battery, and a regiment of uhlans to secure Breitenlee and cautiously poked forward with his remaining force a few hundred yards toward Raasdorf. He did at least station two batteries on a small rise outside Breitenlee from where they opened fire against the left and rear of Massena's men outside Aderklaa. This alone was enough to inspire the grenadiers of the Reserve Corps, the adjacent corps north of Kollowrath's III Corps, to resume their advance against Aderklaa.

Nine grenadier battalions commanded by FML Prochaszka had been holding the ground between Breitenlee and Aderklaa waiting for Karl's right wing to advance. Shortly before 11 A.M. they advanced on a line extended from Aderklaa well beyond Massena's left flank. At the same time Bellegarde launched another assault against the village from the north and northwest. Molitor's division had fought heroically—three of the division's four infantry colonels were hit as were all three of the battalion commanders in the 37th Ligne—but it could not stand up to this. By 11 A.M. Karl's warriors again possessed the key village. Typical of the conduct that carried the Austrian army to the brink of victory was the attitude of Lieutenant Joseph von Osterman. During the grenadier's advance, a cannonball had crushed his legs. His comrades wanted to carry him to the surgeon, but von Osterman replied, "What is the point. . . . No doctor can help me . . . the better thing is to carry me under that tree and there I will die when I see the flying enemy." He lingered for some time and managed to see the Austrian right wing drive Boudet back through Aspern and Essling. "Now you can make my grave," von Osterman announced.[19] Shortly after he died.

By 11 A.M., Karl's entire army except for the two corps defending behind the Russbach were facing east in line between the Danube and Wagram. They had defeated all who faced them. Eugène was the first to appreciate the extent of the French peril. The loss of Aderklaa uncovered the Army of Italy's left flank. He sent word to his stepfather that he could see a heavy Austrian force maneuvering on his left and in his rear. The emperor responded with the order to ignore it. "Keep your eyes on the right," he added, "There is where we will win the battle."[20] In spite of these words of wisdom, Eugène could not overlook the menace. Although the Saxon light cavalry gallantly shielded his flank, they could not arrest Karl's juggernaut. Eugène faced some of Macdonald's men to flank and buttressed his line with all available artillery. Fortunately, at this point Napoleon too recognized the threat. A courier arrived to inform him that the Austrians had captured Aspern. Hard on his heels came another to say that Boudet had lost all his artillery and that the Austrian advance threatened the Danube bridges. It was Napoleon's third shock of the morning. Already substantial elements of his army had proved themselves shaky under the pressure of bombardment and assault. With a massive Austrian assault penetrating the army's rear, the battle's crisis was at hand.

ARTILLERY CHARGE

So far during the 7-hour battle nothing had gone as Napoleon expected. A lesser commander might have lost his balance amidst the succession of surprises and shocks. The French emperor rose to the occasion by an exhibition of superb battle management. The wisdom of his nocturnal decision to concentrate his army in the center now paid dividends. However bad the situation appeared, he retained a formidable proportion of uncommitted troops. Only three of his corps had seriously engaged so far, and of them, only Bernadotte's Corps was out of action. Davout was conducting an offensive that Napoleon believed would eventually turn the Austrian flank. Massena, although much battered, was newly available since his soldiers were no longer enmeshed in the defense of Aderklaa. Perhaps if he had still commanded his Grande Armée, Napoleon would have allowed Klenau to advance along his rear unchecked. After all, if the counterstroke Napoleon planned worked, Klenau would merely be sticking his head further into the noose. But the emperor had seen his army break in panic the previous evening, and major elements had run twice already this morning. He judged his soldiers too fragile to ignore the developments in the rear.

When weighing how to counter the Austrian eruption against his rear, Napoleon had no precise information regarding the extent of the disaster along the Danube. All he knew was that the one division he had left to cover the bridges had been routed. Yet he chose to dispatch Massena's men, three hard-used divisions that so far during the day had experienced defeat and rout, reinforced only by Saint-Sulpice's cuirassiers, and by so doing gave another demonstration of grand tactical genius. Theirs was a formidable assignment. Massena's men had fought hard for Aderklaa and suffered. Now the emperor required them to march 5 miles across the front of a superior and victorious enemy force in order to preserve the vital Danube bridges. Other generals might have sent a much larger force to perform this mission, but Napoleon had calculated it nicely and above all knew the measure of his soldiers and the talent of his marshal.

Massena's departure would uncover Eugène's left flank, so the emperor ordered Macdonald to turn three Army of Italy divisions away from the Russbach and relocate to cover the ground vacated by Massena. Macdonald's maneuver would take time. To buy that time he directed Marshal Bessières to lead his Cavalry Reserve against the enemy forces advancing east from Breitenlee. Eugène, with the remaining Army of Italy troops, would support Macdonald as best he could.

Oudinot would wait until he saw Davout advance past the tower at Neusiedel and then attack. Lastly, Napoleon shifted the Imperial Guard to backstop Macdonald and Bessières. Marmont's XI Corps and Wrede's Bavarian division remained in reserve.

While he prepared these orders, a howitzer shell exploded nearby, its blast causing the emperor's horse to shy. Alarmed, Oudinot exclaimed, "Sire, they are firing on the headquarters." Napoleon replied, "Monsieur, in war all accidents are possible," and continued calmly to finish his dictation.[21] At this juncture the emperor was by no means certain of success. He sent another order to artillery General Songis instructing him to forward artillery ammunition because there well might be another battle tomorrow. Then, showing attention to detail, with each order sent to his infantry, he told the courier to remind his officers not to permit the soldiers to fire off their ammunition haphazardly and then claim they could not perform their duty because they were out of ammunition. A Saxon cavalryman observed Napoleon's conduct at this juncture:

He was surrounded by a numerous General Staff which included a dozen ordinance officers, standing in a row. . . . His face betrayed none of the emotion filling him: it was serious and immobile except for the fiery eyes. He calmly listened to every report made to him. If he wished to send an order, he called "ordinance officer," whereupon the rightmost officer rode up. He was given the order slowly and clearly, then each time was required to repeat it. If this was not satisfactory, he was given the orders again, without an overbearing tone; then he was required to repeat them again. If the officer gave the order word perfect, he heard "Go." Quick as an arrow from the bow, the officer would fly to his destination.[22]

This was done under a punishing bombardment. Twenty-six headquarter officers were hit during the day, almost all by artillery fire. As one imperial doffed his shako to acknowledge that he understood Napoleon's orders, a cannonball knocked it from his hand. Napoleon roared with laughter, commenting, "It's a good job you're not taller!"[23]

The first French troops to implement the emperor's plan belonged to Nansouty's heavy cavalry division, comprising four cuirassier and two carabinier regiments numbering nearly 4,000 troopers. The division was the most powerful, mobile shock force on the field. As they changed front and rode toward the imperiled French left flank they passed beneath a small mound where stood Napoleon and his staff. Each regiment greeted their leader with shouts of "Vive l'empereur!" and Napoleon responded by pointing toward the enemy host whom they must charge and calling out to each colonel to "charge to the hilt."[24]

So desperate was the situation that Bessières did not wait for his precious Guard cavalry to come on line to support Nansouty. As Bessières rode forward to accompany Nansouty's troopers, a cannon ball tore into his thigh and knocked him stunned onto the ground. From a distance it appeared that Bessières had been killed. Weeping guardsmen—Bessières was amazingly popular among the

The Battle of Wagram
(10:00 A.M. to Noon)

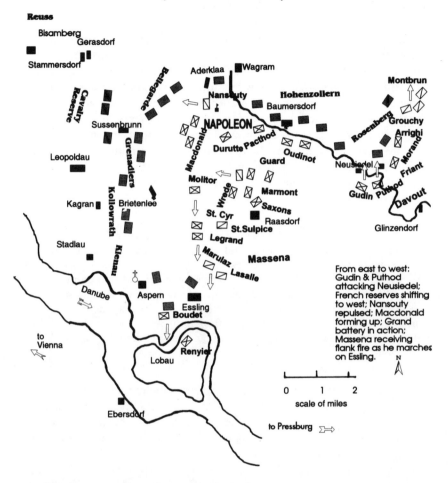

From east to west:
Gudin & Puthod
attacking Neusiedel;
French reserves shifting
to west; Nansouty
repulsed; Macdonald
forming up; Grand
battery in action;
Massena receiving
flank fire as he marches
on Essling.

Imperial Guard—carried him unconscious from the field. Aghast, Napoleon turned away, saying, "I have no time to weep," and, alluding to Lannes's death, "Let us avoid another scene." Bessières's absence left a gap in the French chain of command. As Savary notes, "This untoward cannon-shot left the cavalry without a leader, during the most important quarter of an hour in the day, which was to have an immense influence over the battle."[25] Napoleon himself would later tell Bessières, "That was a fine shot Bessières, it made my Guard cry . . . but it also cost me 20,000 prisoners which you would have taken for me."[26]

Nansouty was fortunate in that his charge struck the Austrians in the seam of an ill-defined boundary between Liechtenstein's Reserve Corps and Kollowrath. Braving a formidable hail of shot and canister—a French carabinier trooper, Jef

Abbeel, recalls that in his regiment only about one in five men managed to penetrate through this barrage— the French heavy horse advanced, only to see the enemy infantry hastily forming square. They managed to rout a grenz battalion but made little impression against the grenadiers. According to one French participant, the Austrians had acquired at Aspern-Essling the confidence that they could repel French cavalry charges. Still, Nansouty had managed to carve a breach between the two Austrian corps. He had no time to look back and see that he was unsupported. Having passed between the enemy squares, Nansouty showed fine tactical control by turning his troopers to the right to charge Liechtenstein's gun line.

During this maneuver a cannonball downed Abbeel's horse. He ran to the rear and seized another mount. Meanwhile, the charge against the Austrian artillery failed when a counterattacking wave of Austrian horsemen, prominently including the Rosenberg Chevaulégers and Kronprinz Cuirassiers, took the carabiniers in flank, wounded their commander, General Defrance, and sent them flying. When Abbeel returned to his comrades, another ball struck his animal, and he fell to the ground. Struggling to extricate himself, Abbeel saw his unit falling back with the enemy in hot pursuit. Terrified, the trooper played dead and watched as the enemy horse swept past him. A shell exploded nearby, covering him with dirt. He crawled behind a small rise and sheltered beneath the bodies of a dead carabinier and his horse. Around him the wheat field began to burn.[27]

Nansouty's repulse was costly. His casualties of 164 men killed and 436 wounded, in addition to 1,141 horses killed or injured, exceeded the totals suffered by either of the other two cuirassier divisions.[28] In the carabinier brigade, fewer than 300 horses remained standing by day's end, an equine loss rate of 77 percent. The 9th Cuirassiers suffered particularly severely in this charge, losing its colonel (who had three horses shot out from under him) and 6 other officers wounded, 31 troopers killed, and 55 wounded.[29] Somehow the cuirassiers had not quite had the same impact on this field as at Aspern-Essling. There were too many enemy guns and too many enemy infantry, and the men of iron had suffered too much in that earlier battle to repeat their May exploits. Nonetheless, Nansouty's charge restored the initiative to the French. Heretofore, the Army of Germany had been reacting to a series of Austrian attacks. Henceforth, the Austrian army reacted to French blows.

Napoleon understood that Nansouty's charge was a stopgap measure. He urgently needed infantry both to fill the space vacated by Massena's departure and because he knew that the appearance of a French force on the flank of the Austrian corps who were advancing along the Danube would impose caution on the heretofore victorious enemy. Napoleon demanded that General Macdonald immediately change front and march to the threatened sector. So great was the emperor's hurry that when he saw that one of the designated assault divisions was fully deployed, he substituted another formation rather than accept the loss of time involved if that division reconcentrated. It was a testament to French flexibility that Macdonald's command, a three-division task force, could operate harmoniously without regard to corps structure and a testament to French tactical skill that Macdonald could march his task force without disruption across the same deadly ground that had been pounded by Hapsburg artillery for close to 8 hours.

So a French-born Scotsman entered center stage at Wagram's decisive moment. Forty-three-year-old Etienne Jacques Macdonald had long believed himself to be a most capable commander. Time and again, by his lights, his skill had retrieved his superiors from the fate appropriate to their blunders. It was deliciously ironic that at the height of crisis, Napoleon had to rely on him. The two had never really gotten on. Macdonald believed that his superior tactical abilities should have earned him membership to the original marshal's list back in 1804. He rightly suspected that Napoleon believed him to be a less than enthusiastic supporter of a Bonaparte dynasty and that this attitude had stalled his career. Consequently, Macdonald had been in rural retirement for the past six years until his assignment to the Army of Italy. July 6 provided him with a great opportunity to redeem himself.

As he marched to his assigned location, some irregularities of the ground prevented Macdonald from seeing the Austrian breakthrough. Not understanding the need for haste, this stubborn general disregarded Napoleon's orders to hurry. Macdonald describes the scene: "The enemy, who were still advancing, halted; and, redoubling their fire, caused us terrible damage . . . .I drew [my lines] closer together, and made them dress as at drill."[30] Although such fine regard for dressing ranks was not what Napoleon had in mind, Macdonald did arrive while the enemy was still recovering from Nansouty's attack. With his shock infantry in place, Napoleon summoned the third element in what he intended would be a decisive combined arms assault. Around 11:30 A.M. he ordered another of his aides, the artillerist General Jacques Lauriston, to concentrate the Imperial Guard guns and to deploy on the plain south of Aderklaa "to erase the enemy masses."[31] What followed was Wagram's celebrated artillery charge.

Eugène's artillery had been in action since the battle began, and it had been a difficult struggle. A battery commander, Captain Noel, relates that he received orders to advance and engage the enemy at Aderklaa. It was the same exposed position where the Saxon guns had so badly suffered, a position that allowed Hohenzollern's artillery to deliver enfilade fire from the higher ground behind the Russbach. The Austrian fire forced Noel to change position frequently. Like most of the other combatants, Noel reports that the dense smoke prevented him from seeing anything beyond his immediate front. As he continued his duel with Hapsburg batteries, he heard an astonishing roar rise above the general din.[32] Europe's foremost gunner had sent in the artillery.

When the emperor ordered Lauriston into action, the guard artillery formed column by battery and galloped toward the enemy. In the lead was Colonel d'Aboville with six horse artillery batteries. Next followed Colonel Bolart with two 8-pound foot batteries and then Colonel Pommereul with two more of the same. Trailing the column was Colonel Drouot with the 12-pound batteries, the emperor's "cherished daughters." The column advanced 600 yards toward the Austrian line. Under a fearful fire, Bolart deployed his foot batteries in succession opposite Breintenlee and Sussenbrunn to provide a central fire base while the horse batteries galloped to the wings. Then the remaining batteries filled in to complete a gun line that extended for more than 2,000 yards. When they finished their deployment, they composed a massive gun line numbering 72 Guard guns and 40 from the Army of Italy. Well within musket range of the white-coated infantry, the Guard gunners stripped to shirtsleeves and opened fire. At such close range neither side could miss, and the resultant carnage was incredible. Bolart writes, "The enemy artillery . . . did us great harm." Men and horses fell constantly. A regiment of infantry and one of cuirassiers supported Bolart's guns, and "they were ruined" by Austrian cannonfire.[33] A near-miss 12-pound shot concussed Boulart himself. Another round tore off d'Aboville's arm. An Austrian canister round struck the right foot of Major Drouot. Bleeding profusely, he refused to relinquish command and provided an imperturbable example for his men.[34] Austrian fire killed 121 Imperial Guard artillery officers and men and wounded 355 more. So painfully thinned were the gunners' ranks that the emperor called for 20 volunteers from each company of his Old Guard infantry to replace the fallen. Easily twice that number responded. Satisfied with their enthusiasm, the emperor took a pinch of snuff, paced back and forth, and awaited results. These infantry gallantly served the guns, providing the brute strength necessary to push the weapons back into position after each recoil.

An eyewitness describes how several horse batteries fell silent, "our brave light artillery was nearly destroyed. Men, horses, cannon, caissons, all pulverized except for one piece served by a solitary gunner."[35] Then a shell descended and blew apart a caisson while this lone sergeant was in the act of removing a cartridge. Horrific as were the losses among the French gunners, the damage they inflicted was even worse. The Guard guns alone fired close to 15,000 rounds during this action, an amazing expenditure of better than 200 round per piece. Napoleon rode forward to his horse artillery to correct their aim. "There," he gestured to the sector between Breitenlee and Sussenbrunn, "is where we will make our breach."[36] And that is what happened. The grand battery quite simply blew a hole in the Austrian line.

Anticipating what was to come, GdK Liechtenstein carefully maneuvered two cavalry regiments to an advantageous position near Aderklaa from where they could charge a French infantry attack. The troopers could not hold their ground in the face of the French bombardment. Baron Prochaszka tried to move some of his grenadiers out of Aderklaa to plug the gap. An overwhelming fire of shot, shell, and canister drove them back to the shelter of the village. GdK Bellegarde dispatched three batteries to fill the void, and they too were forced into precipitous retreat. The French grand battery froze the Austrians in position by interdicting all movement between Breitenlee and Sussenbrunn.

The fire from more than 1,100 artillery pieces produced an unprecedented and overwhelming percussive din. A French veteran relates that the detonations were so loud as to be painful.[37] One of Napoleon's aides recalls that "the artillery of both sides was firing louder than I had ever heard before."[38] Since 6 A.M. the battle had been joined along a front that stretched more than 11 miles from Neusiedel to Wagram to Aspern. The flat ground of the Marchfeld allowed the cannonballs to roll unimpeded. As had been the case at Aspern-Essling, there was little safety even in the rear. A soldier serving with the 1st Battalion of the artillery train recounts how the men in the rear "could see nothing except fire and smoke." Yet even here, "the cannon balls fell like hail."[39] Napoleon's escort cordoned off a small area behind the army's center to serve as field headquarters. Here too the fire was fierce. An imperial aide recalls, "Our ranks suffered greatly under the terrible cannonade."[40] Although the foot soldiers of the Old Guard would not pull trigger on this field, they suffered significant losses as the ball and shell crashed through their serried ranks.

It was the presence of the veterans that enabled the Army of Germany to endure. Wagram was the first battle for one French gunner. In a letter home, he mentioned how he had no time to feel fear after the first enemy ball passed overhead; he was too busy aiming his cannon to notice much else except for the calming presence of his battery commander, an elderly officer who had fought in the early battles of the Revolution and continued to dress in his outdated uniform as if time had stood still. He was one of those "veteran rogues" who had conquered whenever the emperor sent him into battle.[41]

Napoleon could see that opposite the grand battery enemy grenadiers belonging to Liechtenstein's Corps had deployed in a single extended line and lacked reserves. The withering French artillery fire tore holes in their ranks with each discharge. The Hapsburg officers could barely keep their men in formation and freely employed the flats of their swords to drive their wavering men back into the ranks. He saw Liechtenstein scramble to adjust his alignment before the shock by withdrawing his right toward Sussenbrunn. But with the tide turning in his favor, the emperor was not to be hurried. He allowed the battery to continue its fearful work and waited until Davout's flank attack cleared Neusiedel before ordering Macdonald forward. And because he had done all he could do for the moment, the emperor of the French then lay face down on his cape, his head on his arms, and took a nap.[42] He had exerted himself tremendously since his May defeat. He had spent 60 of the past 72 hours on horseback and now was exhausted.[43] A staff officer coursed the field to deliver a report. As he approached imperial headquarters, an emphatic gesture from Berthier caused him to rein in. The officer asked where the emperor was. Berthier motioned to a prone figure lying almost beneath the rider's feet. Napoleon slept while he waited for the situation to ripen.[44]

In centuries past, lookouts had stood atop the square stone tower at Neusiedel to scan the horizon for signs of Hungarian raiders descending from the Carpathian foothills to loot and burn. On July 6, FML Rosenberg used this superb vantage point to watch Davout's men assemble for a major assault. Earlier in the campaign, during the decisive encounter at Eckmuhl in April, he had faced a similar situation. Now as then he arrayed his men with care in an L-shaped line with the tower serving as the hinge. He assigned the defense of the tower and the village to FML Radetzky, who used the dry moat around the tower to shelter some of his infantry. He placed the reliable Stain infantry regiment along the southwest perimeter of the village. Along the village's eastern face was a battalion of the Erzherzog Karl legion and a few hundred landwehr who had remained in the ranks through the dawn assault. In response to Davout's obvious intent to strike the corps' flank, Rosenberg positioned Nordmann's much weakened command in a double infantry line along the plateau, with artillery stationed in the intervals. Farther east still, at the base of the plateau, were 34 squadrons of light cavalry. GM Baron Rothkirch's two dragoon regiments stood on the heights supporting the light cavalry. Rosenberg also had to defend the sloping ground overlooking the Russbach, and this required more than half his strength.[45] This left perhaps 9,000 infantry, 4,000 cavalry, and 60 cannon to resist envelopment by Davout's 28,000 infantry, 6,000 cavalry, and more than 100 artillery pieces. Rosenberg could see that he was substantially outnumbered and keenly felt the absence of any fieldworks facing east toward the pending blow. As he gave his line one last inspection he heard the retort of three measured blasts, obviously signal cannon fired to commit Davout's men to the assault.

Marshal Davout intended to attack Neusiedel from the south and southeast with two divisions, commanded by Gudin and Puthod (who had replaced the undistinguished Démont), while his other two divisions commanded by Morand and Friant outflanked the village from the north. He assigned Grouchy's and Montbrun's cavalry the task of screening the approach march of his enveloping column. The Russbach presented a more serious obstacle than anticipated, and it was not until 10 A.M. that Morand, Friant, and the cavalry had crossed to reach their assault position. Montbrun and Grouchy drove the Hapsburg horse off the plain and up the plateau, thereby creating a safe deployment area for the infantry. Morand formed up on the right, the traditional place of honor for a corps first division. Friant had his right on Morand and his left on the Russbach. As the divisions deployed for battle, an Austrian 12-pound battery shooting from near the tower crossed its fire with another 12-pound battery shooting from the Austrian far left. This crossfire made it clear that an assault would not be easy.

At the sound of the signal cannon, Morand's division, its units formed in battalion column, charged up the slope. The French crossed the beaten zone where the artillery fire struck and penetrated the first defending infantry line. They seemed on the verge of a breakthrough when FML Nordmann sent regiments from his second line in a skillful counterattack against Morand's left flank. The 17th Ligne resisted furiously but had to retire. Here fell Brigadier General Guiot de Lacour with a mortal wound. With him in trouble, the adjacent brigade composing the 61th Ligne also wavered. However, when Nordmann's second line maneuvered for its counterattack, by necessity it had to expose its own flank to Friant. That general was not long in taking advantage.

In an army full of warlike officers, none surpassed blunt and honest General Louis Friant. The son of a wax polisher, he had entered the ranks in 1781. Sterling conduct on numerous fields promoted him to the imperial nobility. He had had three horses killed under him at Austerlitz, an experience that stimulated him to have three horses' heads entered on his family's coat of arms. He often greeted his officers with such words as, "Good morning, comrades, when one sees you, one pines for battle; just think of making peace when one has such regiments!"[46] He was more than just a bluff warrior; he was also an extremely able tactician. Now he put this ability to good use. Friant had already massed 31 artillery pieces to duel with the Hapsburg artillery on the heights. His guns were gaining fire superiority when FML Nordmann committed his second line to attack Morand. Friant launched his veteran 15th Légère and 33d Ligne at the pas de charge. They flanked the flankers and, urged on by a gallant sergeant of the 15th Légère, pressed ahead to overrun a line of shallow Austrian fieldworks. The émigré officer FML Nordmann, one of several dedicated French officers who served the Hapsburg throne in order to restore a French king to rule, rode amid his shattered command to try to rally them and fell dead, a victim of fire delivered by his former countrymen.

Meanwhile, Gudin's veterans and Puthod's conscripts attacked Neusiedel. Progress was slow, Austrian resistance tenacious. In a near mirror image of Nordmann's experience, General Gudin received a wound while rallying one of his wavering infantry battalions. Attrition continued to take a toll as Marshal Davout escaped with a near miss, his horse shot out from under him. Out in the plain, looking up at the combat swirling around the tower, sat the troopers of General Arrighi's cuirassier division. During Rosenberg's 4 A.M. attack, the emperor had assigned this division to Davout. Subjected to a march and countermarch through vineyards occupied by aggressive Austrian skirmishers, with flanks exposed to plunging artillery fire from higher ground, the division had suffered significant losses even though it did not engage the enemy. Then it had spent 6 hours in motionless reserve southeast of Neusiedel, only occasionally bothered by the exploding howitzer shell or bounding cannonball that had been aimed at the infantry in front. Far more tormenting was the troopers' mounting thirst as they baked in their iron helmets and breastplates, tormented by the knowledge that just a little way ahead was the Russbach. From time to time an adventurous cuirassier dodged through the ranks of the infantry and faced closeup canister and skirmish fire to fill a water bottle. Among them were two of Arrighi's aides who risked life and limb to bring their general a refreshing sip. In contrast to Arrighi's somewhat indolent behavior was the conduct of Commandant Romangin, the officer commanding Arrighi's horse battery.

Displaying the kind of junior-level initiative that wins battles, Romangin spurred up to Arrighi to report that he had located a commanding position west of Neusiedel. Arrighi hesitated; he had orders to remain in ready reserve, and

Romangin's scheme would take the battery some distance away. Although it was risky, Arrighi told him to go ahead. Romangin's four 8-pounders and two how-itzers galloped into position and opened fire. Their intervention tilted the balance in the fight for the Neusiedel. First Romangin's fire drove Rosenberg from his tower perch. The Austrian infantry around the tower had stoutly defended against frontal and flank attacks. When cannonballs began striking them from the rear, they abandoned the position. At his moment of triumph, an Austrian cannonball hit the commandant in the chest and killed him.

While Puthod's conscripts stormed Neusiedel's streets, Gudin's men climbed the slope under a still furious fire to carve another breach in Rosenberg's line. Rosenberg's situation was desperate. Many of his cannon had been knocked out by French counterbattery fire. His infantry had fought hard but been unable to hold their position once the French turned their flank. Nordmann's command in particular was shattered, its leader and one of its four brigade commanders killed and another brigade commander grievously wounded. Marshal Davout could see the Austrian line waver. Shortly before noon, he decided to commit the cuirassiers to seal the victory. When Arrighi received this order he hesitated. Several small ravines to his front would make such a charge difficult by chan-neling his troopers onto fireswept ground controlled by the Hapsburg artillery. Perhaps the courier had misunderstood Davout's intentions? Hard on the heels of the first courier came another demanding why the cuirassiers had not charged. Despairing for his men, Arrighi ordered his trumpeters to sound the charge. His brave troopers advanced through the canister fire to reach the summit, where they became entangled among the huts that served as the Austrian camp. Unable to form a line, having suffered serious losses, Arrighi reluctantly ordered a retreat. While he re-formed, he received new orders to march north behind the infantry and join the rest of Davout's cavalry off on the corps' right flank.

The cuirassiers' charge had been premature. Nonetheless, Davout's Corps had achieved an important success. It was noon. A refreshed Napoleon could clearly see that the wall of smoke had passed the tower, thus indicating that his forces had turned the Austrian flank. It was the moment he had been waiting for. Napoleon announced to his staff, "The battle is won."[47] He immediately sent an aide to inform Massena of this fact and to tell marshal that he must join the attack. Another courier went spurring to Davout to hurry him along. Finally he gave the signal to Macdonald to begin his assault.

Sheltered by the bombardment of the grand battery, Macdonald had availed himself of the opportunity to form his three divisions in a most unusual forma-tion. He began in conventional style: two divisions forward, Broussier on the right and Lamarque on the left and Seras's division in support. Each of his two forward divisions deployed two battalions in a first line with two more just to the rear. The balance of these two divisions formed battalion columns to protect the flanks. Macdonald placed Seras in battalion columns behind the leading divisions. This entire formation has been described as an unwieldy, massive "column" necessitated by the lack of experienced soldiers. This was not the case. In fact, it was akin to a corps-sized mixed order, with a line in the center and columns on the flank, chosen because Macdonald judged it best suited for an advance against a combined arms defense.[48] It was, however, an unforgettable artillery target: an 8,000-man formation certain to incur heavy losses once it was underway.

At last the moment came. Scores of French drummers beat the pas de charge, and Macdonald's troops defiled through and to the left of the grand battery. Napoleon, ignoring a barrage of Austrian fire, rode forward to see them off. The Army of Italy responded with tremendous cheers. In a display of courage that thrilled all witnesses, Macdonald, wearing the old-style Republican uniform, led the assault personally. His men followed, marching through a field of summer-ripened wheat. They soon entered into a terrible crossfire from the still numerous Hapsburg cannon. Macdonald's Corps pointed at the vulnerable intersection of Liechtenstein's grenadiers and Kollowrath's Corps. But to penetrate it they had to pass through what they would later describe as "a volcano of fire" from what seemed to be an engulfing semicircle of hostile soldiers.[49]

The leading infantry on the right, Broussier's men, had reached the field over-night after completing an extraordinary four-day forced march through sweltering summer heat.[50] Included in the ranks was the 84th Ligne, whose memorable battle 11 days earlier at Graf had earned a Napoleonic decree that the words *un contre dix* be inscribed on their colors. During this charge all the regiments vied with the 84th Ligne to obtain renown. The entire division won a coveted mention in Napoleon's battle report, with the emperor saying they had "covered themselves with glory." But it was done at terrible cost. Of the 3,700 men who began the advance, 190 died on the field, 184 had an arm or leg amputated, and 1,506 others were hit by Austrian fire. Along with the missing, the division lost a full 60 percent of its strength. Three colonels and ten majors went forward with the infantry. One colonel and two majors died; one colonel and six majors received wounds. Lamarque's adjacent division fared little better. Indicative of the ferocious fire it faced was the fact that Lamarque had four horses shot out from under him, and all six of his orderlies were killed.

Although Macdonald's infantry dented the Hapsburg position, they did not break it. A depleted but still powerful gun line around Sussenbrunn continued to cannonade them. Around Breitenlee FML Graf Saint-Julien struggled to turn his second line to face the French penetration. To buy time, GdK Liechtenstein sent his available cavalry against Macdonald's front. Spearheaded by the Kron-prinz Erzherzog Cuirassiers, the Austrian cavalry braved the French artillery fire and charged Macdonald's foot soldiers. It was to defend against such a stroke that Macdonald had designed his assault formation. His handy battalion columns quickly formed square. His deployed infantry knew that their flanks were secure and likewise confidently deployed into square. The Hapsburg charge crumbled in the face of French battalion volleys.[51] However, by forcing Macdonald's men into square the cavalry had purchased precious moments—time the Austrian infantry used to adjust to Macdonald's near breakthrough.

Although under enormous pressure Karl's lieutenants were clearly maintaining their balance. Near Aderklaa GM Steyrer retired his brigade of grenadiers in echelon to take up a new position on Macdonald's right flank. Off beyond Macdonald's left flank, GM Lilienberg performed a similar maneuver with his fine brigade of regular infantry. Thus the Austrians maintained firm positions on both sides of Macdonald's penetration, allowing the remaining Austrian artillery to keep up a punishing crossfire against Macdonald's men. The cost to Karl's legions was high. During the fighting to stop Macdonald, FML Vukassovich, an officer who had led Austrian troops against Bonaparte during the Italian campaign of 1796–1797, received a mortal wound. As a result of these combinations and because of its own heavy losses, Macdonald's corps ground to a halt. Macdonald would later report that he had been reduced to fewer than 1,500 men, a statement accepted by future historians who wrote about the battle. In fact, this was not so. Although his corps had suffered close to 50 percent losses, it still retained more than 4,000 men.[52] But what Macdonald needed just now was cavalry to enlarge the dent his infantry had made in the enemy position. Although there was cavalry on hand, to the general's considerable vexation, they proved tardy to seize the opportunity.

Nansouty had kept his battered division too far to the rear to support Macdonald promptly. When the Franco-Scotsman summoned them to charge the Austrian guns that were delivering fearful punishment, Nansouty arrived late. Also in reserve was the finest cavalry unit on the field: the division of Imperial Guard heavy cavalry. Their commander, General Frederic Walther, had entered the ranks back in 1781 and only slowly climbed to higher command. A relatively elderly officer at age 48, he did not intend to misstep now. Seeing Walther's men motionless, Macdonald said to the general:

"Do you command that fine and large body of cavalry?"
"I do."
"Then why in the world did you not charge the enemy at the decisive moment?"
"In the Guard we require orders direct from the Emperor himself, or from our chief, Marshal Bessières. Now, as the latter was wounded, there only remained the Emperor, and he sent us no orders."[53]

Thus was missed a great opportunity to exploit Macdonald's success. Bessières's wound and Walther's subsequent failure of nerve had large consequences. Along with Nansouty's conduct, it was a failure that thoroughly annoyed Napoleon. He commented to his staff that his cavalry had "never served me in this manner before; it will be the cause of this battle not being attended with any result."[54] It was almost 2 P.M., and Napoleon's decisive stroke appeared stalled.

THE "INFERNAL COLUMN"

So many cannon were firing so fast that individual retorts could not be heard. Back on Lobau their firing sounded like "a continuous rolling detonation."[55] A French cavalryman wrote that "a shower of bombs and shells split the air and rained with a crash a murderous hail on our heads; the balls whistled, ricocheted in the midst of our ranks and furrowed the ground underneath our feet."[56] A blast of canister toppled six troopers at once; a single ball killed three horses. The fortunate soldiers in Marmont's Corps were in the second line behind the Army of Italy. Early in the battle this allowed them to open their ranks and thus avoid most of the ricocheting balls that bounded their way—most but not all: one soldier in the third rank was sitting on his knapsack and dozing, with his musket cradled between his arms, when a ball struck his weapon and sent a lethal fragment through his heart, killing him immediately. As noon came and passed, the firing intensified. Now even among the reserves, cannon shot carried away entire files of men.

There was very little water to drink, and as the July heat took hold, thirst became intolerable. Soldiers saw skirmishers in the middle of a firefight pause, bend over, and pluck some herbs to chew for relief. Others urinated in bottles and drank. The intense hunger caused by fear and exertion came, yet those fortunate enough to still have some bread found they could not eat it because of their terribly dry mouths. Amid privation and slaughter, many French soldiers retained their renowned sense of humor. Some soldiers were carrying a wounded comrade to the hospital when unbeknown to them another bullet struck and killed the wounded man. They continued and delivered him to the surgeon who upbraided them for bringing a dead man. Their leader replied:

"Major, he is wounded."
"There, look imbecile, don't you see he's dead?"
"That's true, see how one is deceived in this world even by one's best friend. This sly fellow told me he was only wounded."[57]

With Macdonald stalled, more then ever Napoleon relied on Davout. When Rosenberg's Corps had yielded its position around Neusiedel shortly before noon, the left flank of FML Hohenzollern's adjacent II Corps became exposed. Hohenzollern responded rapidly by shifting cavalry and infantry to face Davout. His lone regiment of heavy cavalry, the Hohenzollern cuirassiers, charged against the French infantry. The consequences of the pernicious Austrian practice of scattering their cavalry in penny packets became evident when the Hapsburg cuirassiers picked out the weakest opposing unit, a 258-man battalion of the 85th Ligne, forced it into square, and thereby brought it to a halt. But this result did not slow the forward surge of Davout's infantry. A more serious check came when Erzherzog Karl, ignoring his wound and showing that he too had a sound tactical touch, galloped to his imperiled left flank to commit this sector's last reserve,

The Battle of Wagram
(1:00 P.M. Positions)

five battalions and four squadrons, in a counterattack. Inspired by Karl's presence, most of the surviving Austrian cavalry in the area joined in. The Hapsburg infantry succeeded in stalling the momentum of their French counterparts. GM Wartensleben, who was proving himself this day to be among the best Hapsburg cavalry commanders, took advantage of some screening trees to lead his light cavalry brigade into position on Jacquinot's flank. Wartensleben led the Blankenstein Hussars in a howling charge that routed Jacquinot. The Hapsburg horse almost bagged the Empress Josephine's cousin, Maurice de Tascher, whose horse had been killed by an Austrian ball. Dismounted, he barely escaped the pursuing hussars when two chasseurs reached from their horses to seize him beneath his armpits and half carry, half haul him to safety.

General Grouchy, in turn, led his first line of dragoons into the fray and routed the Austrian hussars. Up came the Hapsburg reserves, the O'Reilly Chevaulégers and Hohenzollern Cuirassiers to force back the French dragoons. This type of swirling cavalry encounter was usually won by whoever held the last reserve, and Grouchy had one final line of dragoons. By nicely coordinating a charge of this reserve line, composed of the 7th Dragoons and the Italian Queen's Dragoons, with Pajol's Brigade, Grouchy finally swept the field, drove off the opposing cavalry, and captured some 400 men in the process.[58]

Impressed by the strength of Karl's counterattack, Marshal Davout realized that he again faced a solid enemy infantry force, so he reacted with his favorite maneuver by once more seeking to outflank his opponents. To ensure success, he sent two couriers to ask General Oudinot to attack Hohenzollern from the front.

General Oudinot had been up at dawn, standing on a small elevation to examine the enemy line. As he readied his command for the expected order to attack, Napoleon sent word to suspend the offensive until the situation along Davout's front clarified. Consequently, for most of the morning, his corps had to stand motionless under an intense bombardment from at least 68 guns firing from the slope behind the Russbach. He had chafed at his enforced inactivity and watched Davout's flank attack intently. When that marshal seemed to be gaining ground, he acted without orders (the account provided by Oudinot's family biographers) or responded to Davout's couriers (the account provided by Davout's family biographers) to order his men forward. What is certain is that this brave man, sword in hand, led from the front as his soldiers stormed Baumersdorf. The evening before, this key village had been overlooked. On July 6 Oudinot targeted it with an overpowering assault. Simultaneously, his artillerist Seruzier advanced his guns to the Russbach. Undaunted by this obstacle, Seruzier had his gunners haul their weapons by main force across the stream. Ordering his cannon loaded with canister, Seruzier spoke to his men: "My friends, we are going to charge the Austrian artillery, and take their position." In an amazing feat, Seruzier ordered the mounted men of the horse artillery to charge in open order against the Austrian gunline. After coordinating the attack with the colonel of the 10th Légère, Seruzier sent them forward. Their charge forced the opposing cannon to withdraw.

Meanwhile, untouched amid a hail of bullets, Oudinot was one of the first to enter Baumersdorf. The Austrians had fought hard for the village on the previous evening. This time they did not fare so well. They had seen the second line redeploy to face Davout's flank attack, and it had made them jumpy. The sounds of French cannon closing on the flank unnerved them completely, and they yielded the village. Next, Oudinot led his men across the Russbach and up the slope. A bullet killed his horse; another nicked his ear. He took the horse of the lieutenant colonel of the 57th Ligne and pressed on. Sensing opportunity, he turned his corps toward Wagram. Then excitement seemed to overcome whatever tactical judgement he possessed, and he galloped along his line yelling,

"Forward, at the run!"[59] Similarly General Grandjean, although behaving bravely enough, seemed overwhelmed by the battle's confusion and was unable to provide the necessary direction to implement Oudinot's directive. Had the soldiers literally followed Oudinot's command, they would have quickly scattered and become vulnerable to any counterstroke. With their superiors gone berserk or rendered incapable, experienced brigade and regimental leaders took over and conducted the advance. Thus, when counterattacking Austrian cavalry threatened the 10th Légère, that veteran regiment calmly closed ranks and saw them off. Likewise, the soldiers of Tharreau's and Claparède's divisions formed square and repelled repeated Austrian cavalry charges.

Re-forming his columns and taking a moment to have a surgeon dress his wound, Oudinot sent Cöehorn toward the road to Znaim—one of the main routes Karl would need if he were to retreat—and placed himself at the head of Albert's brigade for an advance on Wagram. Seruzier, in spite of having his fifth horse shot out from under him, brought up the corps' horse artillery to provide fire support. The artillerist positioned his batteries in echelon formation; while one battery fired, the other advanced and unlimbered, and when the second battery opened fire, the first battery limbered and advanced. These modern fire-and-move tactics helped pave the way for a successful assault. Still, in the end it required naked valor to take Wagram, and none surpassed that of General Oudinot and his staff. Again leading the way, sword in hand, Oudinot rode at the front of his men. A bullet hit his thigh; his chief of staff went down with a mortal wound; his senior aide received a mortal canister wound; four aides-de-camp were hit. Bleeding profusely, Oudinot refused to relinquish command and called upon General Colbert and his "Infernal Brigade" of light horse to clear the way.

Confronting Colbert was a chain of Austrian infantry squares trying to maintain a line of retreat for Rosenberg's people. The trumpeters of the "Infernal Brigade" sounded the charge, and the chasseurs à cheval and hussars "rushed fearlessly forward against the enemy squares on the plain. Led by the general himself, the 7th Chasseurs charged resolutely, but at one hundred paces a terrible volley from the square facing it caused the most fearful confusion in the ranks."[60] Colbert went down with a serious head wound, and the 7th Chasseurs à Cheval fell back. The colonel of the 20th Chasseurs à Cheval showed excellent judgment and converted this setback into opportunity. He had retained control of his men by insisting that they advance at the trot. Instead of attacking straight ahead as ordered, he inclined his regiment toward the square that had just repulsed the 7th regiment. The 20th Chasseurs à Cheval charged home. The Austrian infantry, having emptied their weapons, had no choice but to rely on their bayonets. Although some stood firm—French horses actually received bayonet wounds during this charge—the resolute troopers of the "Infernal Brigade" crushed the square. The men in an adjacent square defending against the 9th Hussars proved unsteady, and they also yielded. Colbert's brigade had carved a breach for Oudinot's infantry.

With the path clear, Oudinot advanced against Wagram and captured it. He sent word to Napoleon that he would not relinquish the village and that the enemy on his front was defeated. With the capture of Wagram, Oudinot's soldiers had completed a splendid transformation from raw conscripts to reliable shock infantry. It was 2 P.M.

Marshal Massena had collected his soldiers outside Raasdorf at 11 A.M. Here many of the soldiers who had run earlier in the battle rejoined the ranks. Massena fortified his men for the coming ordeal by issuing a special reserve, a bracing gulp of gut-roaring army brandy, and arrayed his infantry in column by division at deployment distance, echeloned by regiment. Then he began his march toward the Austrian breakthrough along the Danube. Along with Saint-Sulpice's cuirassier division and the corps' light cavalry, Massena's infantry marched across the front of three Austrian corps to reach a position outside Essling. Although under a heavy flank fire for most of the time, the French IV Corps still completed the march in about 90 minutes. At one point an Austrian hussar regiment attacked the column and swarmed around Massena's carriage. His devoted aides drew sabers to defend him. One aide saw an enemy hussar force his horse close to the carriage and raise his arm to strike the marshal. He shot the hussar with his pistol.

By 12:30 P.M. Massena's "Infernal Column"—the well-chosen words FML Klenau used in his report to describe Massena's approach—had reached Essling. At this point an imperial aide spurred up to Massena's coach with Napoleon's report of Davout's success and an order to drive the enemy. Victory was apparent to neither Massena nor his men. Boudet's survivors were still being hounded by Austrian cavalry as they fled in and about Essling. But if the emperor called for an attack, Massena meant to oblige. Marulaz's light horse, the first of his cavalry to arrive, made a succession of charges to cover Boudet's withdrawal, then turned against the Austrian battery that was firing on the Danube bridges. Marulaz's sudden appearance surprised the Hapsburg gunners, who cut their traces and fled, leaving the French cavalry in possession of a full battery. This was unacceptable to Klenau's cavalry general, Brigadier Walmoden, and he counterattacked with nearly 1,000 hussars, sending Marulaz's troopers flying. But the French cavalry had supports whereas Walmoden did not. Lasalle sent a fresh brigade commanded by General Bruyère to extricate Marulaz. Although the Austrians had managed to pull off most of the battery in the lull between charges, Bruyère captured two guns and, more important, put an end to Klenau's advance. This cavalry attack had the same effect on Klenau that Nansouty's charge had had upon Kollowrath: it reversed the floodtide of Hapsburg advance.

Massena's next objective was Essling, defended by some 1,200 Austrian infantry. In a curious reversal of roles from the situation back in May, a French division stormed the granary and sent the defenders running toward Aspern. By 2 P.M. Massena's men were masters of the village and shortly after regained Aspern as well. This success uncovered Boudet and allowed Massena to reunite his entire corps. His four divisions fanned out, with Molitor's Corps marching toward Breitenlee where it would cooperate with Macdonald's Corps, and the balance of the corps driving northwest toward the heights. The marshal dispatched a courier to Napoleon telling him that his orders had been executed, and all the ground lost during the morning had been regained.

Massena and his men had provided stellar service. In the murky predawn, they had marched 4 miles across the Austrian front to attack and capture Aderklaa. Four hours later, they had repeated the march across the front of three enemy corps in full sway to retrieve the situation along the Danube. Later Marshal Massena would receive the title prince of Essling. It might equally have been prince of Wagram.

Macdonald's Corps was so weakened that he dared not continue into the bowels of the Austrian position. From his vantage point outside Aderklaa, Napoleon could see that Macdonald needed help. The decision when and where to commit reserves is a benchmark of battlefield management. No contemporary military man better understood this than Napoleon. He ordered Eugène to use the two uncommitted Army of Italy divisions to support Macdonald on his flanks and sent Wrede's Bavarians to support Macdonald directly. With these orders Napoleon was sending into battle 7,000 veteran French and 5,500 fresh Bavarian infantry. The emperor also forwarded Reille with the Young Guard, cautioning him to avoid becoming too involved in the fighting because his departure left only two regiments of Old Guard infantry in reserve.[61] The emperor overlooked (perhaps deliberately in order to make a point) the fact that Marmont's completely fresh corps still remained in reserve.

General Pacthod led his understrength division toward Wagram to create a diversion on Macdonald's right. The Austrian infantry in this sector had changed front to face Macdonald and were hugely vulnerable. Outside the village Pacthod surprised one of FML d'Aspré's grenadier brigades in the flank and drove it in confusion toward Aderklaa. There was one last desperate hand-to-hand struggle for Aderklaa's ruins where the grenadiers were nearly surrounded. When d'Aspré, another courageous French émigré officer, fell with a mortal wound, they lost heart and retired. Meanwhile, General Durutte led the other Army of Italy division behind Macdonald's stagnant front to attack Kollowrath's people between Sussenbrunn and Breitenlee. Kollowrath pulled together two artillery batteries to oppose Durutte, but they were not enough. Durutte drove through Breitenlee and headed on toward Leopoldau.

The village of Sussenbrunn stood directly in front of the line of advance chosen by Macdonald. Fire from this bastion had inflicted great damage in the French ranks. Not until Wrede's Bavarian division arrived to reinforce him did Macdonald dare risk an advance against the village. General Broussier consolidated his division's survivors into one battalion numbering about 400 men and massed his eagles in their center. Only one sergeant and four gunners survived to serve a single 3-pound regimental cannon. Around 6:30 P.M. Broussier encountered the Gorgy and Fritch Grenadier battalions, defending a farmyard outside Sussenbrunn. Clearly Austrian morale was on the wane because the grenadiers failed to hold the position. Broussier pressed on to met some 200 Austrian infantry defending the village cemetery. Assisted by the soldiers of the Young Guard (Reille was liberally interpreting Napoleon's directive to avoid joining the fight), Broussier surrounded the cemetery and captured the lot.

The way was now clear for the Bavarian infantry to storm Sussenbrunn. General Wrede led his men forward amid a hail of bullets and fell with a wound. Macdonald galloped up to hear the Bavarian general say: "Tell the Emperor that I die for him. I recommend to him my wife and children." Macdonald laughed and replied, "I think that you will be able to make this recommendation to him yourself."[62] Indeed, Wrede gathered his wits and realized that he had been only lightly grazed. He rose to see that his men had carried the village.

On the opposite flank Davout's men also continued to confront tenacious resistance during the early afternoon. The marshal had sent Friant's division to outflank the new Austrian line. When Friant gained the new Austrian flank at 1 P.M., his division was parallel to the Russbach and in the rear of the original Austrian position. Between Friant and the enemy was a collection of wooden huts built by the Austrians during their long encampment. The French artillery sent their shot bowling through the huts and into the defender's flank. Having run out of reserves, Rosenberg had no choice but to order a retreat. His soldiers retired in good order, with the Hiller and Sztarri Infantry Regiments overcoming the loss of their general to form a solid rearguard to cover the withdrawal. Then they faced about to confront the French once more.

Galvanized by a message from the emperor asking why his corps lagged behind schedule, Davout redoubled his energy. But whenever friendly units converge at right angles (as occurs in a flank charge), there is considerable confusion. In addition, the corps had been fighting and marching for nine hours, and everyone was a little sluggish. Not until close to 4 P.M. did Davout manage to sort out his units on the plateau northwest of Neusiedel. Then the marshal ordered his cuirassiers to break Rosenberg's line. Arrighi's men of iron made a fine left wheel while under artillery fire and drove the opposing infantry from their position, but not without some hard fighting. The 8th Cuirassiers lost one man in eight.[63] The colonels of the other three regiments were all hit, including the 6th's colonel, an officer who had recovered from his wounding at Aspern-Essling to participate in this battle, and Napoleon's brother-in-law, Prince Borghese. A canister fragment gave Arrighi a painful contusion. However, none surpassed Cuirassier Vingelbech who received nine saber wounds during the fighting.

Meanwhile, Grouchy and Montbrun had again turned Rosenberg's open left flank. Montbrun encountered a large force of Hapsburg horse about to deliver a charge. In previous combats beginning early in the morning, Montbrun's troopers had established a morale ascendancy over their opponents. Here again they showed a solid front, which caused the charging Austrians to hesitate, rein up short, and turn about.[64] Having defeated his mounted foe, Montbrun unleashed his light horse in pursuit. His veterans encountered an Austrian skirmish chain deployed among the vineyards. This was difficult cavalry country, prohibiting a charge in line. Accordingly, the chasseurs à cheval formed serried columns, a more compact formation that allowed them to pass between the vines, and charged. The leading squadron was about to saber happily the Austrian skirmishers when a concealed enemy battalion delivered a point-blank fire into its flank, putting an end to the pursuit. During the day Montbrun's division lost 80 killed, 200 wounded, and 400 horses killed or wounded. The check put an end to the very limited French pursuit. By 6 P.M. Davout's weary soldiers were in camp.

Along the Danube, the appearance of Massena's "Infernal Column" had dismayed FML Klenau. One moment his corps had satisfactorily been driving Boudet's people, and the next it had to contend with a powerful and unexpected counterattack. The ease with which the French recaptured Essling and Aspern apparently demoralized Klenau. Although there were numerous easily defensible villages north and west of Aspern, he made little effort to hold them. He contented himself with telling his subordinates to rally upon Stammersdorf, a village from which the corps had departed in the predawn hours, and by sending a courier to Karl reporting that the VI Corps confronted an overwhelming force and that he "feared a disaster" was in the making.[65]

In spite of Klenau's dread his corps retreated in good order. Outside Kagran, two solid squares thwarted Marulaz's efforts to pursue. The French light horse could not continue until the 12-pounders of the corps artillery reserve arrived to blow apart the squares. Meanwhile, Lasalle's division spearheaded the drive on Leopoldau, where the French 8th Hussars charged side by side with the Saxon Prince Clement Chevaulégers, two regiments that had first met on opposite sides during the Battle of Jena. Lasalle was probably the best-known light cavalryman on the field. His rake-hell behavior with its drinking, gambling, and womanizing personified the French light cavalryman. The morning had not begun well for him. Before dawn, his servant had taken his best horse to be watered at a nearby stream, and both had been captured by Austrian pickets. Preparing to mount another horse, he reached up to the saddle holster for a libation from a small brandy flask that he customarily stored there. He found the glass broken and remarked, "What a wretched day! It is the sort of day on which I shall get killed."[66]

Battle fever had lifted Lasalles's spirits. Encountering a battalion of the Duka Infantry Regiment in Leopoldau, Lasalle animated his troopers by telling them that so far during the day they had done very little to contribute to the army's success. They charged with spirit, but the defenders, well sheltered behind a 6-foot-wide village moat, repelled the attack. While Lasalle was rallying his troopers, a bullet—apparently fired by a wounded Austrian infantryman who was lying 15 paces distant—hit him in the chest.[67] Two hours later, at age 33, he was dead.

Marulaz tried to avenge his fallen comrade. He placed himself at the head of his old command: "Hussars of the Eighth Regiment. I have commanded you for twelve years, my name you know. Here is the enemy! I trust you will not sully your ancient reputation. You will charge. Marulaz is at your head!"[68] The regiment charged impetuously, its colonel fell dead, and Marulaz received a serious arm wound. Repulsed, Marulaz persisted until he suffered a stunning fall when a cannon shot killed his horse beneath him.

The cumulative pressure from the general French surge between the Danube and Wagram gradually shredded the Austrian position. With Karl preoccupied on the opposite flank, Klenau, Kollowrath, and Liechtenstein had to fend for themselves. The last two tried to withdraw back to the high ground while detachments slowed the French pursuit by holding hard to the various villages along their line of retreat. With the continuous line now broken, the French sent forward their cavalry. Macdonald had a variety of mounted formations to support him: the Imperial Guard light cavalry, some Bavarian light horse, and a handful of rallied Saxon squadrons. (Whatever criticism the performance of the Saxon infantry merited, the Saxon cavalry displayed great fighting tenacity on this day.) The Guard light cavalry tried several charges against the still-solid Austrian squares covering the Austrian retirement. They could make little impression. A nearsighted French colonel in the Polish Horse almost ruined this elite regiment. Advancing toward a line of Hapsburg uhlans, the colonel misjudged the distance and ordered his unit to right about-face. His subordinate understood that this was disastrous because it would allow the uhlans to charge the unit's rear. He immediately gave the same order again, followed by the command to advance at the trot. Having performed a neat 360-degree pirouette, the Polish Horse was by all rights lost. Fortunately their adversaries belonged to the Schwarzenburg Uhlans, a unit largely composed of Poles recruited from Austrian-held west Galicia, and the uhlans fought halfheartedly against their fellow countrymen. About 150 surrendered at first contact. Thus were the Poles of the Imperial Guard able to convert disaster into triumph.

Stern fighting remained. At Gerasdorf, the detachment that Kollowrath had left behind during the early morning advance offered resistance. A new Austrian gun line, firing from the heights around Stammersdorf, supported this detachment. Their opposition forced Macdonald to pause, deploy a thick skirmish line to provide frontal pressure, and maneuver to outflank the gunline. Even after the Hapsburg gunners withdrew, a stubborn infantry force remained in a stoutly built house overlooking Gerasdorf. They did not yield until massed fire from French howitzers burned them out.

It was much the same north of Wagram. A French artillery captain advanced his battery to the rising ground to see Karl's army retiring "in very good order" without a hint of panic.[69] FML Nostitz covered the plain north of Wagram with the re-formed cavalry of the reserve corps, while FML Radetzky occupied the defiles with his infantry. FML Karl Schwarzenberg saw French cavalry about to capture some abandoned Austrian guns. He galloped to a shaken and disordered uhlan regiment. It was the regiment that carried his name, and the troopers recognized the prince and rallied to him. Schwarzenberg spoke loudly to the uhlans' commander: "There, the enemy is going away with the battery. If the regiment is not going to get it back, it shall never again carry my name."[70] Ten minutes later the Schwarzenberg uhlans had recaptured the guns. Similarly a cavalry battery commander in Bellegarde's corps performed a coolly calculated rearguard action to cover his corps' withdrawal. He positioned his six guns 400 paces behind the retiring infantry, waited until the French drew near, and then drove them off with effective canister fire. Taking advantage of the ensuing lull, he retired to the next favorable firing position. It was actions like these that prompted French Captain Lacombe to write to his father that "the battle did not have the expected success. We defeated the enemy but did not rout him."[71]

In recognition of the fact that even in victory his army had received a severe drubbing, Napoleon did not order an immediate pursuit. As Savary wryly observed, the Austrians had "fought in a manner calculated to instill a cautious conduct into any man disposed to deeds of rashness."[72] The French followed, but did not force the Austrians from the field. They had been under arms for most of the past 40 hours, operating under a hot sun amid heavy artillery fire with little to eat or drink. Indicative of their exhaustion was what transpired shortly after they encamped. Suddenly from somewhere out past Wagram came a burst of fire followed by a throng of running Frenchmen. The grenadiers of the Old Guard hastily formed a square around Napoleon's field headquarters. So alarming was the panic that an exhausted emperor bestirred himself and rode up to Oudinot's men to demand the cause of this commotion. Officers assured him it was nothing more that a few foragers who had strayed beyond the lines, encountered Austrian cavalry, and panicked. For a brief moment (said the officers) they had conveyed their terror to their comrades, but now all was right.

Napoleon returned to his headquarters and shortly after had to address another alarm, this time from the opposite direction. Somehow the people in the army's right rear had decided that Erzherzog Johann had arrived. Faced with a fire from the rear they panicked:

The terrified men were upsetting the saucepans on the fires; mules and horses were being hastily laden anyhow; tents were being overturned, drum and trumpets were sounding on every side. The cavalry mounted, the infantry formed in squares. . . . I galloped at full speed to the emperor's tent, found him as much taken by surprise as any one, and as I drew up he was just flinging himself on to his horse, half dressed, without his cap, and with slippers instead of boots.

The aide assured Napoleon that it was nothing. Another aide arrived to report the same, and Napoleon flew into a rage: "What do you call nothing. I tell you there is no such thing as a small matter in time of war; nothing compromises an army so much as a careless security."[73] He dispatched aides to reconnoiter, and only after they returned with the certain word that it had been a false alarm did he rest. This event, the third major panic of the day, underscored the fact that having conducted a hard fight, the Army of Germany was a spent force.

A voltigeur corporal passes imperial headquarters and realizes that his leader is spent as well. He sees Napoleon slumped over on some straw with his head resting on his hand. A small fire burns nearby. In a gesture characteristic of this army and no other, the voltigeur approaches and asks, "Sire, would your majesty enjoy some of our soup?"

Awakened, Napoleon replies, "Has it steeped?"

The corporal, obviously an expert forager, shows him his thick soup complete with croutons.

"How have you come across white bread and a silver urn? Have you stolen them?" asks Napoleon.

Having faced Austrian fire, this grognard shows he can face the emperor equally well: "I bought the bread from the ambulance train and found the urn on a dead officer." The brazen forager then presents Napoleon with a roasted chicken to complete the meal.[74] For the voltigeur and for the emperor it is a satisfactory ending to a very long day.

Chapter 9

THE SPOILS OF WAR

What my enemies call a general peace is my destruction. What I call peace is merely the disarmament of my enemies.[1]

ARMISTICE

By midafternoon Erzherzog Karl had realized that there was no hope that his brother Johann would reach the field. With Davout's flank attack gaining momentum, Massena driving Klenau back up the river, and his center nearly ruptured by Macdonald's thrust, Karl ordered a general withdrawal from the field. As we have seen, his lieutenants brought this off very well. So exhausted were the French that there was even time for a brief halt on the battlefield's fringe to feed the troops. At 8 P.M. Karl issued instructions for his entire army to retreat into Bohemia. Although he had to abandon his wounded, Karl managed to carry off thousands of French prisoners, 21 cannons, and a handful of captured eagles and standards.

Back on the Marchfeld the huge number of injured soldiers overwhelmed medical capacity. During the morning, Larrey's flying ambulances had coursed the field to carry hurt Imperial Guardsmen to a field hospital. Casualties had been so heavy that by midday Larrey began directing the wounded guardsmen to the general field hospital. The men of the Imperial Guard received first call from the care providers. Because of this, within a few days half of the 1,200 who received wounds at Wagram had returned to the ranks, and only 145 died from their wounds. In contrast was the poor care accorded to the line soldiers. The preponderance of the injured had been hit by cannon fire.[2] These blows caused fearful trauma for which the only answer was amputation. Through the night and during the next day and the next, the surgeons engaged in a frenzy of saw and knife work. Four days after the battle, line soldiers who had had a limb amputated still lay exposed to the elements outside the field hospitals.[3]

Illustrative was the experience of trumpeter Chevillet of the 8th Chasseurs à Cheval who, around 10 P.M. on July 5, had been at his customary position in the forefront of a hack-and-thrust melee. Gripping his reins with his teeth, a pistol in one hand and saber in the other, Chevillet was dealing blows left and right when a tremendous explosion occurred just in front of his horse. It was an Austrian shell fired from the heights behind the Russbach. The blast blew Chevillet from his saddle, killed his horse, and left his right arm dangling by a thread of skin. Although pinned beneath his horse, the trumpeter managed to staunch his bleeding with bandages. Fortunately, the French remained masters of this sector, and his friends found him two hours later, weakened but alive.

Outside of the Guard, the army lacked any kind of systematic casualty clearing. Until a battle ended, an individual had to rely on his own resources to find help, so Chevillet stumbled through the French rear area in search of medical assistance. He finally arrived in Essling to find the village's remaining structures stuffed with wounded soldiers. Overburdened surgeons told Chevillet to wait his turn. Nine hours after being hit, a surgeon amputated his arm and dressed the wound. The trooper returned from surgery to discover that someone had rifled his possessions during his absence. Being a veteran he had wisely retained a money belt, a precaution that was to prove key to his survival. Fatigued by blood loss, Chevillet set off for Lobau where some sympathetic Imperial Guard Marines gave him bouillon and wine. Following a brief slumber, he joined a trail of wounded trekking toward Vienna. The first hospitals Chevillet encountered were full, and he was turned away. Eventually he found a hospital with available space where attendants washed his wound and put him in a makeshift bed of straw and draperies. He slept for 36 hours, to awaken to intense discomfort and a plague of fleas.

For the next eight days he lay unattended, drifting in and out of consciousness. A surgeon finally came and redressed his wound. Chevillet bribed him to continue to provide care and in this manner managed to regain his strength slowly over a 40-day hospitalization. Ahead lay an encounter with the emperor—the trooper asked for the Cross; Napoleon refused but gave him a small annual annuity—a journey home that revealed that the penurious rear echelon troops cared not one whit for the heroes of Wagram, a nearly killing fever and a 50-day convalescence at the hospital in Passau, and a return to France at the end of January 1810. Chevillet had formerly delighted in playing a clarinet and had always been proud of his neat hand writing. Denied music, he taught himself to write left-handed and labored into the next year to complete a transcription of his campaign notes. For all of his suffering, in many ways he had been one of the lucky ones.

July 6 had been a very warm day, and the wounded suffered from the thirst brought on by the dehydrating effect of blood loss. Since the Hapsburg Army had ceded the field, their wounded, who numbered over 10,000, received second call on medical care. Their distressing cries kept many awake through the night. The sound aroused the troopers of the 8th Cuirassiers to form a bucket brigade for passing water to the men who lay in the vines around their bivouac. Most of the French army discovered to their delight that they had encamped among vineyards. In Austria, wine growers located their cellars in the middle of their fields, so naturally the army celebrated its triumph with a stupendous drinking bout. Had Karl been able to deliver one more attack the next morning, history might have been changed.[4] On July 7, cursing and freely employing the flat of his sword, General Oudinot tried to drive the light cavalry from the vineyards and send them off in pursuit. But the troopers, "harassed by fatigue, inflamed by wine, and nearly mutinous," proved balky.[5]

Neither side provided a complete tabulation of the losses suffered on July 5 and 6. Total Hapsburg casualties exceeded 30,000, of whom 24,000 were either killed or wounded and the rest captured. A total of 720 Austrian officers were hit. Among the ranks of brigadier general or higher, excluding Karl himself, losses included 4 killed and 10 wounded. Casualties clearly highlighted which units had fought the hardest. The I, II, and IV Corps all lost 30 percent of their strength, while Klenau's VI Corps endured a rate of 15 percent and the timidly led III Corps suffered only 11 percent losses. In other words, the two corps charged with spearheading Karl's flank attack had fewer than half the percentage losses of the three corps manning the line from Wagram to Neusiedel.

Napoleon's official bulletin stated that his losses had been considerable— "1,500 killed and 3 or 4,000 wounded."[6] This was a bald-faced lie. French losses approximated those suffered by their foe. Reports to Chief of Staff Berthier for the battle on July 6 list 4,230 killed outright, 2,912 mortally wounded, and 18,000 wounded.[7] This tabulation was quite incomplete. Typical of the sloppy French accounting were the reports describing Saxon and Bavarian losses. They listed 3,000 casualties, yet a detailed report furnished on July 8 by General Antoine Andréossy, the man Napoleon had appointed as "governor" of Vienna, states that 5,844 wounded solders from Bernadotte's Corps alone had been admitted to the various hospitals. While this number included Frenchmen from Dupas's division, all of the wounded had yet to be taken to the hospitals. It does not include the corps dead. The report that there had been 3,000 Saxon and Bavarian casualties cannot be squared with known facts.[8] Using the reports handed to Berthier as a base figure, while acknowledging that they are assuredly low, and combining it with an estimate of 3,500 captured and missing—Karl stated that his army carried off 7,000 prisoners, a figure that is certainly too high; half this total seems more accurate—and estimating about 11,000 casualties suffered on July 5, total French and allied casualties of all sorts neared 40,000.

Wagram extracted a high toll from Napoleon's senior leadership. Five generals died, and 38 received wounds, including such notables as Oudinot, Gudin, Vandamme, Marulaz, and Coëhorn. Napoleon's allies had served nobly, as reflected by the casualties among their generals. The Saxon General de Hartitzsch died, and two of his fellow generals received wounds; the Italian Severoli and the

Bavarian Wrede were also hit. A total of 1,822 French officers had been killed or wounded. Coming on the heels of Aspern-Essling, these were staggering figures. Quite simply, the Marchfeld had been a killing ground. Two last examples underscore this point. The 18th Ligne, one of Massena's veteran regiments that had fought in both battles, lost 45 of 54 officers killed and wounded. Molitor's division had a brigadier general lose his arm, one colonel receive a mortal wound, and two colonels and four battalion commanders suffer wounds.[9]

Under the July heat, the battlefield quickly became a stinking abattoir. Whereas the dead soldiers could be buried relatively easily, the bloated bodies of the thousands of dead horses—the Imperial Guard Artillery alone lost 564 riding and draft mounts; Napoleon wrote that "the destruction of horses is immense"— soon putrefied.[10] A month later a soldier walking the field found it "still covered by dead horses and men." He located the Saxon graves carefully memorialized with "hats placed as monuments, weighted with stones."[11] Although looters had gleaned the field, they had left behind headgear and cartridge pouches. Enough of these remained to delineate clearly the battle positions. Between Aderklaa and Wagram, Saxon headgear marked where Bernadotte's soldiers had died before the Austrian cannon fire; cuirassiers' helmets and a set of cuirasses pierced front and back by a hole the size of a 12-pound shot indicated where Nansouty's men had charged; 26 dead Austrian landwehr, victims of French artillery fire during Rosenberg's spoiling attack, remained unburied in a neat rank near Glinzersdorf.

The Battle of Wagram had taken by far the heaviest toll of any other Napoleonic battle to date. About 60,000 combatants on both sides had been hit by lead, the great majority victims of artillery fire.

Napoleon arose on the morning of July 7 to receive reports from his handful of sober vedettes that the Austrians were in retreat. He told the army's chief gunner, General La Riboisière, that his artillery had won the battle. As a special favor, the emperor selected that general's young son to carry the battle news to Paris. At five in the morning he dispatched the young man with two letters: one to a political deputy and one to the Empress Josephine. Riding furiously, the courier made remarkable progress. Three days later the empress received him in her bedroom. She opened her husband's letter to read: "The enemy army is in disorder. . . . My losses have been heavy; but the victory is decisive and complete."[12] The letter said that Eugène had comported himself well and was unharmed. Josephine's son, many of her dear friends, her husband, and her country had all invested much in this battle. The news relieved and delighted the empress. As a token of her esteem, she gave the young man a diamond jewel. The courier received it with a deep bow, clutching his hat firmly with both hands behind his back. After departing, an attendant asked why he had exhibited such a strange posture. Young La Riboisière explained that he did so to hide the rip in his pants caused by 72 hours of hard riding.

So many men had been involved in the battle that any victory could not be easily won. Compounding this was Napoleon's battlefield method, which required the rupturing of the enemy's center. It could not be done without enormous loss. Finally, unlike the Grande Armée, the Army of Germany lacked stamina. For these reasons Napoleon did not order an immediate pursuit after the battle. Instead he set out to inspect his army. Riding among the men of the Army of Italy he paid them a well-deserved compliment: "You are brave soldiers; you have covered yourselves with glory."[13] He rode to Macdonald, embraced him, and said, "You have behaved valiantly, and have rendered me the greatest services. . . . On the battlefield of your glory, where I owe you so large a part of yesterday's success, I make you a Marshal of France."[14] Macdonald was the only Napoleonic officer created marshal on the field of battle. The emperor also sent two staff officers to the hapless Boudet's headquarters to make a formal inquiry into that general's conduct on the previous day, with special attention to the loss of his guns.[15] He ordered another inquiry into why Saint-Cyr's men had routed at Aderklaa on the previous morning.

Meanwhile Karl's army trudged wearily north toward Znaim. The men in the ranks knew they had given their all. Typical was an infantry corporal whose arms had been torn away by a French cannonball. Although he lay dying in a small village while his comrades marched by, the 22-year-old soldier remained cheerful. "I can die," he said, "with great peace of mind because I know that the enemy, even though he won, trembled when he faced our courage."[16] The Austrian Army had rocked Napoleon's legions, but still the battle had been lost. Many wondered why? The Austrian generalissimus had displayed moral courage in preparing for the battle. Instead of seeking a partial victory that might come from defending the Danube and repelling a crossing attempt, he chose to opt for a decisive engagement. He selected well the position for this climactic encounter. With over 40 days to prepare, he then blundered badly by not realizing that his dangling left flank was certain to be a target for a French attack. Had he constructed four or five stout redoubts to defend this open flank, the battle's outcome would have been in doubt. Rosenberg would have retreated to a secure position after his attack or could have fought on the defensive from the start.

As we have seen, Rosenberg's offensive well served Karl as a spoiling attack. But this had not been his intention. He conceived of a double envelopment, which was much too ambitious given the discrepancy in numbers. The wisdom of leaving FML Reuss's corps defending the Danube opposite Vienna is debatable. On the one hand, it was the army's smallest corps, and assigning it the task of flank defense can be viewed as a wise precaution. On the other hand, the corps composed nearly 9,000 men, including three fine, veteran infantry regiments. Given that Karl intended to risk all for a decisive battle and that his observers on the Bisamberg had not detected any signs of a French crossing from Vienna, not summoning Reuss to the field was an avoidable error. The weight of another 9,000 men driving against the French bridges or turning to deflect Macdonald's blow also would have altered the battle. Last, Johann's failure to arrive on the field, a failure caused by an unnecessary 11-hour delay, had a significant impact.

Had Johann arrived when ordered, it would have placed Napoleon in a most awkward bind. Johann's appearance in Davout's rear must have checked that marshal's advance. Although the emperor retained in hand a large and fresh reserve consisting of Marmont's Corps and the Imperial Guard, and these men could have blocked Johann's eruption into the French right rear, in their absence Macdonald would have been unable to progress. And there we must leave it, except to say that for Karl the Battle of Wagram was a winnable proposition.

Karl's choice of line of retreat, was faulty. Had he withdrawn northwest toward Prague, he would have been on Napoleon's line of communications and have had access to a better logistical base. By retiring toward Znaim, he worked himself into a cul de sac. Napoleon had comprehensively studied this terrain during his Austerlitz campaign. He immediately realized that he could use the March River as a strategic barrier to limit Karl's options while hounding his army closely with a force that directly pursued him. Napoleon assigned Marmont to command the pursuit with 20,000 men. Marmont's own XI Corps had never engaged at Wagram. Having merely lost somewhat more than 600 men to artillery fire, it was the natural choice for this mission. In addition to his corps, Marmont commanded Wrede's relatively intact Bavarian division and three light cavalry brigades, with the latter being directed by the skilled Montbrun. The chase effectively began on July 8. Both the pursuers and the pursued toiled beneath a blazing July sun.

Although Karl had conducted a clean retreat, leaving behind few unwounded prisoners and little artillery, during the succeeding days the morale blow to his army became apparent as the Hapsburg rear guard fought a series of listless blocking actions. The generalissimus despondently informed his brother the Kaiser that each day witnessed straggling and desertion, particularly among the landwehr. Meanwhile Napoleon masterfully directed his various corps along multiple lines of advance to bring Karl to bay. Then his old comrade Marmont almost ruined everything when Karl turned to confront his pursuers on July 10 near the town of Znaim. Marmont, who keenly felt the knowledge that his corps had done little to contribute to victory, proved overly zealous. He advanced his unsupported corps against a force of unknown strength. During the ensuing battle— and battle it was, with Marmont's Corps alone losing more than 1,200 men and Massena's Corps, once they arrived, suffering 2,000 more—it became clear that the Austrians had superior numbers and were deployed on a formidable ridgetop position. Darkness put an end to the fighting before Marmont suffered defeat. Overnight, substantial French reinforcements arrived including Napoleon himself. The next day the skirmishers engaged, the artillery opened fire, and both sides braced for another stern fight. Much as had been the case during the first hours at Friedland in 1807, the French aim was to pin Karl's army until sufficient reinforcements arrived to win the battle. Heavy skirmishing continued until 7 P.M. Suddenly a cavalryman appeared waving a white flag. The word spread rapidly, "Peace! Peace!" and the order came to cease fire.

The next day, July 11, Napoleon and Karl negotiated an armistice that was to last for one month. No sooner had the armistice been agreed to than certain high-ranking French officers fell to one of their favorite pastimes, quarreling. Generals Nansouty and Arrighi disputed rights to a small farm pond, each wanting it reserved for his troopers. They argued strenuously, and at one point it appeared that matters would not be resolved without a duel. Finally Nansouty, by virtue of his seniority, won out. A trooper in Arrighi's division erected a small, sarcastic sign with the message "Nansouty's fishpond."[17] More serious was the behavior of the contentious Marshal Bernadotte who had had the remarkable audacity to deliver a proclamation, two days after the battle, praising his Saxons for their conduct on July 5. Bernadotte wrote that by "piercing the enemy's center," fighting until midnight, and "bivouacking in the midst of the Austrian lines," his men had virtually won the battle. The wording made no mention of the French and suggested that the Saxons had captured and retained Wagram. Regarding July 6, Bernadotte commended his men for their perseverance as their columns "remained stationary" amid a withering artillery fire.

The proclamation infuriated Napoleon, who immediately responded: "It belongs to him [the emperor] alone to assign to each one the share of glory to which he may be entitled." Napoleon wrote that Wagram was won by the French and not by foreigners, and it had been because "Massena and Oudinot . . . had pierced the enemy center at the same time Davout turned their flank." Napoleon continued with a point-by-point refutation of Bernadotte's claims, concluding with the scathing observation that instead of remaining steady under fire, the Saxons had been the first to run on July 6. In sum, Bernadotte had given "false pretensions" to "mediocre" soldiers.[18] Besides underscoring Napoleon's contempt for his allies—they were useful cannon fodder and little else; he dissolved the Saxon Corps the next day, distributing its men to other commands—his public chastisement of the proud Gascon marshal was sure to rile, and it did.

On the field of Znaim, Bernadotte reports to Napoleon to ask the Emperor for leave to return to Paris. His effrontery amazes Napoleon, who responds, "But the cannon are still firing."

"So what!" replies Bernadotte. "Is not a French brigadier sufficient to command that which is called my army corps?"[19]

Instead of losing his patience, Napoleon tried to persuade Bernadotte to attend to his duty, but the marshal was adamant. Napoleon appreciated that Bernadotte's departure widened the breach between them. He did not realize the extent of the schism. Only later would he understand that "Bernadotte was the snake we sheltered in our bosom."[20]

So one marshal departed the field in a cloud of controversy. But two other men were about to receive the coveted marshal's baton. The day after Wagram, Napoleon had been furious at Oudinot for his unauthorized assault against the Russbach. He shouted, "Do you know what you did yesterday?"

Oudinot replied, "I trust, Sire, I did not too badly do my duty."

"What you did was . . . you deserved to be shot!"[21]

But the emperor wanted to gild the lily, and so his battle report ignored Oud-inot's impetuous insubordination. Instead he made him a marshal on July 12. At Wagram Oudinot had displayed his one surpassing talent: his courageous front-line leadership.

In an earlier campaign, Napoleon had publicly cut the vain Auguste Marmont to the quick with the comment, "You have maneuvered like an oyster." At that time Marmont believed he stood no chance of ever being promoted again. The day after the armistice Napoleon closely questioned Marmont about his opera-tions in Illyria. For two hours he offered pointed criticisms. Marmont departed exhausted and despondent. Back at his tent, he began to unwind when one of Berthier's aides appeared and asked if he might embrace him. Marmont replied that he could not understand why anyone would want to embrace a dirty, un-shaven, and discredited fellow like himself. Then the aide explained: "Here is your nomination for marshal."[22] Marmont was totally surprised and delighted. However, the notice that he would become a marshal came with a deflating personal letter from the emperor that said, "Between ourselves, you have not yet done enough to justify entirely my choice."[23] This proved to be one of Napoleon's most accurate prognostications. After becoming a marshal and while serving in independent command, Marmont would fail to win any battle. In 1814 he took failure one step further by betraying Napoleon.

So the Wagram campaign saw three ascensions to the rank of marshal. In their campfire gossip, the French soldiers showed that they clearly understood what had taken place and circulated a little ditty:

> Macdonald is France's choice
> Oudinot is the army's choice
> Marmont is friendship's choice.

To celebrate the great victory at Wagram, the emperor lavishly distributed other favors and rewards. Davout became Prince of Eckmuhl; Massena, Prince of Essling; Berthier, Prince of Wagram. Imperial Guard colonels received 6,000-franc bonuses. Underscoring his awareness that his artillery above all had won the battle, Napoleon awarded the Imperial Cross to all the surviving noncom-missioned artillerists in his Imperial Guard. He elevated Drouot to colonel. On Saint Helena he would say that Drouot was a superb artillerist and overall su-perior to many of his marshals. He also named Colonel Seruzier, the "father of the cannon shot," to the imperial nobility by making him a baron.

Promotion-seeking officers excepted, few men who fought at Wagram wanted to fight again. Henri-Joseph Pasteger, a trooper in the 1st Carabiniers, spoke for many survivors when he wrote his father to marvel at the fact he remained alive: "I have had extremely good fortune to escape from this battle. I had two horses killed underneath me. [The second time] a cannon ball entered the [horse's] shoulder and exited through the opposite leg carrying with it a portion of my blanket roll and my stirrup. I had nothing except a slight tear of the skin."[24] Upon learning of the armistice, a French captain wrote his father, "We will have peace. God willing."[25]

A DURABLE PEACE

Rumors of the victory at Wagram circulated around Paris on July 11. When confirmation came, joy was near universal. Pages read the official bulletins at theaters amid an uninterrupted ovation. On the twenty-third, by order of Napoleon, Parisian churches held a massive Te Deum. However, the dying did not end with the armistice at Znaim. In the Viennese hospitals, wounded soldiers fought for life as tenaciously as they had fought to capture the rubble of Ebelsberg, Aspern, and Aderklaa. The campaign's hardships had weakened some, making them more vulnerable to disease. On August 28, soldier Bonfond succumbed to fever. Cumulative exhaustion, and perhaps the taint of disgrace, killed General Boudet on September 14, 1809. Jean-Lambert Saive of the 4th Sapper Battalion started home, only to die in the Linz hospital in December. And it continued into the next year. Jean-Joseph Delfosse of the 12th Battalion of military trains and equipment died in a Viennese suburb on February 4, 1810.

The battle left many men crippled for life. For some their wounds began a downward spiral of poverty and despair. Others accepted it as their lot. For a spirited few it mattered very little. Napoleon visited 32-year-old Major Daumesnil, a squadron leader in the Imperial Guard Chasseurs à Cheval and one of his favorite cavaliers. The major had lost a leg to an Austrian cannonball at Wagram, the twentieth wound of his career. During his amputation, he had joked with surgeon Larrey that he "would rather live with three limbs than die with four."[26] The emperor inquired if he regretted having served. Daumesnil replied, "If I have a wooden leg, I still have an iron arm!"[27] In spite of this stout response, Napoleon could not have a cripple leading his most cherished cavalry formation. When Berthier presented a list of candidates to replace him, Napoleon selected Major Lion, an officer who had come to his attention because of his gallantry during the Eckmuhl campaign.[28] Relegated to rear echelon command, Daumesnil had one last moment of glory. In 1814, during the final desperate defense of France, the allies summoned him to surrender the fortress of Vincennes. He replied, "You may tell [them] that when they give me back my leg, then I shall give up the keys of the fortress."[29]

The campaign to liberate the German-speaking peoples from the French yoke, begun so hopefully in the spring, had failed dismally. Erzherzog Karl was particularly despondent, and his brother, the kaiser, removed him from command. The clear-sighted Clemens Metternich, released from his internment in France, became Kaiser Franz's main adviser. In the Austrian camp, the weeks following the armistice were full of debate and dissension. Many in the kaiser's entourage looked to the events of 1805 for precedent. On that field Austria had shared in a crushing defeat. Metternich assailed the logic that equated Austerlitz with

Wagram. Militarily, because Austria retained an armed force of nearly one-quarter million men, the nation was in better shape than in 1805 when the army had been crippled and nearly destroyed. Politically the situation was far worse. Metternich explained that in contrast to 1805, "Now Prussia is destroyed, Russia is an ally of France, France the master of Germany. Austria also stands alone, without any support but in herself."[30]

Metternich added that the monarchy could not afford the type of concessions it had made in 1805. The Hapsburg Empire was in a precarious state; if it lost much more valuable territory it would become bankrupt. During the coming peace negotiations, Napoleon was sure to demand a reduction in the army. Metternich argued that this was tolerable—in fact, even necessary for financial reasons. In conclusion, he recommended that his kaiser be prepared for some territorial concessions. However, if Napoleon demanded too much—he warned that the French leader might even ask Franz to relinquish his title as kaiser—then Austria should fight to the death. Stiffened by Metternich's resolve, Franz instructed his diplomats to prolong the negotiations through the end of August in order to smoke out the French position. As they had shown before the war began, the Austrians proved better at diplomatic cut and thrust than at war management.

In the period following Wagram, Napoleon too was in a delicate position. He badly needed a peace treaty to conclude the war. He would later confide that had Austria resumed hostilities and defeated him in battle, he would have lost his empire.[31] Consequently, he showed surprising patience while French and Austrian negotiators haggled over peace terms. In the absence of a treaty, Napoleon continued to attend closely to his army. His order of the day on August 13 chastised the lack of discipline in Tharreau's division and noted that since Wagram, the unit had attended neither battalion school nor target practice. Henceforth, the emperor ordered, the men would perform the basics of the soldier's school and practice platoon drill each morning. They would fire 12 cartridges daily at the marks and for two hours in the evening perform battalion maneuvers. Publicly embarrassing Tharreau and his officers and assigning them remedial instruction was a clear reminder to all officers not to allow discipline to slip.

To keep his army in fighting trim, there were numerous inspections and reviews. The 3d Cuirassier division passed in review at the Schönbrunn. As was his custom when honoring gallant units, Napoleon stood before the 8th Cuirassiers and asked who was the unit's bravest trooper. The colonel replied that the entire regiment was brave. The emperor directed his question to the troopers, and they answered "Millot." When that worthy stepped forward, Napoleon, exhibiting his formidable memory that so delighted his grognards, inquired if they had not already met. "Yes," replied Millot, "at Heilsberg" (during the 1807 Polish campaign).[32] Napoleon awarded him with the cherished Cross and would later promote him into the Imperial Guard Grenadiers à Cheval. The emperor also looked toward the future and issued orders to Bertrand to destroy the walls of various Austrian fortresses. After all, the French might have to march this way again. Included in the list cited for destruction were the walls of Vienna, and so disappeared the ramparts that had defied the Turks back in 1684.

On August 15 the French occupiers staged a large festival in honor of Napoleon's birthday. A dragoon officer recalls how each trooper received a 2-franc bonus, a double food ration consisting of three loaves of white bread and variety of meats, and two bottles of Austrian wine.[33] The emperor, in his munificence, did not forget those who had lost an arm or leg during the campaign. He announced that he would provide a cash payment to recompense their services ranging from 500 francs for a private to 4,000 francs for a general. In addition, in keeping with his previous practice, he would "adopt" all children orphaned by the battle deaths of their fathers. These children received 500 or 2,000 francs, depending on their father's seniority. Any titles and associated tithes passed from the deceased to the oldest surviving male child.[34] To mark this day the French bent every effort to stimulate Austrian enthusiasm; music, contests, fireworks, all were met with a chilly response from the Viennese. Marie-Louise noted in her diary that the people did not even bother to look out their windows at the parades.

On this day Napoleon also announced the creation of a new order, the Three Golden Fleeces. Throughout history the expansion of a system of honors, awards, and medals frequently parallels martial decline, and so it was in Vienna in 1809. The new order was intended to honor the bravest officer in each regiment and by so doing partially duplicated the Légion d'honneur. It could not help but cheapen the Cross and increase army-wide cynicism toward medal awards. In the event, Napoleon never followed through with the order, but it was symptomatic of decline. Henceforth more men would receive more medals, but this would no longer make them fight harder. On September 17 Napoleon returned to the battlefield of Austerlitz, where elements of Davout's Corps restaged some of that engagement's memorable maneuvers. He continued to dispense medals broadcast style, awarding some simply on the recommendation of a unit's colonel without verifying that that recipient was truly worthy. Still, from time to time, he scrutinized the candidate more closely. When he asked about one trooper's qualifications, the colonel replied that the candidate had been wounded during the campaign. The emperor interjected, "Wounded? That is not enough! Did he wound any of the enemy? That is the point!"[35]

During the morning parade Napoleon made himself available to those who wished to present a petition. Most frequently the petitioner believed himself deserving of promotion, the cross, or entrance into the Imperial Guard. It was uncommon for a foreigner to request an audience, so when a young Austrian student pressed forward through the crowd on the morning of October 12 he attracted attention. Colonel Dupin, of the Guard Chasseurs, intercepted him to ask what was his business. He explained that he was a student at the University of Jena and that he must personally present a petition to the emperor. Dupin could not fob him off, and the commotion attracted General Rapp. The man explained that he wanted to speak with the emperor. Rapp replied in German to stand back; the matter would be taken care of in due course. Something in his fixed stare alarmed Rapp, who then noticed that the student kept one hand inside of his jacket. Rapp ordered an officer of the gendarmerie to seize him and discovered that concealed in his jacket was a large carving knife.

The review proceeded as if nothing had happened. Later Rapp interrogated the student but could learn nothing. The man said he would speak only to Napoleon. Intrigued, Napoleon visited the prisoner. His name was Friederich Stapps, he was a Saxon, he was 18 years old, and he told Napoleon that he had intended to kill him. Thoroughly puzzled by Stapps's combination of ineptitude and bloody-minded determination, Napoleon asked, "What harm have I done you?" Stapps replied, "You oppress my country."[36] This was too incredible for the emperor to comprehend. He insisted Stapps must be mad, or ill, or belong to some secret conspiracy, but he was not. Stapps was one of an increasing number who, inspired by the original tenets of the French Revolution, believed that violence was justified against the forces of tyranny. Revolutionary ideals, spread ironically by Napoleon and his Grande Armée, had given birth to a nationalist spirit that was one of Napoleon's most threatening opponents.

The entire incident shocked the emperor, and more so when Stapps displayed iron resolution by declining his offer that if he apologized, he could avoid death. Stapps assured his jailers that if freed he would seize every future opportunity to try to assassinate Napoleon. For three days Stapps refused all food, telling his jailers he would "be strong enough to walk to the scaffold." On the day of his scheduled execution, Napoleon remarked, "This affair is beyond my comprehension." Napoleon asked an aide to inquire how Stapps died. He learned that on the scaffold Stapps had loudly exclaimed, "Liberty for ever! Germany for ever! Death to the tyrant."[37]

The people inhabiting the Tyrol felt much the same as young Friederich Stapps, and like Stapps they put their lives on the line to achieve liberation from the French. In June and July, while Napoleon strained every nerve to concentrate his forces near Vienna, Andreas Hofer and his fellow Tyrolese guerrillas had enjoyed considerable success by mounting daring attacks against French and French-allied columns, camps, and bases. They briefly captured Constance, feinted against Bavaria and Bohemia, and under cover of these diversions launched simultaneous forays against numerous towns and cities. The summer months featured fierce combats pitting dedicated guerrillas against less than enthusiastic Bavarians and troops from the Confederation of the Rhine. A Württemberg soldier, Jakob Walter, describes the heavy fighting outside the city of Lindau. His battalion of the Franquemont Infantry Regiment, along with detachments of French and Baden soldiers, had chased a Tyrolese force up a mountain slope in an effort to recapture some men who had been taken prisoner. Suddenly the Tyrolese turned the tables, routed the pursuers, and chased them in turn. Walter continues the story:

Now the detachment retreated slowly until near the city, and then took up again the position for firing. Here we held out for half an hour, everyone firing as much as he could.

The cannon were hauled out, but the grapeshot fire did not help either, since the enemy formed a half-moon line and only a few could be hit, for they lay down on the ground behind the hedges, trees, and hills, while every shot of theirs could hit our compressed column.[38]

Driven back into Lindau by the fierce Tyrolese fighters, Walter relates that his comrades still found time during their retreat to kick and hit the hapless peasants, who, conscripted to drive ambulance wagons, were cowering in fear.

   In sum, this little combat contained many of the classic elements of a failed antiguerrilla policy: poor intelligence (the detachment blindly stumbled into an ambush), fighting on unfavorable terrain, inappropriate tactics (formed in unwieldy column to fight an opponent in loose skirmish order), and brutalization of the civilian population.

   The armistice at Znaim did not put an end to the war in the Tyrol. But cut off from any outside support, confronting an ever increasing number of French and French allied units, the guerrilla bands inevitably began to succumb. Napoleon's legions, released from the contest against Karl's field army, flooded the valleys of the Tyrol. They noted that the guerillas periodically had to descend from the heights to the villages below to obtain food. Consequently, instead of chasing them to their near-invulnerable aeries, they guarded the villages and waited.[39] Finally in January 1810, someone betrayed Hofer. Following a long chase through the mountains, French patrols captured him. They hauled him to Mantua, in northern Italy, to face trial for his life. Although the Hapsburg government tried to intercede on his behalf, Napoleon was implacable. He wanted to make an example of this man. After a rigged court-martial and the predictable death sentence, French soldiers dutifully executed the 43-year-old innkeeper by firing squad.

   On October 14, France and Austria signed a peace agreement at the Schönbrunn Palace. As might be expected, it was completely one-sided. Austria had to pay a huge monetary indemnity to the victors. The empire ceded the Inn region and Salzburg to Bavaria. Maritime Croatia and the ports of Fiume, Istria, and Trieste, along with Carinthia and Carniola, went to France. The king of Saxony received some territory in Bohemia and an equal share with the Austrians and Poles of some important West Galician saltworks. The Grand Duchy of Warsaw reincorporated Lublin and Cracow. As a sop to Napoleon's Russian "ally," the Tarnopol region went to Russia. Overall, the Hapsburg Empire lost 3.5 million inhabitants and its direct access to the Adriatic.

   Although this was a staggering loss, the crucial fact to Metternich and the kaiser was that the monarchy endured. Wagram had completely discredited the Hapsburg war party. Kaiser Franz concluded that Napoleon was invincible and accepted Metternich's conciliatory policy: "We must confine our system to tacking, and turning, and flattering. Thus alone may we possibly preserve our existence, till the day of general deliverance."[40] That day, predicted Metternich, would not arrive until Russia once again fought France. Franz was a deeply conservative man and had never felt comfortable with reforms and appeals to nationalism. Thus he happily administered a restoration of the monarchy's old-fashioned bureaucracy complete with its "clumsy, intricate formalities . . . masses of paper and empty stupidity and laziness" instead of "any form of free activity."[41]

Until 1813, nascent German nationalism would be superseded by Metternich's policy of coexistence with Napoleon. Yet its embers still glowed. On the day the papers announced the treaty, unsigned placards appeared throughout Vienna urging the people to act like Spanish and Prussian patriots and kill all Frenchmen and put their heads on pikes. The manifesto ended with the call for "vengeance against the French!"[42] Vengeance would be difficult because the crushing French-imposed indemnity combined with the war's cost to reduce Austria's economy by one-third and because treaty terms limited army size to 150,000 men. It would also have to take place without Karl's assistance. He formally retired from most military life, to be replaced eventually by Prince Karl Schwarzenberg, the officer who had led his uhlan regiment to rescue the Austrian guns on the field at Wagram.

Wagram had also put an end to British subsidy payments. The October peace accord between Austria and France completely severed Vienna's ties with London, a fact underscored by the murder of the British diplomat (probably by French agents) who had negotiated the short-lived Anglo-Austrian alliance. One other notable feature of the Peace of Schönbrunn was Napoleon's refusal to support Czar Alexander's claim to Galicia. Russian failure to live up to its pledges to intervene on the French side if Austria attacked France displeased Napoleon. He showed his displeasure by not backing the czar's Galician claim.

With the signing of the Peace of Schönbrunn, Imperial France had reached its greatest extent. One French mother wrote to her son who had served in Austria a remarkably prescient letter: "All the victories, all of the spilt blood mean nothing unless they earn a durable peace! . . . The peace with Germany means nothing at all for Spain. . . . The day you leave me for that country will be the saddest of all."[43]

PERFIDIOUS ALBION

Great Britain, the nation Napoleon sneeringly referred to as "perfidious Albion," had pledged some enterprise in northern Europe in order to distract French resources away from Austria. During the six weeks between Aspern-Essling and Wagram, the Austrian ambassador in London protested about the slow pace of British preparations. The lack of British energy contrasted notably with French activity along the Danube corridor. He relayed Foreign Minister Johann Stadion's point that since Napoleon had stripped his empire to concentrate force in Vienna, surely there was opportunity for a British blow. Austrian pleas met with sympathetic shrugs and little else. To the Austrian ambassador's consternation, the government was already showing a keener interest in the rumors (which turned out to be accurate) about war profiteering by Mrs. Mary Anne Clarke, the Duke of York's mistress, than in accelerating preparations for a cross-channel attack.[44]

British strategists had devised a plan to seize Walcheran, an island located at the mouth of the Scheldt River, and use it as a base of operations for an advance up the river to capture the great French naval base at Antwerp. When the 300-ship fleet, an armada that included 35 ships of the line and 23 frigates, began assembling in the Scheldt estuary during the last week of July 1809, the Austrians had already fought and lost at Wagram. But the Admiralty knew that during the four years since Trafalgar, continental shipyards had been constructing scores of superb warships, apparently with the intent of trying conclusions with the Royal Navy one more time. This building program represented a serious threat. Consequently by British lights, regardless of what took place around Vienna, the capture of Antwerp—the most important port north of Brest—would be quite a coup. So, at 4 P.M. on July 30, small boats began shuttling red-coated infantry to Walcheran's low-lying shore.

Confronting them was a thoroughly motley collection of soldiers belonging to two battalions of the Prussian Regiment (an essentially mercenary unit composed of ex-Prussian soldiers, drifters, and ne'er-do-wells), the "Flushing Chasseurs" (a unit of returned French deserters), the 1st Colonial Battalion (another penal unit, their vision of a sunny colonial billet squashed beneath Dutch clouds and rain), assorted artillerists, and 480 men of the 1st Irish Battalion. The Irish Battalion had originally formed in hopes of spearheading an overthrow of the British yoke via a French amphibious invasion of Ireland, but that vision had long receded. Since the fall of 1807 the unit had garrisoned Walcheran and seen its strength depleted by the malarial fevers that afflicted this region. So weakened had the Irish core of this once-proud unit become that half its manpower was composed of Poles. And now, instead of invading Ireland to overthrow the British, the hated redcoats had come to fight them.

The island was barely above sea level, dead flat, and poorly drained. It offered few defensive positions, yet the Irish and Colonial battalions fought a determined rearguard action to cover the preparation of the town of Flushing to withstand a siege. The British commander, John Pitt, the earl of Chatham, advanced cautiously with his 13,893-man army. The French took advantage to send slightly more than 3,000 reinforcements to Flushing. By August 7, British gunboats had isolated Flushing from outside help. Meanwhile, reinforced to nearly 20,000 men, Chatham began a siege. The French commander, General Lows-Claude Monnet, made the serious decision on August 6 to open the dikes (Napoleon had instructed him to inundate the island if necessary to save Flushing) but then only halfheartedly implemented his decision. The resultant flooding inconvenienced the British but did little more. A bungled French sortie on August 7 that subtracted 340 men from the defender's ranks failed to stop Lord Chatham's inexorable advance. When British ships worked close inshore on the morning of August 14, the end was near. An Irish officer describes the bombardment:

Seven ships of the line . . . approached to within half a cannon shot of the town and gave the signal for the general bombardment to the ten frigates, gunboats, and all the land batteries and incendiary rockets. . . . In a very short time, many of our pieces were dismounted; a number of the gun carriages were very old and shattered after one report. . . . In less than an hour, we lost half of our artillerymen. Finally, our batteries were reduced almost to silence by the extraordinary fire of the enemy.[45]

With his guns silenced and flames threatening to consume the entire town, General Monnet asked for terms, and on August 15 he surrendered. Because of their history of insurrectionary behavior, surrender was out of the question for some Irish officers. Among those who escaped was Major William Lawless. Although seriously wounded, for six weeks the major dodged British patrols until finally taking an open boat to Antwerp. Lawless carried with him the eagle that Napoleon had given the Irish Legion back in 1804. Delighted with his conduct, Napoleon summoned Lawless to Paris and rewarded him with entrance into the Légion d'honneur.

The capture of Flushing gave Chatham an opportunity for fame. If he hurried, few French forces stood between him and Antwerp. Instead he dawdled and by so doing allowed Minister of the Interior Joseph Fouché to appoint Bernadotte (conveniently on hand and unemployed following his disgrace at Wagram) to take command. Whatever he was and was not, Bernadotte could exhibit energy and martial ability when he chose. The marshal proceeded to seal off Walcheran with a patchwork of units, including numerous National Guards. Fever did the rest. The unfortunate redcoats camped amid Walcheran's waterlogged polders through the height of malaria season. By the time Chatham reembarked his army, he had lost 106 men killed in action and 4,000 dead through disease.

So the British descent on Walcheran ended as an unrelieved disaster. Prime Minister Spencer Perceval managed to survive by forcing Chatham to resign. The debacle did lead to a bitter feud between Canning, who resigned from the government, and Castlereagh that ended in a celebrated duel and Canning's wounding. Then the Walcheran Inquiry began to produce unsavory details of royal misconduct involving the Duke of York's mistress, although in the end the Inquiry accomplished little more beyond inflicting embarrassment. Naturally it was the soldiers who continued to suffer for their leaders' misconduct. For the next several years, British officers noticed that the men who had served at Walcheran lacked campaign endurance and experienced a fearful sickness rate, due to the debilitating exposure to the island's fevers.

The Walcheran expedition had taken place simultaneously with a climactic campaign in Spain that featured the best opportunity French forces would ever have to destroy the major British force in the Iberian Peninsula. Long after the event, military analysts and historians would severely criticize Napoleon for issuing orders from afar to his peninsular marshals—orders that were hopelessly out of date, confusing, and worse than useless. Indeed, such was his fixation on the Wagram campaign that when a weary staff officer arrived from Spain on July

1 bearing urgent dispatches from Marshal Soult, he gave his papers to Berthier and was then left cooling his heels for nearly three weeks before the emperor interviewed him.[46] Yet before Lieutenant General Arthur Wellesley had begun his summer offensive into Spain, Napoleon wrote Soult that "Wellesley will probably advance by the Tagus against Madrid; in that case, pass the mountains, fall on his flank and rear, and crush him."[47]

During the first weeks of July, Wellesley's campaign indeed seemed to be following the emperor's prediction. For the British commander, it had been a rude introduction to the realities of allied warfare. Before leaving Portugal, Wellesley thought he had arranged a campaign plan with his Spanish allies. The Spanish pledged cooperative armies, provisions, and local guides. It proved a parcel of lies. As his 20,997-man army marched into Spain, Wellesley rode ahead to confer with his erstwhile ally. He arrived on the evening of July 10—the day that the Army of Germany caught up with Karl near Znaim some 1,300 miles to the northeast— to meet General Gregorio García de la Cuesta and inspect his army. Cuesta was a most unimpressive figure: a fat, infirm, and old man of feeble intellect and little energy. He chose to march to war in a heavy carriage drawn by nine mules and had the distressing habit of falling asleep at virtually any time of the day. His redeeming feature was his hatred of the French. Wellesley rode among Cuesta's 35,000-man army and saw an infantry barely capable of performing rudimentary maneuvers and a cavalry more akin to a mob than a trained fighting force. An overly large artillery train of 70 guns further limited this army's mobility. During his service in India, Wellesley had encountered some wretchedly inefficient fighting forces, but this introduction to the Spanish army was truly dismaying. Still, his own army was too small to accomplish much on its own, and so he needed Cuesta's assistance.

In spite of all difficulties, July 23 found the British and Spanish forces with a great opportunity near the town of Talavera in the Tagus valley. Marshal Claude Victor stood before them with an unsupported force of 22,000 men. Outnumbering Victor two to one, Wellesley worked out a dawn attack to crush the French. Three hours of daylight passed, and the Spanish did not budge. Wellesley rode to Cuesta's headquarters, found that officer asleep, roused him, and learned that the Spanish general had decided his army was too tired to fight this day. Overnight Victor withdrew. Thoroughly disgusted, Wellesley declined to pursue. But Cuesta, having been stimulated by the sight of his enemy's heels, impetuously took out after the French. Then when Victor received reinforcements, Cuesta retreated back toward Talavera. On the morning of July 27, Wellesley felt compelled to forward some of his army to support him. By so doing he left himself hugely vulnerable to a French counterstroke.

Napoleon's eldest brother, Joseph, was a man of admirable talents, overwhelmed by his brother's genius. One year before he had reluctantly acceded to Napoleon's desire and ascended to the Spanish throne. Joseph had found that his just instincts had little chance of flourishing in that war-torn country. Unhappily elevated to war chief—he much preferred crafting a new liberal rule for the downtrodden Spanish people to attending to war matters—Joseph tried to interpret his brother's wishes and to harmonize his marshals' quarrels while squashing a ferocious guerrilla insurgency and operating against a British expeditionary force. When he learned of Wellesley's junction with Cuesta, he saw a threat against his capital at Madrid. In his muddle-headed panic, he overlooked his brother's sagacious advice to operate against the British rear and instead departed for the field near Talavera where he intended to bring his foe to battle.

The morning of July 27—22 days after the Battle of Wagram began—found a French army of 46,000 men confronting Cuesta's disordered Spanish supported by two British divisions. Wellesley had strongly urged his Spanish counterpart to retreat—tradition has it that the proud Spaniard would not consider a withdrawal until Sir Arthur begged him on bended knee—and at last Cuesta had concurred. The French pressed the retiring enemy hard. During a spirited action, veteran French light infantry almost bagged Wellesley himself and managed to inflict 440 casualties on the inexperienced British for the loss of about 100 men. By day's end they had driven the British and Spanish back to a position at Talavera.

This position blocked the Tagus valley, and there was no need to assault it. It would have been preferable to have waited until flanking operations threatened the British line of communications, the plan promoted by Napoleon. Wellesley would have had to conduct a retreat in the face of an aggressive pursuit, and experience had shown that while his army was steadfast in battle, it could all too easily disintegrate under the pressure of a forced retreat. Marshal Jean-Baptiste Jourdan, fulfilling his role as Joseph's military adviser, argued against an attack, but his appeal fell on deaf ears. The long-sought British army was here offering battle, offering the chance for the veterans of the Grande Armée to destroy it, for Marshal Victor and King Joseph to demonstrate surpassing martial ability. Joseph, enthusiastically seconded by Victor, resolved to attack.

Wellesley chose to defend a 2.5-mile-long front between the Tagus River and the mountains. He anchored his right on the town of Talavera. The ground from Talavera north for three-quarters of a mile was easily defensible, and accordingly Wellesley assigned Cuesta's Spanish this sector. Cuesta arrayed his men in two lines, with his left resting on the Pajar mound and his right in Talavera itself. His front extended through farming land criss-crossed by ditches, hedges, and mud walls. A convent, felled trees, and breastworks added to the sector's natural defenses. Wellesley placed a brigade of British light cavalry to backstop the Spanish and, confident that Cuesta's position was near impregnable, turned his attention elsewhere.

Two miles north of Talavera stood two hills, the Medellín on the west and the Cascajal on the east. They dominated the plain and were the tactical key to the battle. A north-south running mountain torrent, the Portina brook, passed through a severe ravine between them before continuing on to Talavera. The British commander chose to concede the Cascajal and defend behind this brook. He formed his men so they extended the Spanish line parallel to the brook, with its left flank dangling at the base of the Medellín. Wellesley intended to occupy the Medellín, but for the moment the designated unit was well forward in support of the Spanish. In turn, probably due to the confusion of trying to coordinate a battle with the Spanish, Wellesley overlooked the fact that another division, which was supposed to secure the British left flank, had yet to occupy its position and was instead in camp. Thus Wellesley, who outside of India had never commanded such a large force, made several errors that opened the way for a French victory.

About 10 P.M., while the allied army lay about its camps, an entire French division crossed the Portina and began to climb the Medellín. This advance caught the British by surprise. Wellesley's army composed many inexperienced soldiers, some of whom had been so recently drafted from the militia that they still wore militia accoutrements. They and their equally green officers performed poorly. In a confusing affair, the French first captured and then lost the crucial heights during a close-range, blundering combat. Wellesley realigned his troops as best he could in the dark and awaited the next blow.

At 5 A.M. on July 28 a French signal cannon fired to announce the battle's resumption. A furious cannonade came from the Cascajal, the type of bombardment that had had such lethal effect on the Marchfeld. The combination of the more rugged terrain and Wellesley's orders to his infantry to retire behind the hill crest and lie down negated much of the artillery's power. The French infantry columns advanced with their artillery batteries in the interval. They marched across closed terrain full of hayfields and olive orchards, across the ravine separating the two hills, and clambered up the Medellín. Suddenly, only 40 yards distant, a line of British soldiers rose up and fired, catching the French before they had deployed and punishing them terribly. Likewise, before the accompanying artillery unlimbered, it received "a terrible musket fire" that killed their leader, a Dutch artillery major, wounded a Baden battery commander, and killed enough horses so that the gunners had to abandon two guns.[48] The second French blow aimed at the crucial high ground had been repulsed.

With that, King Joseph was ready to call off the battle. He had just received alarming news that another Spanish army threatened his capital, and Marshal Jourdan counseled a retreat. But Marshal Victor's fighting blood was up. Although his men had twice failed against the Medellín, he promised success if he received support from adjacent formations. He concluded, "If such a combination fails it is time to renounce war."[49] Joseph was not a trained military man. With his two marshals disputing what to do, the decision was his to make. Lurking in the back of his mind was a concern over appearances. How would it look if his brother agreed with Victor's argument that here lay a great opportunity, and then he, Joseph Bonaparte, had failed to seize it? So he ordered another attack.

This time the French delivered hard blows all across the British-held portion of the line. After stern fighting, the initial attacks failed. However, in the valley on the British right flank, a British counterattack plunged out of control. So far in the battle, the French infantry had failed to deploy from column into line before entering combat range. As the British infantry surged forward, one French division did deploy and shot apart the British advance.[50] Here the British Guards lost one man in four in a matter of minutes. Then the French advanced to rout several British brigades and to overrun their cannon in the front line. It was the battle's crisis. Wellesley had been watching from the commanding heights and had anticipated the likely outcome. In contrast, the French commanders and King Joseph were too far away to comprehend tactical developments. Displaying a wonderful sense of tactical timing, Wellesley sent the largest battalion in his army, the 48th Regiment, in an inspired attack against the flank of the French breakthrough. The 48th cleared the front. Had it been a French unit, dispatches certainly would have trumpeted the fact that the regiment had covered itself with glory. Although the battle continued to rage over different sectors of the field, the outcome was no longer in doubt.

It was a glorious victory won by the British infantry, but won at a steep price. During the two-day combat, Wellesley's army lost more than 6,200 men, nearly 30 percent of its strength. Wellesley's postbattle report to Secretary of State Castlereagh glossed over all of the battle's difficult, harrowing moments. However, in his conclusion, Wellesley spoke the simple truth: "I have reason to be satisfied with the conduct of all the officers and troops."[51] Given Wellesley's retreat to Portugal following the Battle of Talavera, Britain could hardly celebrate a major triumph. Still, in comparison to Austria's collapse and the failure at Walcheran, Talavera symbolized a ray of hope. It was also a signpost pointing to the future. Austria's defeat left Britain alone. If it hoped to defeat Napoleon, it would have to pour treasure and manpower into the last remaining arena available, the Peninsula. If Wellesley could keep a field army intact, he could force the French to concentrate to check his army. The act of concentration prevented the French from sending mobile columns against the guerrillas. It weakened French control of the all-important countryside and provided opportunity for the guerrillas to gather their strength and expand their control over the hinterland. In essence, Wellesley's field army deflected attention away from the guerrillas. It was a successful strategy, one that George Washington had practiced in the American Revolution and Vo Nguyen Giap would practice in Vietnam more than 150 years later.

Before the Talavera campaign, Marshal Nicholas Soult had told King Joseph: "Under present circumstances we cannot avoid some sacrifice of territory. Let us concentrate on a few points. . . . the moment we have beaten and dispersed the enemy's masses we shall recover all our ground."[52]

It did not work that way. When evaluating Talavera, Napoleon wrote to Joseph that a battle should be risked only as a last resort, since battles, by their very nature, were chancy things. He recommended engaging only if the odds in favor of success were at least 70 percent. Spanish guerrillas frequently intercepted Napoleon's dispatches and handed them to Wellesley. Whether or not he read this missive, to the enormous frustration of the French generals in the Peninsula, Wellesley evaded battle for the next 14 months.

Napoleon was furious when he learned of the Battle of Talavera. By his lights a tremendous opportunity had been lost when Wellesley risked his small army in the midst of "10,000 of the best troops in the world."[53] From the Schönbrunn Palace he sent a scathing critique to Marshal Jourdan, rightly complaining that the French had failed to concentrate before the battle, failed to reconnoiter before attacking, failed to take advantage of Wellesley's open left flank, and failed to commit available forces to the fight. He concluded that the fate of Spain was endangered through ignorance of the rules of war. It seemed that after the emperor completed his accords with the Austrians, he would have to go to Spain to crush the land forces of perfidious Albion once and for all.

Chapter 10

AN END TO GLORY

My power is dependent on my glory, and my glory on my victories. My power would fall if I did not base it on still more glory and still more victories. Conquest made me what I am; conquest alone can keep me there.[1]

DYNASTIC IMPERATIVE

Napoleon returned to France on October 24, 1809. He found a people pleased with victory but increasingly war-weary. Madame Junot observed that "the campaign had been so murderous, the victory so obstinately disputed, that France began to consider her laurels too dearly purchased."[2] In all theaters of operation in 1809, the French army lost 45,000 killed, 70,000 wounded, and 20,000 prisoners. French-allied forces suffered 45,000 casualties.[3] The great majority of these losses came in the war against Austria. These grim figures far surpassed any previous totals under Napoleon's reign and were to be exceeded only twice between the years 1792 and 1815: during the disastrous Russian campaign of 1812 and during the bloodiest year of them all, 1813. While the losses of 1809 touched more French households than ever before, people also pondered one fairly modest wound. They wondered what might have transpired had the ball that hit the emperor in his heel at Ratisbonne struck two feet higher. They understood that in the absence of an heir, Napoleon's death could return France to the turmoil of the Revolution.

Napoleon himself was keenly aware how everything he had worked for depended on his own existence. Whereas his rivals could lose battles, and indeed could lose wars, the tradition of monarchical rule would retain the leaders as head of the state. With him, this was not the case. To protect France against turmoil should he fall in battle, to cement his accomplishments for future generations, he needed an heir. And by 1809 it was clear that his beloved wife was not able to produce one. Napoleon questioned whether this inability was his own fault. Then he learned that his devoted mistress, Marie Walewska, was pregnant.

Napoleon often said that he could not afford to be sentimental. Unless one had a firm heart, he "had no business mixing in war and government."[4] He boasted that if his wife suddenly died, it would not interfere for fifteen minutes with the execution of his plans. So he cast about to replace Josephine, and his eye turned toward St. Petersburg. Russia was the sole remaining great continental power. A closer attachment with that country, cemented by the bonds of family and marriage, would be a strategic stroke of immense value. But the czar prevaricated, and this angered Napoleon. In a huff he turned to his second choice, Austria.

It was a turnabout covertly encouraged by the newly appointed Austrian Foreign Minister, the brilliant Clement Lothar Wenceslas Metternich. Metternich was one of the handful of men capable of matching strategic wits with Napoleon. For the near future, Metternich appreciated that Austria must rest and rebuild. If the nation had to accommodate itself to the victor, what better way than to offer an Austrian archduchess as bride? If callous toward the feelings of 18-year-old Marie-Louise, it was in keeping with the traditional saying, "Others wage war. You, happy Austria, marry." If it overlooked the fate of the last Austrian who wed a French ruler, Marie Antoinette, then so be it. As Metternich remarked, "Our princesses are little accustomed to choose their husbands according to the dictates of their hearts." He concluded that Marie-Louise was a "good and well-brought-up" child and would obey her father's wishes.[5] Metternich found an ally for his scheme in a surprising place. The Empress Josephine, in a last act of devotion, summoned Metternich's wife to inform her that she was pressing on her husband the idea that he should marry Marie-Louise. She accepted her divorce with stunning dignity.

So it was in March 1810 that the newly titled Prince of Wagram, Marshal Berthier, came to Vienna to escort Marie-Louise to France. First there would be a proxy wedding in which Erzherzog Karl represented the French emperor. Surrounded by the Hungarian noble guard, Austrian grenadiers, Bohemian dragoons, and the Hofburg halberdiers, Berthier conveyed Napoleon's request for Marie-Louise to become his wife. A sad and very pale Kaiser Franz answered, "I grant my daughter's hand to the French emperor." Forward stepped a French hussar to deliver the first of what would become a supremely extravagant series of gifts for the new wife. A jewel-encrusted box held Napoleon's miniature in a frame set with twelve colossal diamonds. Marie-Louise gazed at the image of her husband-to-be with keen interest. As she later confided to a friend, at least Napoleon physically did not appear to be a monster.

At the royal banquet to celebrate the marriage, no Viennese dignitary except Karl would talk to Berthier. The patriots in Vienna could not help but notice that in the imperial ballroom where one year earlier they had sung bloody-minded songs about their landwehr and gave poetic tribute to Spanish guerrillas, they now toasted the marriage of their sovereign's daughter with the Corsican ogre. A ditty appearing in one Viennese shop window well represented the feelings of many:

> Louise's skirts and Napoleon's pants
> Now unite Austria and France.

With an escort of French hussars—Napoleon had given Montbrun and his 7th Hussars this honor—Marie-Louise traveled to France to meet her husband. Because the marriage united the parvenu Bonaparte clan with the oldest reigning monarchy in Europe, Napoleon was keenly sensitive toward legitimizing it. Consequently, everything about the journey was heavy with ceremony. At the Bavarian border near Passau, French engineer-architects had built a pretentious, neoclassical structure divided into three chambers. Here Austrian plenipotentiaries were to hand Marie-Louise over to Napoleon's representatives. Orders went out to a regiment of hapless French soldiers who had been garrisoning the Tyrol: arrive at Passau before the wedding cortege. The regiment conducted a killing march through melting snow, mud, and floodwater, overcoming all obstacles in what one grognard recalls was the hardest march of his career. Men perished and horses drowned, but they arrived at the specified time. The military being the military, they then waited two weeks for Marie-Louise's arrival. A soldier recalls:

When Her Majesty appeared, the artillery made a terrific noise, the music of the regiments played out of tune; the drums rumbled dully, for it was pouring, we had mud to our knees, and the Paris journals went into ecstasies on the good fortune we had had of being the first to salute our august and gracious sovereign. . . . The next day the Empress left for Paris; we again took by short stages the road to our mountains, trying to persuade ourselves that we had had a very good time.[6]

This soldier did not see the high drama staged inside. To symbolize the transition, the eastern chamber was in Austrian territory, the western chamber in French, and the middle chamber was neutral ground. The eastern chamber witnessed a sad scene as tearful Austrians filed past their archduchess to bid farewell. The neutral chamber featured an undignified French rush as men and women alike elbowed and pushed to find a place to glimpse their new empress before she entered the room. One French dignitary had drilled three peepholes in the door to the Austrian chamber in order to catch a first glimpse of Marie-Louise. After she was officially handed over to the "court" of France, Napoleon's sister Caroline bundled the young woman off to have her stripped of her tainted Austrian clothing, bathed, perfumed, her hair redressed by a French coiffeur, and outfitted in the latest Parisian fashion. Then the journey continued in carefully staged increments.

Although the bridegroom himself had specified exactly how all of this should take place, the slow pace of her approach drove him to distraction. He could not concentrate. He became snappish and ill-tempered. Although the union with Austria satisfied his political aspirations, his manhood caused him to wonder what lay ahead. His adult love life had been full of the age's most splendid women. Rumor had it that his virgin bride was no beauty. He asked an aide who had met her, did she have "enough of this and that?" When a dispatch rider came to announce that the procession had entered France, the emperor closely questioned him regarding her looks. The miserably embarrassed young man stuttered and stammered. Napoleon turned to his brother-in-law and said, "Obviously my wife is hideous as not one of these young rips has dared say the contrary." He consoled himself with the hope that she would bear him fine sons and resolved to try to love her as if she were beautiful. He concluded, "After all, it is a womb that I am marrying."[7]

Marie-Louise drew near, and the emperor could stand it no longer. Instead of waiting for the stage-managed introduction, he would ride to meet her en route. His valet brought him a gold-braided suit designed for the formal occasion. His good humor restored, Napoleon laughed. He would wear his green chasseur uniform and the grey frock coat he had worn at Wagram. Riding through a pelting rain, Napoleon encountered outriders near the little village of Courcelles at dusk. He hoped to surprise his bride, but a shocked escort officer recognized him and announced, "The Emperor!"

"Imbécile!" hissed Napoleon as he climbed into the coach carrying Marie-Louise.

On Saint Helena Napoleon would say that his first glimpse of his bride agreeably surprised him. Prepared for the worst, he saw a young woman's face (mercifully the fading light hid her smallpox scars), an ample bosom, and best of all tiny feet (he loathed women with large hands and feet).

A brief introduction, "Madame, I am delighted to see you," a shower of caresses and kisses, and all plans for a stately formal procession fled with the wind. Napoleon wanted to take this woman to bed as quickly as possible. And he did. The following morning Napoleon was in high spirits. He advised an aide, "Marry a German girl. They make the best wives in the world; sweet, good, naive and fresh as roses."[8]

From Napoleon's perspective, the year 1810 brought fine promise. Wedlock had merged the interests of his most obstinate continental foe with his own. Prussia was a nonentity, having "neither sovereign, nor people, nor minister, nor money." During the critical weeks following Napoleon's first defeat at Aspern-Essling, the fate of the empire had hinged on Czar Alexander. It was a tense strategic position Napoleon did not want to recur. Russia was obstinate and troublesome and would have to be dealt with. England too, of course, required attention. Napoleon found particular delight in the elevation of French marshal Bernadotte to Crown Prince of Sweden. It was "one of the best possible tricks that could be played on England."[9] The emperor considered Bernadotte a very smart man and a good soldier, but he was glad to be rid of him to distant Sweden.

The marriage between the emperor and Marie-Louise had begun on the crudest basis: a conqueror demanding the daughter of the defeated warlord and then taking her to bed at first meeting. Yet, in the coming months, Napoleon experienced genuine happiness with his young wife, and it was a feeling she seemed to share. People remarked on how the marriage changed the husband.[10] Napoleonic dining had always been a shockingly brief affair, with the guests often unable even to taste their food before the great man had finished and risen from the table. Marie-Louise liked to eat; henceforth meals stretched out for hours, and Napoleon did not seem to mind. He tended less often to the burden of administrative detail, delegating important decisions to subordinates for the first time. Instead he lavished gifts and attention on his new bride. In 1810 he changed the uniform of his elite carabiniers à cheval by replacing their fur hat with a helmet and giving them a bronze-colored cuirass. The new uniform resembled that worn by the Austrians, and it was said the emperor designed it as a gallantry to Marie-Louise.

When he had first learned of the French defeat at the Battle of Talavera, Napoleon had commented, "My God! What is an army without a leader?"[11] He had intended to return to Spain to provide that leadership and to finish the war. In the event he could not quite bring himself to leave his new family. Instead, from a distance he marveled at Wellington's campaign skills. When he retreated before Marshal Massena's offensive in 1810, the emperor commented: "There's a man for you." He marveled at Wellington's understanding the need to retreat before a stronger army he dare not fight, all the while employing stratagems to weaken the pursuer. Napoleon concluded that in "all of Europe, only Wellington and I are capable of carrying out such measures."[12]

Napoleon had tried to campaign against Austria while leaving numerous experienced leaders and about 290,000 men, including many veteran formations, in Spain. After Wagram, many units from the Army of Germany went to Spain, and it proved a graveyard. About 50,000 and 20,000 allies were lost in Spain and Portugal, respectively, during each of the years 1810 and 1811. Steady attrition also sapped at the dwindling pool of leadership talent. On October 26, 1809, General Alexander Senarmont, Napoleon's ablest artillery commander, died while siting siege guns at Cadiz. Sainte-Croix, the officer whose remarkable ability to anticipate the emperor's intentions prompted Napoleon to predict that he would go far and whom he had promoted to brigadier general on July 19, died while campaigning with Massena in 1810.

Yet Napoleon steadfastly refused to conduct meaningful peace negotiations with England. He believed that Lord Richard Wellesley had a dominant influence in British councils and that as long as his brother Arthur continued to enjoy success in the peninsula, there was no point negotiating. On Saint Helena Napoleon at last understood what he had lost in Spain: "The roots of my disasters were attached to this fatal knob; it destroyed my moral standing in Europe, complicated my every position, opened a school for the English soldier."[13] In 1810 he did not understand this. So taken was he by the ardent embrace of a young woman that he willingly left his Spanish problem to his marshals. Not until the great Russian campaign of 1812 would Napoleon depart from his wife. During the ensuing disaster, one of the grumblers of the Imperial Guard remarked, "He hadn't ought to have left the old one [Josephine]. . . . She brought him luck, and us too!"[14]

The much-anticipated event began on the evening of March 19, 1811. The empress underwent a prolonged labor that proved exceedingly stressful to Napoleon. During the long night, groans escaped the bedroom and could be heard both by guests in the billiard room and by a nervously pacing Napoleon in the antechamber. When the labor pains eased, the attending physician announced there was no urgency and he was going to bed.

Shortly after 5 A.M., while the emperor refreshed himself with a scalding bath, in burst the assistant physician, pale, sweating, and barely coherent. "What is it?" shouted Napoleon. "Is she dead?"

"No," replied the assistant. He proceeded to explain that it was a breech presentation and he would have to operate. It might become a question of saving either the mother or the child. To Napoleon's great credit, he decisively ordered the physician to save the mother. As they gathered in the bedroom, and after reassuring a near hysterical Marie-Louise that she was not to be sacrificed for the child's sake, the assistant physician became totally unhinged. He refused to operate until the senior physician returned. Napoleon lost his temper: "What can he tell you that you don't know already. . . . I've had enough of this, Dubois. I order you to deliver the empress."[15] Fortunately, the senior man appeared, and in a 26-minute operation—so excruciating to observe that it sent a shaken Napoleon fleeing from the room—a boy emerged. The birth of an heir was the triumphant culmination of months of diplomacy. Yet when the physician approached the emperor with his report, again Napoleon's first concern was for his wife. She had survived.

The news of his son's birth—he was introduced to the world as the King of Rome—went by Chappe's telegraph to all parts of the empire. The French people greeted it with genuine enthusiasm. Parisians from humble Seine waterman to bourgeois banker and lawyer celebrated into the night while a city-wide illumination gaily lit the quarters of the poor and wealthy alike. A doting Napoleon believed that he would play the role of Philip of Macedon to his son, who would become another Alexander the Great. Instead, at age 3, following the 1814 defeat of the gallant "Marie Louises"—the nickname for the teen-aged conscripts brought into French service after the failure in Russia—the boy would retrace his mother's 1810 journey in reverse, leave France forever, be raised in the Hapsburg court where he was known as the Duke of Reichstadt, and die in relative obscurity at age 21.

Napoleon liked a woman who was blond and curvaceous, and Marie-Louise filled the bill, but Josephine remained special and it was something he retained to the last. On his deathbed, as his mind wandered, he suddenly told his entourage with extraordinary emotion that he had seen her and that "she told me we were going to see each other again and never again leave each other. She has promised me—Did you see her?"[16]

ASSESSMENT

The Austrian campaign of 1809 marks a turning point in the history of warfare. It was the world's last campaign in which cavalry shock action had decisive tactical importance. At the Battle of Eckmuhl in April and again at Aspern-Essling in May, French cavalry leaders conducted brigade- and division-size charges that overthrew formed infantry and overran well-served artillery. Their charges routinely stopped cold the advancing Austrian columns and carved breaches in defending lines. Because they maneuvered at speed, Napoleon called upon them to plug holes, redress setback, create opportunity, and exploit tactical success. Frequently all of this was done at high cost. By Wagram it could barely be done at all because of the cumulative losses and, more important, the tremendous concentration of artillery. There would be only one more field on which cavalry had close to the same tactical impact: Borodino, the fearfully bloody battle of attrition that decided the Russian campaign in 1812. At Borodino, as at Wagram, French and French-allied heavy cavalry braved near overwhelming artillery fire to breach the Russian line. The slaughter on that field, the ruinous loss of horses during the winter retreat, and the large number of guns and howitzers employed by all contestants during the subsequent campaigns involving continental armies thereafter relegated cavalry to a secondary importance.

From the late days of the Roman Empire until the Battle of Agincourt, cavalry shock action had dominated field battles. Agincourt began an era when infantry, with bow, pike, and then musket, was of at least coequal importance. Wagram marks the end of cavalry domination and the rise of the artillery arm. Europe's generals were slow to appreciate this change. In the next great encounter between French imperialism and German nationalism, the 1870 war, both sides organized, equipped, and dressed thousands of troopers in the Napoleonic style. Their saber and lance charges could not contend with the era's more efficient shoulder arms and artillery's improved technology. Still Europe's generals did not learn. Again in 1914 thousands more troopers went to war armed and trained in almost the same manner as Espagne's cuirassiers and Marulaz's chasseurs. Confronted with machine guns, modern explosive shells, and barbed wire, they quickly demonstrated their uselessness.

Just as Wagram is the end of the cavalry shock era, so it marks artillery's ascension toward battlefield domination. Napoleon, who began his career as an artillerist, appreciated better than any of his contemporaries artillery's potency. In 1796, while conducting his first campaign, Bonaparte had organized a massed battery (led by Marmont) to win the decisive Battle of Castiglione. During one

of his ruminations to Eugène in 1809, he told his stepson to support an attack
with a massed battery of 30 to 36 guns since "nothing can resist it."[17] He added
that the same guns evenly distributed along a line would fail to give the same
result. The emperor's reliance on massed artillery reached its apogee on July 6
when his Imperial Guard artillerists formed the core of the 112-gun Grand Battery. Reflecting on the nature of combat and undoubtedly recalling those perilous
two days in May 1809, Napoleon in later life said, "A good infantry is without
doubt the soul of the army; but, it cannot long maintain a fight against a superior
artillery, it will become demoralized and then destroyed." He added, "The fate
of a battle, of a state, often follows the [route] taken by the artillery."[18]

Napoleon's continental adversaries had begun to comprehend artillery's value.
Although they seldom managed the knack of massing guns at a decisive sector,
they made up for this by the sheer number of weapons they brought to the
battlefield. Karl had 452 guns at Wagram. The Russian Field Marshal Mikhail
Kutusov fought the Battle of Borodino with 640 guns. On the third day of Leipzig
in 1813, the allies concentrated an incredible 1,500 artillery pieces on the field.
Clearly Napoleon's enemies had concluded that the tactical counter to French
battlefield maneuverability was a crushing weight of artillery fire. Allied leaders
extended their infantry masses across a wide front and buttressed the line with
scores of cannon. The sheer extent of the front meant that if Napoleon tried an
outflanking maneuver, it would be too difficult to coordinate and take too long
to complete. Alternatively, if Napoleon chose to attempt a blow against the
center, the artillery guaranteed that it could not be done without such high losses
that there could be no significant exploitation.[19] Wagram revealed that a battle
won by a frontal breakthrough would be so costly that there could be no pursuit.
Subsequent campaigns would verify this lesson. In time Napoleon's adversaries
appreciated this. After Napoleon defeated the Prussians at Ligny in 1815, a Prussian officer who was familiar with the emperor's war machine informed Wellington that the French would not pursue early the next morning because they
required time to rest and refit.

After Wagram, artillery's tactical domination of the battlefield negated battles
of maneuver. In their stead came grinding battles of frontal attrition. Napoleon
would "win" many of these, but they were devoid of strategic significance. From
Napoleon's foes' perspective, reliance on infantry masses buttressed by a colossal
artillery might not earn victory, but it ensured that a defeat would be of minimal
significance.

The musket's inefficiencies dictated the era's shoulder-to-shoulder infantry tactics. As we have seen, closed ranks made an unmistakable artillery target. During
the Battle of Wagram, more Frenchmen were struck by enemy fire on a single
day than on any other field during the Napoleonic Wars. It would take the Battle
of the Somme 107 years later to surpass their loss rate.[20] Yet within the era's
tactical permutations there were formation choices that would limit vulnerability
to artillery fire: lines instead of columns, open instead of closed order. The uneven
quality of the troops in the Army of Germany precluded much tactical finesse.

Writing about Aspern-Essling, Savary observed that if "instead of having had the troops composed of very young soldiers, we had had troops trained like those from the camp of Boulogne, we could have boldly formed and deployed under fire without fear of disorder."[21] Marmont made the same point, noting that the several panics of July 6 would never have occurred among the men of Austerlitz and Jena.[22]

Included in the French losses during the 1809 campaign against Austria were many irreplaceable Grande Armée veterans. Three regiments in Saint-Hilaire's division—the 3rd, 72d, and 105th Ligne—whose exploits began on the ridgetop of Teugen-Hausen and continued through Aspern-Essling and Wagram demonstrate this point.[23] In spite of incorporating substantial numbers of conscripts into their ranks during the campaign, they still suffered so severely that following the Armistice at Znaim, they had to consolidate their survivors, with three battalions' becoming two and a cadre returning to the regimental depots in France. The 57th Ligne and 10th Légère fared even worse. Never again would these once-superb units display exceptional battlefield performance. The value of the Grande Armée veterans can hardly be overstated. The Russian campaign would slaughter thousands more, yet their influence could still be detected during the 1813 campaign when officers often attributed a unit's particularly valorous performance to the presence of a remaining handful.

But the brilliant maneuver battles that typified Bonaparte's Italian campaign of 1796–1797, the bold strokes characteristic of the glory campaigns of 1805–1806 were not to be seen again. In large part this was because "the days of Essling and Wagram had massacred the flower of the French army."[24]

July 6, 1810, witnessed a moving scene at the Panthéon in Paris when Marshal Jean Lannes was laid to rest. Marshal Davout, who delivered the funeral eulogy, spoke of the man's qualities that had earned him the sobriquet "bravest of the brave." In his conclusion, Davout revealed how far he had descended toward becoming the ultimate toady. He said that the best way for Lannes's friends and for the army as a whole to honor the deceased's memory was by being like the dead marshal, always "ready to spill . . . the last drop of our blood in the service and the glory of our great and good friend the Emperor!"[25]

Lannes was one of several excellent officers who had shown the potential to rise to the challenge of independent action and had fallen during the 1809 campaign. Such men were exceedingly hard to replace. Writing from the perspective of an officer who had served in many capacities, Marmont noted that "It is infinitely easier to command 40,000 men in a subordinate capacity than to lead 10,000 alone."[26] None of the three new marshals would ever gain battlefield success while at the head of an army. Their unblemished record of defeat suggests that they should not have been promoted. Too late Napoleon would recognize the mistake. He reflected, "I should not have made either Marmont or Oudinot marshals. We needed to win a war."[27]

The campaign had also witnessed exceptional carnage among the emperor's

cavalry leaders. Lasalle's death in particular "left a great gap in our light cavalry.
... A man did not think himself a chasseur, still less a hussar, if he did not model
himself on Lasalle, and become, like him, a reckless, drinking, swearing rowdy.
Many officers copied the faults of this famous outpost leader, but none of them
attained to the merits which in him atoned for the faults."[28] This became quickly
evident during the pursuit after Wagram, when Lasalle's replacement proved too
impetuous and led his light cavalry into an untenable position where they were
unnecessarily cut up.

Napoleon never came to grips with his defeat at Aspern-Essling. He would jest
to his toadies that "the Austrians had this day met with an ally they had not
reckoned upon, and that General Danube had proved himself the best officer of
their army."[29] But keen listeners noted that Napoleon would follow this comment
with an insincere laugh, as if somewhere deep within he too recognized its false-
ness. Likewise, he glossed over the failure on the evening of July 5. More than
anything else, the July 5 setback had been caused by overconfidence. The artillerist Seruzier observed, "In brief, we had not adequately reconnoitered the point
of attack."[30] But the stern Austrian effort during those two July days did make
an impression on Napoleon. At least once during the 1813 campaign, the emperor's candid attitude emerged. A young officer was denigrating Austrian ability.
The emperor brought him up short with the comment, "You, sir, were not at
Wagram."

French writers, then and thereafter, dismissed the setbacks at Wagram by blaming the Saxons. Typical was the account in Oudinot's *Memoirs*. Referring to the
failure around Baumersdorf on July 5, the author wrote, "But at the same moment
a portion of Macdonald's troops fired by mistake upon our allies the Saxons, and
the latter, seized with panic, gave way on all sides. This incident compelled us
to abandon the attack."[31] As we have seen it was no such thing. Piecemeal
assaults and tactical errors account for the failure. It was even easier to point a
finger at the Saxons for the rout the next day, but, as we have seen, even more
Frenchmen ran. The battle's artillery inferno was more than many could bear.

During the 1809 campaign the Austrian army demonstrated vast improvement
over its prior performances. The Hapsburg officer corps risked itself to a heretofore unprecedented extent. Officers and men alike well deserved their great
victory at Aspern-Essling. Even in defeat at Wagram the army conducted a poised
retreat and managed to maintain an intact field army. The French captured few
unwounded prisoners at Wagram. As Marmont observed, "The time where clouds
of prisoners fell into our hands ... had passed."[32]

Some of the tactical changes Erzherzog Karl introduced before the war paid
dividends. The practice of arranging units with half the men in a first line and
the remainder in a second line repeatedly dislocated French attacks. Time and
again assaults overcame the Austrian first line only to fall afoul of a still intact
second line. The battalion mass proved a useful formation. The Austrian light
infantry, while never equaling that of the French, performed better than ever
before. Problems remained. Coordinated, multiregiment cavalry charges contin-

ued to be beyond Hapsburg capabilities. This inability greatly reduced the combat effectiveness of the Austrian cavalry. The creation of advance guard divisions composed of all three arms was an inefficient allocation of resources. Few commanders of any nationality had the ability to lead both infantry and cavalry effectively. One of Napoleon's maxims stated that the "habit of mixing small bodies of infantry and cavalry together is a bad one."[33] The combat fate of the advance guard divisions proved the emperor's point. These formations lacked enough cavalry to resist an enemy cavalry division and enough foot soldiers to stand up to an opposing infantry division.

Britain contested French expansion from the Revolution through to Waterloo. The Royal Navy carried the burden of this battle. Napoleon never thoroughly comprehended naval warfare in the age of sail. He was a soldier, not a sailor, and thus his armies carried his destiny. The defeat of Napoleon required massive land forces, and it fell to Austria to provide more than its share. The Hapsburg monarchy proved Napoleon's most implacable foe. The two battles fought outside Vienna in 1809 represent the zenith of Austrian participation in the Napoleonic Wars. Austria would make important contributions to the great alliance that ultimately defeated the French emperor in 1813–1814. But, as a French veteran observed, "Never again did the Austrians fight with so much vigor as at Wagram."[34]

The valor display by Austrian volunteers and landwehr, Stapps's icy resolve, the cold reception the people of Vienna displayed to the conqueror in contrast to their 1805 conduct, the Tyrolese insurrection, Schill's Saxony adventure, and above all the vastly improved Austrian battlefield conduct all pointed to the emergence of a new force in Europe: Germanic nationalism. Napoleon saw it with a blind eye. When a candid imperial aide observed that "the people were everywhere tired of us and of our victories," Napoleon snarled and refused to listen.[35] Yet during a more reflective moment in 1808, the emperor had observed that there were two powers in the world, the sword and the spirit, by which he understood civil and religious institutions. He had concluded, "In the long run the sword is always beaten by the spirit."[36] Part of Napoleon's confusion stemmed from the fact that he still retained some Revolutionary ideals. He believed that the German people, as opposed to their rulers, had a surpassing desire to live in a meritocracy where the peasant had the same rights and opportunities as the nobleman. He did not understand that nationalism was a force stronger than the desire for personal freedom.

His was a failure that is shared today as resurgent nationalism promises conflict throughout the world.

APPENDIXES

Appendix I
Order of Battle Aspern-Essling, May 21–22, 1809[+]

Generalissimus: FM Erzherzog Karl
Generaladjutanten: Phillipp Grunne

Avantgarde (5,907 and 6 guns)		btn/sq
Division FML Klenau		
Brigade Hardegg	1st Jager Battalion	(1)
	Erzherzog Karl IR#3	(3)
	Stipsicz Hussars	(8)
	Schwarzenberg Uhlans	(8)
	6lb cavalry baty	(6 guns)

I ArmeeKorps GdK Heinrich Graf Bellegarde(24,594 and 50 guns)		
Division FML Dedovich		
Brigade Henneberg	Reuss-Plauen IR#17	(3)
	Kollowrath IR#36	(3)
	6lb brigade baty	(8 guns)
Brigade GM Wacquant	Erzherzog Rainer IR#11	(3)
	Vogelsang IR#47	(3)
	6lb brigade baty	(8 guns)
Division FML Fresnel		
Brigade GM Clary	Anton Mittrowsky IR#10	(2)
	Erbach IR#42	(2)
	6lb brigade baty	(8 guns)
Brigade GM Lutzel	Argenteau IR#35	(3)
	4th E. Karl Legion	(1)
	6lb brigade baty	(8 guns)
Brigade GM Stutterheim	2d Jager Battalion	(1)
	3d Jager Battalion	(1)
	Blankenstein Hussars	(10)
	6lb cavalry baty	(6 guns)
Reserve Artillery: one 12lb position baty		(6 guns)
one 6lb position baty		(6 guns)

II ArmeeKorps FML Franz Furst zu Hohenzollern-Hechingen (21,590 and 50 guns)		
Division FML Brady		
Brigade GM Buresch	Zach IR#15	(2)
	Joseph Colloredo IR#57	(3)
	6lb brigade baty	(8 guns)
Brigade GM Paar	Zedtwitz IR#25	(3)
	Froon IR#54	(3)
	6lb brigade baty	(8 guns)
Division FM Ulm		
Brigade GM Alstern	Stuart IR#18	(3)
	Rohan IR#21	(3)
	Frelich IR#28	(3)
	6lb brigade baty	(8 guns)
Brigade GM Wied-Runkel	Stain IR#50	(2)
	Wurzburg IR#23	(1)
	Wurttemberg IR#38	(1)
	6lb brigade baty	(8 guns)

```
Brigade FML Segenthal       2d Bat. E. Karl Legion      (1)
                            7th Jager Battalion         (1)
                            8th Jager Battalion         (1)
                            Klenau Chevaulegers         (8)
                            6lb cavalry baty         (6 guns)
     Reserve Artillery:  one 12lb position baty      (6 guns)
                         one 6lb position baty       (6 guns)
```

```
IV ArmeeKorps  FML Franz Furst v. Rosenberg(21,702 and 50 guns)
     Division FML Bartenstein
     Brigade GM Hessen-Homburg  Hiller IR#2            (3)
                                Sztarrai IR#33         (3)
                                6lb brigade baty    (8 guns)
     Brigade GM Neustadter      Czartoryski IR#9       (3)
                                Reuss-Greitz IR#55     (2)
                                6lb brigade baty    (8 guns)
     Division FML Rohan
     Brigade GM Riese            Bellegarde IR#44      (3)
                        Chasteler IR#64        (3)
                                6lb brigade baty    (8 guns)
     Brigade GM Swinburne       Erzherzog Ludwig  IR#8  (3)
                                Koburg IR#22           (3)
                                6lb brigade baty    (8 guns)
     Brigade GM Gratze          Wal. Illyrian Grenz    (2)
                                2d Mahrisch Freiwilliger  (1)
                                Carneville Freicorps Ft  (1/3)
                                Carneville Freicorps Cav  (1)
                                Vincent Chevaulegers   (6)
                                E. Ferdinand Hussars   (8)
                                6lb cavalry baty    (6 guns)
     Reserve Artillery:  one 12lb position baty     (6 guns)
                         one 6lb position baty      (6 guns)
```

```
VI ArmeeKorps  FML Johann von Hiller (12,858 and 54 guns)
     Division FML Hohenfeld
     Brigade GM Alder           Klebek IR#14           (2)
                                Jordis IR#59            (2)
                                3 Mahrisch Landwehr    (1)
                                6lb brigade baty    (8 guns)
     Brigade GM Bianchi         Gyulai IR#60           (3)
                                Duka IR#39              (3)
                                6lb brigade baty    (8 guns)
     Division FML Kottulinsky
     Brigade GM Hoffmeister     Benjowsky IR#31        (2)
                                Spleny IR#51           (3)
                                3 Vienna Freiwilliger   (1)
                                4 Vienna Freiwilliger   (1)
                                6lb brigade baty    (8 guns)

     Brigade GM Nordmann        War. St. George Grenz   (1)
                                Broder Grenz          (1/3)
                                1 Vienna Freiwilliger   (1)
```

	2 Vienna Freiwilliger	(1)
	3lb brigade baty	(6 guns)
Brigade GM Wallmoden	Liechtenstein Hussars	(8)
	Kienmayer Hussars	(8)
	6lb position	(6 guns)
	6lb cavalry baty	(6 guns)
Reserve Artillery:	12lb position baty	(6 guns)
	6lb position baty	(6 guns)

I Reservekorps GdK Johannes Liechtenstein (11,152 and 12 guns)
    Division FML d'Aspre

Brigade GM Merville	Grenadier Bat. Scharlach	(1)
	Grenadier Bat. Puteani	(1)
	Grenadier Bat. Brezeczinsky	(1)
	Grenadier Bat. Scovaud	(1)
Brigade GM Hammer	Gren. Bat. Kirchenbetter	(1)
	Grenadier Bat. Bissingen	(1)
	Grenadier Bat. Oklopsin	(1)
	Grenadier Bat. Mayblumel	(1)
	6lb brigade baty	(6 guns)

    Division FML Prochaszka

Brigade GM Murray	Grenadier Bat. Leiningen	(1)
	Grenadier Bat. Portner	(1)
	Grenadier Bat. Georgy	(1)
	Grenadier Bat. Wieniawsky	(1)
Brigade GM Steyrer	Grenadier Bat. Hohenlohe	(1)
	Grenadier Bat. Legrand	(1)
	Grenadier Bat. Demontant	(1)
	Grenadier Bat. Hahn	(1)
	6lb brigade baty	(6 guns)

Cavalry Corps (9,039 and 42 guns)
    Division FML Hessen-Homburg

Brigade GM Kroyher	Kaiser Cuirassiers	(4)
	Liechtenstein Cuirassiers	(6)
	6lb cavalry baty	(6 guns)
Brigade GM Lederer	Kronprinz Cuirassiers	(6)
	Hohenzollern Cuirassiers	(6)
	6lb cavalry baty	(6 guns)
Brigade GM Siegenthal	E. Albert Cuirassiers	(6)
	E. Franz Cuirassiers	(6)
	6lb cavalry baty	(6 guns)

    Division FML Kienmayer

Brigade GM Vecsey	Vincent Chevaulegers	(6)
	Klenau Chevaulegers	(8)
Brigade GM Provencheres	Rosenberg Chevaulegers	(6)
	O'Reilly Chevalegers	(5)
	6lb cavalry baty	(6 guns)
Brigade Rottermund	Riesch Dragoons	(6)
	E. Johann Dragoons	(6)
	6lb cavalry baty	(6 guns)
Brigade GM Wartensleben	Blankenstein Hussars	(10)
	6lb cavalry baty	(6 guns)
Brigade GM Clary	Knesevich Dragoons	(6)

```
                              61b cavalry baty              (6 guns)
Summary:
                  btns.  sqds.  guns   inf.    cav.      total*

Avantgarde          4     16     6    4,129   1,778      5,907
I Armeekorps       22     10    50   23,555   1,039     24,594
II Armeekorps      27      8    50   20,810     780     21,590
IV Armeekorps      26 1/3 15    50   20,220   1,682     21,702
VI Armeekorps      21 1/3 16    54   10,360   1,165     12,858
I Reservekorps     16      87    54   11,152   9,039     20,191
total             116 2/3 128   264   90,226  12,918    103,144
```
+from Krieg 1809, Bowden & Tarbox, Gachot
*does not include artillerists, specialists, and train.

Determining an accurate French Order of Battle is extremely trying.
Consider the case of Nansouty's division. His three brigades with
six regiments are included in most OBs. Eyewitness accounts
describe his carabiniers and cuirassiers in action. Martinien's
tabluation of officer casualities names individual officers in all
three brigades, namely the 2nd, 3rd, and 12th cuirassier and the 2d
carabinier. Yet Saski's reproduction of the entire army's positions
on May 24 shows three of Nansouty's regiments on Lobau and three
near Ebersdorf indicating that the balance of three regiments did
not cross to participate in the fighting. What to make of it.
Thus is history!

L'Armee d'Allemagne at Aspern-Essling, May 21-22, 1809+
Sa Majeste L'Empereur Napoleon
Chef d'etat-major du Armee d'Allemagne:
Marechal Louis-Alexander Berthier, Prince de Neuchatel

Garde Imperial **(9,491 and 8 guns)**
```
                                                           btns/sqs
1st ("Young Guard") Division Curial
     Brigade Rouget          Tirailleur chasseurs        (2)
                             Tirailleur grenadiers       (2)
     Brigade Gros            Fusilier chasseurs          (2)
                             Fusilier grenadiers         (2)
2nd ("Old Guard") Division Dorsenne
                             Chasseurs a pied            (2)
                             Grenadiers a pied           (2)
3rd ("Cavalry") Division Arrighi de Casanova
     Brigade Guyout          Chasseurs a cheval          (2)
                             Grenadiers a cheval         (1)
                             Dragons de l'Imperatrice   (1)
     Brigade Krazinski       Chevaulegers polonais       (3)
                             Gendarmie d'elite          (1/2)
     Guard artillery  [Boulart]                    (8 guns)
```

II Corps Marechal Jean Lannes Duc de Montebello(**22,788 and 56 guns**)
1st Division Tharreau
```
     Brigade Conroux     6,24,25,9,16,27 Legere  1 btn ea.
```

```
        Brigade Albert          18,24,45,94,95,96 Ligne 1 btn ea.
        Brigade Jarry           4,18,54,63 Ligne        1 btn ea.

                                8lb baty               (6 guns)
                                4lb horse baty         (6 guns)
2d Division Claparede
        Brigade Coehorn         17,21,26,28 Legere     1 btn ea.
                                Tirailleurs du Po         (1)
                                Tirailleurs Corses        (1)
        Brigade Lesuire         27,39,59,69,76 Ligne   1 btn ea.
        Brigade Ficatier        40,88,64,100,103 Ligne 1 btn ea.

                                8lb baty               (6 guns)
                                4lb horse baty         (6 guns)
 3d Division Saint Hilaire
        Brigade Marion          10 Legere                 (3)
        Brigade Lorencez        3 Ligne                   (3)
                                57 Ligne                  (3)
        Brigade Destabenrath    72 Ligne                  (3)
                                105 Ligne                 (3)
                                8lb baty               (8 guns)
                                6lb horse baty         (7 guns)
     Corps Reserve Artillery    two 12lb baty          (17 guns)

IV Corps Marechal Andre Massena Duc de Rivoli(32,450 and 64 guns)
1st Division Legrand
        Brigade Ledru           26 Legere                 (3)
                                18 Ligne                  (3)
                                 6lb baty              (8 guns)
                                6lb horse baty         (6 guns)
        Baden Brigade            3 Infantry Regiment         (2)
                                1 Infantry Reg.        (4 coys)
                                6lb baty               (8 guns)
2d Division Carra Saint-Cyr
        Brigade Cosson          24 Legere                 (3)
        Brigade Dalesme         4 Ligne                   (3)
                                46 Ligne                  (3)
        Hesse-Darmstadt Brigade Leib-Garde musketeers    (2)
        (Generals Schiner       Leib musketeers          (2)
          and von Nagel)        6lb baty               (6 guns)
                                6lb baty               (8 guns)
                                6lb horse baty         (6 guns)
3d Division Molitor
        Brigade Leguay          2 Ligne                   (2)
                                16 Ligne                  (3)
        Brigade Viviez          37 Ligne                  (3)
                                67 Ligne                  (3)
                                6lb baty               (6 guns)
4th Division Boudet
        Brigade Fririon         3 Legere                  (2)
        Brigade Valory          56 Ligne                  (3)
                                93 Ligne                  (3)
```

```
                                  6lb baty            (6 guns)
IV Corps Cavalry Brigade           3 Chasseurs a cheval   (2)
Marulaz                           14 Chasseurs a cheval   (3)
                                  19 Chasseurs à cheval   (3)
                                  23 Chasseurs a cheval   (3)
                                  Baden Light Dragoons    (4)
                                  Hesse Gd. Chevaulegers    (1)
Corps Reserve Artillery           12lb baty           (8 guns)
                                  baty                (8 guns)
Light Cavalry Division Lasalle (attached to IV Corps)
     Brigade Pire                  8 Hussars              (4)
                                  16 Chasseurs a cheval   (4)
     Brigade Bruyere              13 Chasseurs a cheval   (4)
                                  24 Chasseurs a cheval   (3)
     attached:                    Wurttemberg Chasseurs a ch.(1)
Reserve Division Demont
     1st Brigade                  17,30,61,65 Ligne   1 btn ea.
     2d Brigade                   33,111 Ligne        1 btn ea.
     3d Brigade                   7 Legere,21,12,86 Ligne 1 btn ea.
                                  two 4lb baty        (12 guns)
Reserve Cavalry Corps Marechal Jean-Baptiste Bessieres Duc d'Istria
1st Heavy Cavalry Division Nansouty
     Brigade Defrance              1 Carabiniers           (4)
                                   2 Carabiniers           (4)
     Brigade Doumerc               2 Cuirassiers           (4)
                                   9 Cuirassiers           (4)
     Brigade Saint Germain         3 Cuirassiers           (4)
                                  12 Cuirassiers           (4)
                                  two 8lb horse baty  (12 guns)
2d Heavy Cavalry Division Saint Sulpice
     Brigade Lagrange              1 Cuirassiers           (4)
                                   5 Cuirassiers           (4)
     Brigade Guiton               10 Cuirassiers           (4)
                                  11 Cuirassiers           (4)
                                  8lb horse baty      (6 guns)
3d Heavy Cavalry Division d'Espagne
     Brigade Raynaud               4 Cuirassiers           (4)
                                   6 Cuirassiers           (4)
     Brigade Fouler                7 Cuirassiers           (4)
                                   8 Cuirassiers           (4)
                                  8lb horse baty      (6 guns)
```

Summary:

	btns.	sqds.	guns	inf.	cav.	*total
Imperial Guard	12	7 1/2	8	7,878	1,305	9,491
II Corps	46		56	21,428		22,788
IV Corps	40 2/3	32	58	27,889	4,561	32,450
Demont	10		12	3,998		4,100
Reserve cavalry		72	24		11,000	11,438
total	108 2/3	111 1/2	158	61,193	16,866	80,267

+Gachot, Bowden and Tarbox, Saski III, Gill
*includes field artillery, parks, and engineers

Appendix II
Order of Battle Wagram, July 5–6, 1809[+]

```
Generalissimus:  FM Erzherzog Karl
Avantgarde FML Nordmann                              btns/sqs
     Brigade GM Riese         Bellegarde IR#44          (3)
                              Chasteler IR#46           (3)
                              Beaulieu IR#58            (2)
                              1st Vienna Woods Landwehr (1)
                              2nd Vienna Woods Landwehr (1)
                              3rd Vienna Woods Landwehr (1)
                              6lb brigade baty      (6 guns)
     Brigade GM Meyer         Deutchmeister IR#4        (3)
                              Kerpen IR#49              (3)
                              5th Vienna Woods Landwehr (1)
                              6th Vienna Woods Landwehr (1)
                              6lb brigade baty      (6 guns)
     Brigade Vecsey           Wallach-Illyrian Grenz    (2)
                              Hessen-Homburg Hussars    (6)
                              6lb cavalry baty      (6 guns)
     Brigade GM Frelich       1st Jager Battalion       (1)
                              7th Jager Battalion       (1)
                              Stipsicz Hussars          (8)
                              Primatial Hussars         (6)
                              6lb cavalry baty      (6 guns)
I ArmeeKorps  GdK Heinrich Graf Bellegarde
     Division FML Dedovich
     Brigade GM Henneberg     Reuss-Plauen IR#17        (3)
                              Kollowrath IR#36          (3)
                              6lb brigade baty      (8 guns)
     Brigade GM Wacquant      Erzherzog Rainer IR#11    (3)
                              Vogelsang IR#47           (3)
                              6lb brigade baty      (8 guns)
                              6lb position baty     (6 guns)
     Division FML Fresnel
     Brigade GM Clary         Anton Mittrowsky IR#10    (2)
                              Erbach IR#42              (2)
                              Hradisch Landwehr         (1)
                              6lb brigade baty      (8 guns)
     Brigade Motzen           Argenteau IR#35           (3)
                              4th E. Karl Legion        (1)
                              6lb brigade baty      (8 guns)
     Brigade GM Stutterheim   2d Jager Battalion        (1)
                              Klenau Chevaulegers       (8)
                              6lb cavalry baty      (6 guns)
                              6lb position baty     (6 guns)
     Reserve Artillery:  two 12lb position baty   (12 guns)
                         one 6lb position baty     (6 guns)
II ArmeeKorps FML Friedrich Franz Furst zu Hohenzollern-Hechingen
     Division FML Brady
     Brigade GM Buresch       Zach IR#15                (2)
                              Joseph Colloredo IR#57    (3)
                              1st Brunner Landwehr      (1)
                              3rd Brunner Landwehr      (1)
```

```
                                6lb position baty    (6 guns)
                                6lb brigade baty     (8 guns)
        Brigade GM Paar         Zedtwitz IR#25            (3)
                                Froon IR#54               (3)
                                2nd Znaimer Landwehr      (1)
                                3rd Hradischer Landwehr   (1)
                                6lb brigade baty     (8 guns)
        Division FML Ulm
        Brigade GM Alstern      Rohan IR#21               (3)
                                6lb brigade baty     (8 guns)
        Brigade ?               Frelich IR#28             (3)
                                d'Aspre IR#18             (3)
                                6lb brigade baty     (8 guns)
                                6lb position baty    (6 guns)
        Division FML Segenthall
                                2d Bat. E. Karl Legion    (1)
                                8th Jager Battalion       (1)
                                Vincent Chevaulegers      (6)
                                6lb cavalry baty     (6 guns)
Reserve Artillery:          two 12lb position baty (12 guns)
                            one 6lb position baty   (6 guns)
III ArmeeKorps FZM Karl Graf Kollowrath-Krakowsky
        Division FML Saint Julien
        Brigade GM Lilienberg   Kaiser IR#1               (2)
                                Manfredini IR#12          (3)
                                Wurzburg IR#23            (2)
                                6lb brigade baty     (8 guns)
        Brigade GM Bieber       Kaunitz IR#20             (3)
                                Wurttemberg IR#38         (2)
                                6lb brigade baty     (8 guns)
                                6lb postion baty     (6 guns)
        Division FML Vukassovich
        Brigade GM Grill        Wenzel Colloredo IR#56    (3)
                                Karl Schroder IR#7        (3)
                                6lb brigade baty     (6 guns)
        Brigade Wratislaw       Prager Landwehr           (1)
                                1st Berauner Landwehr     (1)
                                3lb brigade baty     (6 guns)
        Brigade GM Schneller    Lobkowitz Jagers          (1)
                                2nd Berauner Landwehr     (1)
                                Schwarzenberg Uhlans      (6)
                                6lb cavalry baty     (6 guns)
                                6lb position baty    (6 guns)
Reserve Artillery:        two 12lb position baty (12 guns)
IV ArmeeKorps  FML Franz Furst v. Rosenberg
        Division FML Bartenstein
        Brigade GM Hessen-Homburg Hiller IR#2            (3)
                                Sztarri IR#33             (3)
                                6lb brigade baty     (8 guns)
        Division FML Rohan
            Brigade GM Swinburne Erzherzog Ludwig  IR#8  (3)
                                Koburg IR#22              (3)
```

```
                              1st Iglauer Landwehr      (1)
                              1st Znaimer Landwehr      (1)
                              6lb brigade baty     (8 guns)
                              6lb position baty    (6 guns)
        Division FML Radetzky
        Brigade GM Weiss      Erzherzog Karl IR#3       (3)
                              Stain IR#50               (3)
                              2nd O.M.B. Landwehr       (1)
                              4th Vienna Woods Landwehr(1)
                              6lb brigade baty     (8 guns)
        Brigade ?             2d Mahr. Freiwil. Jager  (1)
                              Carneville Freicorps Ft (1/3)
                              Carneville Freicorps Cav(1/2)
                              Waltrich Jagers           (1)
                              E. Ferdinand Hussars      (8)
                              6lb cavalry baty     (6 guns)
                              6lb position baty    (6 guns)
    Reserve Artillery:  two 12lb position baty     (12 guns)
                        one 6lb position baty      (6 guns)
VI ArmeeKorps  FML Johann Graf Klenau
        Division FML Hohenfeld
        Brigade Alder         Klebek IR#14              (2)
                              Jordis IR#59              (2)
                              3rd E. Karl Legion        (1)
                              3rd Mahrisch Landwehr     (1)
                              Outer Austrian Landwehr   (1)
                              6lb brigade baty     (8 guns)
        Brigade  Bianchi      Gyulai IR#60              (3)
                              Duka IR#39                (3)
                              6lb brigade baty     (8 guns)
                              6lb position baty    (6 guns)
        Division FML Kottulinsky
        Brigade Splenyi        Benjowsky IR#31          (2)
                               Spleny IR#51             (3)
                              3 Vienna Freiwilliger     (1)
                              4 Vienna Freiwilliger     (1)
                              combined Mahr. Landwehr   (1)
                              6lb brigade baty     (6 guns)
        Division FML Vincent
        Brigade August Vecsey Ward. St. George Grenz  (1)
                              Broder Grenz            (1/2)
                              3lb brigade baty     (6 guns)
        Brigade Mariassy      1 Vienna Freiwilliger    (1)
                              2 Vienna Freiwilliger    (1)
                              3rd Lower Austria LW.    (1)
                              3lb brigade baty     (6 guns)
        Brigade Wallmoden     Liechtenstein Hussars    (8)
                              Kienmayer Hussars        (8)
                              6lb position baty    (6 guns)
                              6lb cavalry baty     (6 guns)
    Reserve Artillery:        12lb position baty   (6 guns)
                              6lb position baty    (6 guns)
```

Reservekorps GdK Johannes Furst Liechtenstein
```
     Grenadiers Division FML d'Aspre
     Brigade GM Merville        Scharlac,Puteani,Brezeczinsky
                                Scovaud              1 btn ea.
                                6lb brigade baty     (8 guns)
     Brigade GM Hammer          Kirchenbetter, Bissingen
                                Oklopsin, Locher     1 btn ea.
                                6lb Brigade Baty     (8 guns)
                                3lb brigade baty     (8 guns)
     Division FML Prochaszka
     Brigade GM Murray          Leiningen, Portner, Georgy
                                Frisch               1 btn. ea.
                                3lb brigade baty     (8 guns)
     Brigade GM Steyrer         Hromada, Legrand, Demontant
                                Hahn, Berger         1 btn. ea.
                                6lb brigade baty     (8 guns)
                                3lb brigade baty     (8 guns)
Cavalry Corps
     Division FML Hessen-Homburg
     Brigade GM Kroyher         Kaiser Cuirassiers        (4)
                                Liechtenstein Cuirassiers  (6)
                                two 6lb cav. baty    (12 guns)
     Brigade GM Lederer         Kronprinz Cuirassiers     (6)
                                Hohenzollern Cuirassiers   (6)
                                two 6lb cav. baty    (12 guns)
     Brigade GM d'Hurbal        E. Albert Cuirassiers     (6)
                                E. Franz Cuirassiers      (6)
                                two 6lb cav. baty    (12  guns)
     Division FML Schwarzenberg
     Brigade GM Teimern         Rosenberg Chevaulegers    (8)
                                Knesevich Dragoons        (6)
                                6lb cavalry baty      (6 guns)
     Brigade Kerekes            Neutra Insurrection Hus.  (6)
     Division FML Nostitz
     Brigade GM Rothkirch       Riesch Dragoons           (6)
                                E. Johann Dragoons        (6)
                                6lb cavalry baty      (6 guns)
     Brigade GM Wartensleben    O'Reilly Chevaulegers     (8)
                                Blankenstein Hussars     (10)
                                two 6lb cav. baty    (12 guns)
```

Summary:	btns.	sqds.	guns	inf.	cav.	total*
Avantgarde	23	20	24	11,837	2,528	14,365
I Armeekorps	22	8	68	20,892	801	21,693
II Armeekorps	26	6	68	25,434	517	25,951
III Armeekorps	22	6	58	15,929	667	16,596
IV Armeekorps	24 1/3	8.5	60	17,395	792	18,187
VI Armeekorps	25.5	16	64	12,465	1,275	13,740
Reservekorps	17	84	108	9,882	8,554	18,436
total:	160	148.5	450	113,834	15,134	137,563

+from Krieg 1809, Bowden & Tarbox, Gachot
*does not include artillerists, specialists, and train.
grand total includes artillerists

```
L'Armee d'Allemagne Sa Majeste L'Empereur Napoleon
Garde Imperial                                    btns/sqs
1st ("Young Guard") Division Curial
      Brigade Rouget            Tirailleur chasseurs          (2)
                                Tirailleur grenadiers         (2)
      Brigade ?                 Fusilier chasseurs            (2)
                                Fusilier grenadiers           (2)
2nd ("Old Guard") Division Dorsenne
                                Chasseurs a pied              (2)
                                Grenadiers a pied             (2)
3rd ("Cavalry") Division Walther
      General Guyout            Grenadiers a cheval           (4)
      General Thiry             Chasseurs a cheval            (4)
      General Letort            Dragons de l'Imperatrice      (4)
      General Krazinski         Chevaulegers polonais         (4)
      General Savary            Gendarmie d'elite             (2)
      Guard artillery           one 6lb foot, three 12lb foot baty
      General Lauriston         six 6lb horse baty      (60 guns)
II Corps General de Division Oudinot
1st Division Tharreau
      Brigade Conroux           6,24,25,9,27 Legere      1 btn ea.
                                Tirailleurs corse             (1)
      Brigade Albert            8,24,45,94,95,96 Ligne   1 btn ea.
      Brigade Jarry             4,18,54,63 Ligne         1 btn ea.
                                8lb baty                 (6 guns)
                                4lb baty                 (6 guns)
2d Division Claparede
      Brigade Coehorn           17,21,28,26 Legere       1 btn ea
                                Tirailleurs du Po             (1)
      Brigade Razout            27,39,59,69,76 Ligne     1 btn ea.
      Brigade Ficatier          40,88,64,100,103 Ligne   1 btn ea.
                                8lb baty                 (6 guns)
                                4lb baty                 (6 guns)
3th Division Grandjean
      Brigade Marion            10 Legere                     (3)
      Brigade Lorencez          3 Ligne                       (3)
                                57 Ligne                      (3)
      Brigade Brun              72 Ligne                      (3)
                                105 Ligne                     (3)
                                8lb baty                 (8 guns)
                                6lb baty                 (8 guns)
      Portuguese Legion         Infantry                      (3)
      General Logo              Cavalry                       (2)
      Cavalry Brigade Colbert    7 Chasseurs a cheval         (4)
                                20 Chasseurs a cheval         (3)
                                 9 Hussars                    (4)
      attached:                 Prinz Johann Chevaulegers     (4)
      Corps Reserve Artillery   three 12lb baty         (24 guns)
III Corps Marechal Louis Davout, Duc de Auerstadt
1st Division Morand
      Brigade Lacour            13 Legere                     (3)
                                17 Ligne                      (3)
```

```
                                30 Ligne                   (3)
          Brigade l'Hullier     61 Ligne                   (3)
                                8lb baty             (8 guns)
                                6lb baty             (8 guns)
                                4lb horse baty       (6 guns)
2nd Division Friant
     Brigade Gilly              15 Legere                  (3)
                                33 Ligne                   (3)
     Brigade Barbanegre         48 Ligne                   (3)
     Brigade Grandeau           108 Ligne                  (3)
                                111 Ligne                  (3)
                                8lb baty             (8 guns)
                                6lb baty             (8 guns)
                                4lb horse baty       (6 guns)
3rd Division Gudin
     Brigade Leclerc            7 Legere                   (3)
     Brigade Boyer              12 Ligne                   (3)
                                21 Ligne                   (3)
     Brigade Dupellin           25 Ligne                   (3)
                                85 Ligne                   (3)
                                two 8lb baty        (16 guns)
                                4lb horse baty       (6 guns)
4th Division Puthod
     Brigade Girard             17 Legere,30,33,61,65 Ligne 1 btn ea.
     Brigade Desailly           7 Legere,111,25,21,85 Ligne 1 btn ea.
                                two 4lb baty        (12 guns)
                                4lb horse baty       (6 guns)
Corps Cavalry Brigade Pajol     11 Chasseurs a cheval      (4)
                                12 Chasseurs a cheval      (3)
                                5 Hussars                  (3)
Corps Reserve Artillery         three 12lb baty     (24 guns)
                                4lb baty             (6 guns)
IV Corps Marechal Andre Massena, Duc de Rivoli
1st Division Legrand
     Brigade Ledru              26 Legere                  (3)
                                18 Ligne                   (3)
     Baden Brigade              1 Infantry Reg. Grossherzog    (2)
     von Neuenstein             2 Infantry Reg. Erbgrossherzog (2)
                                3 Infantry Reg. Graf Hochberg (2)
                                Jager Battalion Lingg      (1)
                                6lb baty             (8 guns)
                                6lb horse baty       (4 guns)
2d Division Carra Saint-Cyr
     Brigade Cosson             24 Legere                  (3)
     Brigade Dalesme            4 Ligne                    (3)
                                46 Ligne                   (3)
     Hesse-Darmstadt Brigade    Leib-Garde musketeers      (2)
     (Generals Schiner          Leib-Garde Fusilier battalion (1)
     and von Nagel)             Leib musketeers            (2)
                                1st Leib Fusilier Battalion (1)
                                6lb baty             (6 guns)
                                6lb baty             (8 guns)
```

```
                              6lb horse baty         (6 guns)
3d Division Molitor
     Brigade Leguay            2 Ligne                  (2)
                              16 Ligne                  (3)
     Brigade Viviez           37 Ligne                  (3)
                              67 Ligne                  (2)
                              6lb baty              (6 guns)
                              4lb baty              (6 guns)
                              6lb horse baty        (6 guns)
4th Division Boudet
     Brigade Fririon           3 Legere                 (2)
     Brigade Valory           56 Ligne                  (3)
                              93 Ligne                  (2)
                              6lb baty              (8 guns)
                              6lb horse baty        (6 guns)
IV Corps Cavalry Brigade Marulaz
                               3 Chasseurs a cheval      (4)
                              14 Chasseurs a cheval      (4)
                              19 Chasseurs a cheval      (4)
                              23 Chasseurs a cheval      (3)
                              Baden Light Dragoons       (1)
                              Hesse Darm. Gd. Chevaulegers  (2)
                               1 Bavarian Chevaulegers   (4)
Corps Reserve Artillery       12lb baty             (8 guns)
Light Cavalry Division Lasalle (attached to IV Corps)
     Brigade Pire              8 Hussars                 (4)
                              16 Chasseurs a cheval      (4)
     Brigade Bruyere          13 Chasseurs a cheval      (4)
                              24 Chasseurs a cheval      (3)
Armee d'Italie Prince Eugene de Beauharnais
Royal Italian Guard (General de Division Lecchi)
     Brigade Fontanelli       Guard Velites             (1)
                              Guards d'Honneur          (1)
     Brigade Guerin           Guard chasseurs           (1)
                              Guard grenadiers          (1)
                              Guard Dragoons            (2)
                              Guard Horse Baty      (6 guns)
Corps Macdonald
1st Division Broussier
     Brigade Dutruy            9 Ligne                   (3)
                              84 Ligne                   (3)
     Brigade Dessaix          92 Ligne                   (4)
                              baty                  (6 guns)
2d Division Lamarque
     Brigade Huart            18 Legere                  (2)
                              13 Ligne                   (3)
     Brigade Almeiras         23 Ligne                   (2)
                              29 Ligne                   (4)
                              baty                  (6 guns)
Corps Grenier
1st Division Seras
     Brigade Garraud           1 Legere                  (1)
```

```
                              35 Ligne                        (1)
                              53 Ligne                        (3)
        Brigade Roussel       42 Ligne                        (1)
                              106 Ligne                       (3)
                              baty                       (6 guns)
2d Division Durutte
        Brigade Valentin      22 Legere                       (1)
                              23 Ligne                        (3)
                              60 Ligne                        (1)
        Brigade Bruch         62 Ligne                        (3)
                              102 Ligne                       (3)
                              baty                       (6 guns)
3d Division Pacthod
        Brigade Teste         8 Legere                        (2)
                              1 Ligne                         (3)
        Brigade Abbe          52 Ligne                        (4)
                              baty                       (6 guns)
Cavalry Division Sahuc
                              6 Chasseurs a cheval            (4)
                              8 Chasseurs a cheval            (4)
                              9 Chasseurs a cheval            (3)
Army of Italy Artillery Reserve
                              12lb baty                  (8 guns)
2d Bavarian Division Wrede
        Brigade von Minucci   6 Light battalion               (1)
                              3 Infantry Prinz Karl           (2)
                              6 Infantry Herzog Wilhelm       (2)
        Brigade von Beckers   7 Infantry Lowenstein           (2)
                              13 Infantry                     (2)
        Cavalry Brigade        2 Chevaulegers Konig           (4)
        von Preysing          3 Chevaulegers Leiningen        (4)
        Artillery             6lb light baty            (6 guns)
                              four 6lb batys           (24 guns)
                              12lb baty                 (6 guns)
IX Corps Marechal Jean-Baptiste Bernadotte, Prince de Ponte Corvo
Advant Guard GM Gutschmid     Prince Clemens Chevaulegers     (4)
                              Herzog Albrecht Chevaulegers    (1)
                              Hussars                         (3)
1st Division GL v. Zezschwitz
        Brigade von Hartitzsch Leib Grenadier Garde Battalion  (1)
                              2 Grenadier Battalion           (1)
                              2 Schutzen Battalion            (1)
        Brigade von Zeschau   Konig Infantry Battalion        (1)
                              von Niesemeuschel Infantry Btn.  (1)
                              combined infantry battalion     (1)
                              two 8lb baty              (16 guns)
2d Division GL von Polenz
        Brigade von Lecoq     Prinz Clemens Infantry Battalion (1)
                              von Low Infantry Battalion      (1)
                              von Cerrini Infantry Battalion  (1)
        Brigade von Steindel  Prinz Anton Infantry Battalion  (1)
                              Prinz Maximilian Infantry Btn.  (1)
```

```
                              Prinz Friedrich August Inf. Btn. (1)
                              two 8lb baty              (16 guns)
Cavalry Brigade               Leib-Garde Kuirassier          (4)
von Feilitzsch                Garde du Corps                 (2)
                              Karabinier                     (2)
                              8lb horse baty            (6 guns)
Division Dupas
     Brigade Gency            5 Legere                       (2)
     Brigade Veau             19 Ligne                       (3)
     attached:                1 Saxon Grenadier battalion    (1)
                              1 Saxon Schutzen battalion     (1)
XI Corps Marechal Auguste Marmont, Duc de Raguse
1st Division Montrichand
     Brigade Soyez            18 Legere                     (2)
                             5 Ligne                        (2)
     Brigade Launay           79 Ligne                      (2)
                             81 Ligne                       (2)
                             two 6lb baty           (12 guns)
2d Division Clauzel
     Brigade Delzons          8 Legere                      (2)
                             23 Ligne                       (2)
     Brigade Bachelu          11 Ligne                      (3)
                             two 6lb baty           (16 guns)
                             24 Chasseurs a cheval          (1)
Cavalry detached to screen army's right wing:
Division Grouchy             7 Dragoons                     (4)
                             30 Dragoons                    (4)
                             Italian Dragoons de la Reine   (4)
Division Pully               23 Dragoons                    (4)
                             28 Dragoons                    (3)
                             29 Dragoons                    (4)
Division Montbrun
Brigade Jacquinot            1 Chasseurs a cheval           (4)
                             2 Chasseurs a cheval           (3)
                             7 Hussars                      (3)
                             4lb horse baty          (6 guns)
Reserve Cavalry Corps Marechal Jean-Baptiste Bessieres Duc d'Istria
1st Heavy Cavalry Division Nansouty
     Brigade Defrance         1 Carabiniers                 (4)
                             2 Carabiniers                  (4)
     Brigade Doumerc          2 Cuirassiers                 (4)
                             9 Cuirassiers                  (4)
     Brigade Saint Germain    3 Cuirassiers                 (4)
                             12 Cuirassiers                 (4)
                             two 8lb horse baty     (12 guns)
2d Heavy Cavalry Division Saint Sulpice
     Brigade Fiteau           1 Cuirassiers                 (4)
                             5 Cuirassiers                  (4)
     Brigade Guiton           10 Cuirassiers                (4)
                             11 Cuirassiers                 (4)
                             8lb horse baty          (6 guns)
```

```
3d Heavy Cavalry Division Arrighi de Casanova
    Brigade Raynaud            4 Cuirassiers              (4)
                               6 Cuirassiers              (4)
    Brigade Bordesoule         7 Cuirassiers              (4)
                               8 Cuirassiers              (4)
                               8lb horse baty        (6 guns)
Lobau Island General de Division Reynier
                               Artillery            (123 guns)
```

Summary:

	btns.	sqds.	guns	inf.	cav.	*total
Imperial Guard	12	18	60	7,351	3,366	12,363
II Corps	50	17	64	26,011	2,049	28,060
III Corps	52	10	114	31,614	2,090	36,571
IV Corps	45	37	74	27,184	3,764	30,948
Armee d'Italy	53	13	44	19,594	2,012	23,306
Wrede	9	8	36	5,544	1,103	6,647
IX Corps	19	16	38	14,800	2,050	16,850
XI Corps	15	1	28	9,747	280	10,700
Right Wing Cavalry		33	6		4,077	4,177
Reserve cavalry		56	24		8,235	8,778
Renyier			123			8,475
total:	255	209	611	141,845	29,026	186,875

```
+Krieg 1809, Bowden and Tarbox, Exner, Gill
*includes field artillery, parks, and engineers
```

NOTES

INTRODUCTION

1. J. Christopher Herold, ed., *The Mind of Napoleon: A Selection from His Written and Spoken Words* (New York, 1955), p. 241.

2. This altogether representative sampling comes from *Unpublished Correspondence of Napoleon I* (New York, 1913), 3:37, 41–43.

3. Ibid., pp. 30, 35–36, 46.

4. C.G.L. Saski, *La Campagne de 1809* (Paris, 1899–1902), 2:375.

CHAPTER 1

1. David G. Chandler, *The Military Maxims of Napoleon* (New York, 1988), maxim IX, p. 58.

2. J. W. Ridler, "Ruekerinnerung an Oesterreichische Helden," *Archiv fuer Geographie, Histories, Staats- und Kriegskunst* (Vienna, 1811), p. 198.

3. Ibid., p. 198.

4. Twelve officers and 215 men died in the misconceived defense of the Ebelsberg approaches, while another 400 had been wounded.

5. Baron Lejeune, *Memoirs of Baron Lejeune* (London, 1897), 1:240–241.

6. Ridler, "Ruekerinnerung an Oesterreichische Helden," p. 200.

7. Ibid., p. 199.

8. See James R. Arnold, *Crisis on the Danube* (New York, 1990), p. 148.

9. Charles A. Fare, *Lettres d'un Jeune Officier à sa Mère* (Paris, 1889), p. 201.

10. Edouard Gachot, *1809 Napoléon en Allemagne* (Paris, 1913), p. 128. Gachot must be consulted with caution, but this rings true since it well accords with Massena's blame-seeking personality.

11. General Baron Pouget, *Souvenirs de Guerre du Général Baron Pouget* (Paris, 1895), p. 145.

12. J. J. Pelet, *Mémoires sur la Guerre de 1809* (Paris, 1824), 3:211.

13. C.G.L. Saski, *La Campagne de 1809* (Paris, 1899–1902), 3:136.

14. Pouget's gripping account of this battle appears in his *Souvenirs de Guerre*, pp. 146–150.

15. Lejeune, *Memoirs* 1:243–244.

16. Ridler, "Ruekerinnerung an Oesterreichische Helden," p. 201.

17. Typical of the problems reconstructing French losses is the example of one French general who wrote 11 days later that his unit had lost 100 men killed just during the charge across the bridge, whereas in fact his total killed for the entire action did not exceed 30 men.

18. Wien Kriegsarchiv, *Krieg 1809* (Vienna, 1907–1910) 2:420–423.

19. The exploits of the Vienna Volunteers are honored by a fine statue near the castle in Ebelsberg.

20. Cited in F. L. Petre, *Napoleon and the Archduke Charles* (London, 1976), p. 242.

21. Philippe-René Girault, *Les Campagnes d'un Musicien* (Paris, 1901), p. 212.

22. See Saski, *La Campagne*, Napoleon to Lannes, May 4, 1809, 3:145–146.

23. Pouget, *Souvenirs de Guerre*, p. 151.

24. Ibid., p. 152.

25. Ibid., p. 153. For details about the battle see Pelet, *Mémoires*, 2:202–217; Saski, *La Campagne*, 3:132–146; General Stutterheim, *La Guerre de l'An 1809* (Vienna, 1811), pp. 52–63; Moriz Edlin von Angeli, *Erzherzog Carl* (Vienna, 1896–1897) 4:226–233. Gachot, *Napoléon en Allemagne*, pp. 123–137, provides an entirely unreliable account as revealed by comparing his account of the battle's timing, duration and of Massena's participation with the other accounts. For a very interesting discussion of the losses at Ebelsberg, see *Empires, Eagles and Lions* 78 (March, 1984), 83 (Oct., 1984), 85 (Jan., 1985), and 103 (Nov.-Dec., 1987).

26. Baron de Marbot, *Mémoires of Baron de Marbot* (London, 1892) 1:405.

27. Ridler, "Ruekerinnerung an Oesterrichische Helden," p. 197.

28. Walter Langsam, *The Napoleonic Wars and German Nationalism in Austria* (New York, 1930), p. 131.

29. Emile Fairion and Henri Heuse, *Lettres de Grognards* (Paris, 1936), p. 108.

30. Maurice de Tascher, *Journal de Campagne d'un Cousin de l'Impératrice* (Paris, 1933), p. 216.

31. Elzear Blaze, *Recollections of an Officer of Napoleon's Army* (New York, 1911), p. 19.

32. Girault, *Les Campagnes d'un Musicien*, p. 219.

33. Archives, Musée de L'Emperi, Salon de Provence, France.

34. This success is still honored today by a lineage commemorated by the 10th Austrian Tank Battalion.

CHAPTER 2

1. Peter G. Tsouras, *Warriors' Words: A Quotation Book* (London, 1992), p. 29.

2. Aymar Oliver Gonneville, *Recollections of Colonel de Gonneville* (London, 1875), 1:120–123.

3. Elzear Blaze, *Recollections of an Officer of Napoleon's Army* (New York, 1911), p. 215.

4. See Lt. Col. Ernest Picard, ed., *Préceptes et Jugements de Napoléon* (Paris, 1913), p. 139.

5. *Napoleon's Own Memoirs* (London, 1823), pp. 176–177.

6. Cited in J. Colin, *La Tactique et la Discipline dans les Armées de la Révolution* (Paris, 1902), p. lxli.

7. In Picard, *Préceptes*, Napoleon to Eugène, December 5, 1806, p. 106.

8. Marc Desboeufs, *Souvenirs du Capitaine Desboeufs* (Paris, 1901), p. 115.

9. Austrian and French drill specified march and attack rates of 70 to 140 paces per minute, with a pace equal to 22 inches. These rates presume peacetime passage over featureless terrain. My estimate is based on a battalion line charge over unequal, but not rough, terrain.

10. Tsouras, *Warriors' Words*, p. 41.

11. Jean François Bon Boulart, *Mémoires Militaires du Général Bon Boulart* (Paris, 1892), p. 219.

12. The artillery on the second day at Aspern-Essling had 12 4-pounders, 48 6-pounders, 30 8-pounders, 21 12-pounders, 14 6-pouce howitzers, and 10 24-pouce howitzers. C.G.L. Saski, *La Campagne de 1809* (Paris, 1899–1902), 3:406.

13. Picard, *Préceptes*, p. 33.

14. J. W. Ridler, "Ruekerinnerung an Oesterreichische Helden," *Archiv fuer Geographie, histories, Staats- und Kriegskunst* (Vienna, 1811), p. 199.

15. Dezydery Chlapowski, *Memoirs of a Polish Lancer* (Chicago, 1992), p. 66.

16. Charles A. Thoumas, *Le Général Curely: Itinéraire d'un cavalier Léger de la Grande Armée* (Paris, 1887), p. 225.

17. Chlapowski, *Memoirs*, p. 67.

18. Lt. General Reiset, *Souvenirs du Vicomte de Reiset* (Paris, n.d.), p. 95.

19. De Brack, noted in an exhibit at the Musée de l'Emperi, Salon de Provence, France.

20. Raoul Dupuy, *Historique de 12e Régiment de Chasseurs de 1788 à 1891* (Paris, 1891), p. 165.

21. "Voici pourquoi de Beaux Uniformes Sont Si Utilités." Picard, *Préceptes*, p. 138.

22. "Tous les régiments qui sont à Naples sont des corps perdus, parce qu'on en a ôté la crème," Napoleon to Murat, March 20, 1807, in ibid., p. 139.

23. Henry Lachouque, *Anatomy of Glory* (Providence, R.I., 1961), p. 145.

24. *Unpublished Correspondence of Napoleon I* (New York, 1913), vol. 3: order 3185 of May 25, 1809, and 3278 of June 28, 1809, respectively, p. 65 and p. 106.

25. Blaze, *Recollections*, p. 40.

26. Jean-Baptiste Barres, *Memoirs of a Napoleonic Officer* (London, 1925), p. 134.

27. Blaze, *Recollections*, p. 195.

28. See Kellerman's report in F. L. Petre, *Napoleon's Campaign in Poland 1806–07* (New York, 1907), p. 19 n. 1.

29. J. Christopher Herold, ed., *The Mind of Napoleon: A Selection from His Written and Spoken Words* (New York, 1955), p. 215.

30. Etienne-Denis Pasquier, *The Memoirs of Chancellor Pasquier* (Cranbury, N.J., 1968), p. 95.

31. Emile Fairion and Henri Heuse, *Lettres de Grognards* (Paris, 1936), p. 365.

32. Much of the information for this section comes from the Musée de la Poste in Amboise, France.

33. Herold, *Mind of Napoleon*, p. 216.

34. This was 20 above the authorized strength; all companies received a special prewar augmentation of 20 men. See General Stutterheim, *La Guerre de l'An 1809* (Vienna, 1811), p. xxiii.

35. Guillaune Peyrusse, *Lettres Inédites de Guillaune Peyrusse* (Paris, 1894), p. 18.

36. Edouard Gachot, *1809 Napoléon en Allemagne* (Paris, 1913), Johann to Karl, July 5, 1809, pp. 262–263.

37. Maximilian von Thielen, *Erinnerungen* (Vienna, 1863), p. 51.

38. The army entered the 1809 campaign with 76 batteries, 12,976 men, and 518 tubes including 64 3-pound, 308 6-pound, 56 12-pound, and 90 howitzers. Stutterheim, *La Guerre*, p. liii.

CHAPTER 3

1. J. Christopher Herold, ed., *The Mind of Napoleon: A Selection from His Written and Spoken Words* (New York, 1955), p. 221.

2. Various sources describe the length of this second bridge differently. I have gone with Paulin, who was on the scene.

3. A point noted by Baron Lejeune, one of the imperial aides charged with constructing the bridges. See Baron Lejeune, *Memoirs of Baron Lejeune* (London, 1897), 1:293.

4. Philippe-René Girault, *Les Campagnes d'un Musicien* (Paris, 1901), p. 226.

5. Marcel Doher, *Charles de la Bedoyère: Aide de Camp de l'Empereur* (Paris, n.d.), p. 45.

6. See Appendix I, Order of Battle.

7. Girault's letter is on display at the Musée de l'Emperi, Salon de Provence, France.

8. F. L. Petre, *Napoleon and the Archduke Charles* (London, 1976), p. 271.

9. Manpower strength is difficult to ascertain. Estimates range from 75,000 in the Austrian official report (surely too low a figure) to around 100,000, a figure given by Pelet, and Buat's 105,000. French sources exaggerate and Austrian sources understate strengths. Even "neutral" sources are unreliable. The *West Point Atlas*, for example, says 80,800 infantry and 15,000 cavalry. Adding in another 12,000 gunners gives the implausible total of 107,800. While the battalion, squadron, and battery totals in my text come from the official Austrian report, the manpower strength represents my best estimate.

10. The attack order is in MR 671 at the French archives at the Chateau de Vincennes under the jurisdiction of the Service Historique de l'Armée.

11. See Napoleon's notes on the Battle of Essling in Count de Montholon, *Memoirs of the History of France during the Reign of Napoleon Dictated by the Emperor at Saint Helena* (London, 1823), 6:75.

12. MR 664, Chateau de Vincennes archives.

13. J. W. Ridler, "Ruekerinnerung an Oesterreichische Helden," *Archiv fuer Geographie, histories, Staats- und Kriegskunst* (Vienna, 1811), p. 201.

14. From the Austrian official report translated into the French, in MR 671, Chateau de Vincennes archives.

15. Jules A. Paulin, *Les Souvenirs du Général Bon Paulin* (Paris, 1895), p. 188.

16. Jean Michel Chevalier, *Souvenirs des Guerres Napoléoniennes* (Paris, 1970), p. 105. Chlapowski also describes this incident on p. 69.

17. The French translation of the German is "en masse par battalion, sur le demi division du centre." See MR 671, Chateau de Vincennes archives.

18. A sixth regiment, the 23d Chasseurs à Cheval, remained in reserve at this time.

19. Maximilian von Thielen, *Erinnerungen* (Vienna, 1863), p. 48.

20. Baron de Marbot, *Mémoires of Baron de Marbot* (London, 1892), 1:421.

21. Ibid., pp. 423–424.

22. J. J. Pelet, *Mémoires sur la Guerre de 1809* (Paris, 1824), 3:301.

23. Ridler, "Ruekerinnerung an Oesterreichische Helden," p. 201.

24. Molitor reported 79 officers and 2,107 men killed or wounded during the two-day combat, the vast majority of which occurred on the twenty-first.

25. General Baron Pouget, *Souvenirs de Guerre du Général Baron Pouget* (Paris, 1895), p. 156.

26. Marbot, *Mémoires*, p. 426.

27. Slightly more than 65,000 French crossed to the far shore. Perhaps 7,000 fell on the battle's first day. Songis's report breaks down the artillery into 21 12-pounders, 30 8-pounders, 48 6-pounders, 12 4-pounder, 15 24-pound howitzers, and 18 lighter howitzers. See Edouard Gachot, *1809 Napoléon en Allemagne* (Paris, 1913), p. 173.

CHAPTER 4

1. Baron Lejeune, *Memoirs of Baron Lejeune* (London, 1897), 1:268.

2. Robert M. Epstein, *Prince Eugène at War* (Arlington, Texas, 1984), Napoleon to Eugène, April 30, 1809, p. 73.

3. Joachim Delmarche, *Les Soirées du Grenadier* (Musée de Cerfontaine, 1980), p. 21. A saber wound to the right arm would end this grenadier's day. Two years later he would receive his reward when he became a member of the Légion d'honneur.

4. The official IV Corps report (MR 661, Chateau de Vincennes archives) of the two-day battle makes frequent mention of the terrible Austrian cannon fire.

5. In his May 24 report, Songis lists 24,300 French shots. Karl reports 51,000. See C. G. L. Saski, *La Campagne de 1809* (Paris, 1899–1902), 3:406; and Edouard Gachot, *1809 Napoléon en Allemagne* (Paris, 1913), p. 186, respectively.

6. Rovigo, who accompanied Lannes's men, attests to this formation. See Duc de Rovigo, *Mémoires du Duc de Rovigo* (Paris, 1901), 3:121.

7. See Saski, *La Campagne*, 3:252.

8. Rovigo, *Mémoires*, pp. 121–122.

9. See James R. Arnold, *Crisis on the Danube* (New York, 1990), p. 174.

10. Lejeune, *Memoirs*, 1:283–284.

11. Noted in Raoul de Cisternes, ed., *Journal de Marche du Grenadier Pils* (Paris, 1895), p. 71.

12. Count de Montholon, *Memoirs of the History of France during the Reign of Napoleon Dictated by the Emperor at Saint Helena* (London, 1823), 6:82.

13. Berthier to Davout, May 22, 1809, in *Correspondance de Napoléon Ier* (Paris, 1866), 19:33.

14. P. Berthezène, *Souvenirs Militaires* (Paris, 1855), 3:235.

15. Baron Seruzier, *Mémoires Militaires du Baron Seruzier* (Paris, 1823), p. 133.

16. Cisternes, *Journal*, p. 70.

17. Dezydery Chlapowski, *Memoirs of a Polish Lancer* (Chicago, 1992), p. 75.

18. Jean François Bon Boulart, *Mémoires Militaires du Général Bon Boulart* (Paris, 1892), p. 216. Chlapowski, *Memoirs*, testifies to the effectiveness of even the errant Austrian shots on p. 73.

19. Davout, in a May 23 letter to his wife, writes, "Glory always costs something," and proceeds to relate the news of Lannes's injury.

20. See Boulart, *Mémoires*, p. 216.

21. See Arnold, *Crisis on the Danube*, pp. 146–147.

22. General Count Rapp, *Memoirs of General Count Rapp* (London, 1823), pp. 137–138.

23. Seruzier, *Mémoires*, p. 136.

24. Chlapowski, *Memoirs*, p. 72.

25. General Marquis de Bonneval, *Mémoires Anecdotiques du Général Marquis de Bonneval* (Paris, 1900), p. 28.

26. Elzear Blaze, *Recollections of an Officer of Napoleon's Army* (New York, 1911), p. 279.

27. Jules A. Paulin, *Les Souvenirs du Général Bon Paulin* (Paris, 1895), p. 190.

28. Rovigo believes that Lannes dismounted to avoid enemy fire. He was there. I accept his version over those who claim Lannes dismounted because he was grief-stricken over the death of his friend Pouzet. See Rovigo, *Mémoires*, p. 125.

29. Paul Triaire, *Dominique Larrey et les Campagnes de la Révolution et de l'Empire* (Tours, France, 1902), pp. 475–477.

30. This dramatic dialogue is variously reported. Pelet was present and I've taken his version, which includes the " . . . ," which undoubtedly represent pauses in the dialogue. See J. J. Pelet, *Mémoires sur la Guerre de 1809* (Paris, 1824), 3:335; and Larrey to Ribes, July 18, 1809, in Triaire, *Dominique Larrey*, pp. 478–479.

31. Lejeune, *Memoirs*, 1:294–295.

32. General Koch, *Mémoires de Massena* (Paris, 1850), 6:259.

33. Cited in Gachot, *Napoléon*, p. 191.

34. Wounded Austrian generals included Bobau, Dedovich, Weber, Fresnel, Winzergerode, Geille, Neusstader, Siegenthal, Colloredo, Maxer, Bobenfield, and Buresch. Casualty totals are from the official Austrian report in MR 671, Chateau de Vincennes archives.

35. Gachot, *Napoléon*, p. 192.

36. See Maximilian von Thielen, *Erinnerungen* (Vienna, 1863), p. 58.

37. The official Austrian report claims 3,000 cuirasses. Probably this represents 1,500 front and back pairs.

38. For example, see Jean Michel Chevalier, *Souvenirs des Guerres Napoléoniennes* (Paris, 1970), pp. 107–108.

39. See Bonneval, *Mémoires*, p. 30.

40. Chevalier, *Souvenirs*, p. 110.

41. Triaire, *Dominique Larrey*, p. 482.

42. Charles A. Thoumas, *Le Général Curely: Itinéraire d'un Cavalier Léger de la Grande Armée* (Paris, 1887), p. 229.

43. See: Arnold, *Crisis on the Danube*, pp. 153–154.

44. Berthier to Daru, 23 May, 1809, in *Correspondance de Napoléon Ier*, 19:34. This order was given at 1 A.M.

45. MR 664, Château de Vincennes archives.

46. Saski, *La Campagne*, 3:402, for initial strength; Aristide Martinien, *Tableaux par Corps et par Batailles des Officiers Tués et Blessés pendant les Guerres de l'Empire* (Paris, 1899) for losses.

47. Regimental officer losses: 3d, 27 casualties out of 51 present (27/51); 57th, 31/41; 72d, 25/42; 105th, 23/52; 10th Leg., 24/66. Saski, *La Campagne*, 3:398; and Martinien, *Tableaux*.

48. Regimental losses: 4th, 17/29; 6th, 16/29; 7th 9/19; 8th, 19/32. Saski, *La Campagne*, 3:402–403; and Martinien, *Tableaux*.

49. Pelet, *Mémoires*, 3:259.

50. General Vincent J. Esposito and Colonel John Elting, *Military History and Atlas of the Napoleonic Wars* (New York, 1964), report losses of 19,000 to 20,000; and Pelet, *Mémoires*, 15,000 to 20,000 wounded.

51. Herold, *Mind of Napoleon*, p. 218.

52. Ibid., p. 221.

53. David G. Chandler, *The Military Maxims of Napoleon* (New York, 1988), maxim XXV, p. 63.

54. Thomas Graham, *The History of the Campaign of 1796 in Germany and Italy* (London, 1800), 1:337.

55. Rovigo, *Mémoires*, pp. 127–128.

CHAPTER 5

1. J. Christopher Herold, ed., *The Mind of Napoleon: A Selection from His Written and Spoken Words* (New York, 1955), p. 242.

2. Patrick Turnbull, *Napoleon's Second Empress* (New York, 1971), p. 26.

3. Napoleon to Clarke, May 17, 1809, *Unpublished Correspondence of Napoleon I* (New York, 1913), 3:61.

4. Baron Seruzier, *Mémoires Militaires du Baron Seruzier* (Paris, 1823), pp. 97–112, relates Schill's fate.

5. Madame Junot, *Memoirs of the Emperor Napoleon* (London, 1901), 3:147.

6. Herold, *Mind of Napoleon*, p. 109.

7. Ludwig Compte de Lebzeltern, *Mémoires et Papiers de Lebzeltern; un Collaborateur de Metternich* (Paris, 1949), p. 68.

8. See General Count Rapp, *Memoirs of General Count Rapp* (London, 1823), p. 139.

9. Herold, *Mind of Napoleon*, p. 185.

10. Ibid., p. 190.

11. Ibid., p. 132.

12. Junot, *Memoirs*, 3:147.

13. For a typical mention of their depredations, see Cambacères to Napoleon, May 14, 1809, in Jean Cambacères, *Lettres Inédites à Napoléon* (Paris, 1973), no. 837.

14. See Cambacères to Napoleon, July 3, 1809, in ibid., no. 868.

CHAPTER 6

1. David G. Chandler, *The Military Maxims of Napoleon* (New York, 1988), maxim LXX, p. 78.

2. For a discussion of Karl's strategic formulations see James R. Arnold, *Crisis on the Danube* (New York, 1990), pp. 56–58.

3. Most of the "Notes" are reproduced in Robert M. Epstein, *Prince Eugène at War* (Arlington, Texas, 1984), pp. 22–28.

4. Original document displays at the Musée de l'Emperi, Salon de Provence, reveal this.

5. The following is largely based on General Stutterheim, *La Guerre de l'An 1809* (Vienna, 1811).

6. Cited in Epstein, *Prince Eugène*, p. 63.

7. Ibid., p. 72.

8. J.N.A. Noël, *Souvenirs Militaires d'un Officier du Premier Empire* (Paris, 1895), p. 59.

9. This phenomenon is apparently a diurnal effect of alpine snow melt.

10. Colonel de Gonneville, *Recollections of Colonel de Gonneville*(London, 1875), 1:264

11. Ibid.

12. Ibid., p. 267.

13. "An imprudent position offering the enemy two targets at a time," according to Noël whose battery stood in front of this cavalry. Noël, *Souvenirs*, p. 62.

14. J. Chevillet, *Ma Vie Militaire* (Paris, 1906), p. 200.

15. Ibid., pp. 205–206, for whom this was the first campaign, provides a two-page, blow-by-blow description in a letter to his father that well captures the terrifying confusion of a cavalry combat.

16. Ibid., p. 203.

17. Etienne MacDonald, *Marshal Macdonald's Recollections* (London, 1892), p. 315.

18. Moritz Exner, *The Participation of the Royal Saxon Army in the Campaign against Austria* (Dresden, 1894), p. 58.

19. Ibid., p. 67.

20. Ibid., p. 60.

21. Ibid., pp. 61–63.

22. J. Christopher Herold, ed., *The Mind of Napoleon: A Selection from His Written and Spoken Words* (New York, 1955), p. 168.

23. Colonel Paszkowski lays out the elements of Poniatowski's partisan war in his April 21 letter to Bernadotte. See Wladyslaw de Fedorowicz, *1809 Campagne de Pologne* (Paris, 1911), 1:317.

24. Emile Fairion and Henri Heuse, *Lettres de Grognards* (Paris, 1936), p. 110.

25. C. Pelleport, *Souvenirs Militaires et Intimes du Général Vte. de Pelleport* (Paris, 1857), 1:277.

26. Alexandre Alville, *Un Suisse Officier d'Ordonnance de Napoléon* (Lausanne, 1956), p. 75.

27. Paul Britten Austin, "Oudinot: The Father of the Grenadiers," in David G. Chandler, ed., *Napoleon's Marshals* (New York, 1987), p. 390.

28. *Unpublished Correspondence of Napoleon I* (New York, 1913), 3:99.

29. Berthier to Davout, May 24, 1809, in *Correspondance de Napoléon Ier* (Paris, 1866), 19:39.

30. Lieutenant-Général Compte Friant, *Vie Militaire* (Paris, 1857), p. 186.

31. P. Berthezène, *Souvenirs Militaires* (Paris, 1855), 3:243.

32. "To General Clarke," June 11, 1809 in *Unpublished Correspondence of Napoleon I* 3:86.

33. Chevillet, *Ma Vie Militaire*, p. 261.

34. Marquis de Grouchy, *Mémoires du Maréchal de Grouchy* (Paris, 1873) 3:35.

35. General Camon, *La Manoeuvre de Wagram* (Paris, 1926), Napoleon to Marmont, May 28, 1809, p. 50. Marmont's infantry exclusively was composed of the 1st, 2d, and 3d battalions.

36. Marc Desboeufs, *Souvenirs du Capitaine Desboeufs* (Paris, 1901), pp. 98–99.

37. Ibid., p. 101.

38. "Marmont to Napoleon" May 29, 1809, contains Marmont's battle report. See Auguste Marmont, *Mémoires du Maréchal Marmont, Duc de Raguse* (Paris, 1857), 3:204–207.

39. L. Loy, *La Campagne de Styrie* (Paris, 1908), p. 68.

40. Jules A. Paulin, *Les Souvenirs du Général Bon Paulin* (Paris, 1895), p. 201.

41. Exner, *Participation*, p. 15.

42. A point emphasized in ibid. See p. 5.

43. Desboeufs, *Souvenirs*, p. 110.

44. Marmont, *Mémoires*, 3:225.

45. Paulin, *Souvenirs*, p. 193.

46. Ibid., p. 197.

47. Attributed to Napoleon, this bridge was in fact designed by a junior engineer. It consisted of 12-meter sections joined by heavy cordage.

48. Berthezène, *Souvenirs*, 3:247.

49. Henry Lachouque, *The Anatomy of Glory* (Providence, R.I., 1961), p. 161.

50. Paul Ollendorff, ed., *Souvenirs de Roustam, Mamelouck de Napoleon Ier* (Paris, n.d.), p. 235.

51. Napoleon's correspondence to La Riboisière is in Etienne Aubrée, *Le Général de la Riboisière* (Paris, 1948), pp. 29–37. They underscore how much importance Napoleon placed on this aspect of the crossing.

52. See Paulin, *Souvenirs*, p. 212.

53. Philippe-René Girault, *Les Campagnes d'un Musicien* (Paris, 1901), p. 250.

54. A total of 23 landwehr and 11 volunteer battalions, these latter featuring select landwehr soldiers. Only 8 battalions had been in the ranks at Aspern-Essling. The Hungarian insurrection also contributed one landwehr-like, 600–man force of light cavalry for field duty.

55. This document is mentioned in several French accounts, including General Comte Roguet, *Mémoires Militaires du Lieutenant Général Comte Roguet* (Paris, 1865), 4:70.

CHAPTER 7

1. J. Christopher Herold, ed., *The Mind of Napoleon: A Selection from His Written and Spoken Words* (New York, 1955), p. 45.

2. "Projet de Proclamation à l'Armée," in *Correspondance de Napoléon Ier* (Paris, 1866), 19:217.

3. See François-Joseph Jacquin, *Carnet de Route d'un Grognard de la révolution et de l'Empire* (Paris, 1960), pp. 70–71.

4. J. Chevillet, *Ma Vie Militaire* (Paris, 1906), p. 285.

5. Ibid., p. 284.

6. Auguste Marmont, *Mémoires du Maréchal Marmont Duc de Raguse* (Paris, 1857), 3: 229.

7. Paul Ollendorff, ed., *Souvenirs de Roustam, Mamlouck de Napoléon Ier* (Paris, n.d.), p. 236.

8. See the General Order of June 28, 1809 in *Unpublished Correspondence of Napoleon I* (New York, 1913), 3:110. Napoleon tinkered with the details of the crossing, issuing additional orders at 11 P.M. on July 2 and final orders on July 4.

9. Baron Seruzier, *Mémoires Militaires du Baron Seruzier* (Paris, 1823), p. 156.

10. "Ordre Pour le Passage du Danube," July 2, 1809, in *Correspondance de Napoléon Ier*, 19:205.

11. F. L. Petre, *Napoleon and the Archduke Charles* (London, 1976), p. 333.

12. Baron Lejeune, *Memoirs of Baron Lejeune* (London, 1897), 1:315.

13. Jean Thiry, *Wagram* (Paris, 1966), p. 175.

14. Moritz Exner, *The Participation of the Royal Saxon Army in the Campaign against Austria* (Dresden, 1894), p. 5.

15. Ibid., p. 33. French historians refused to acknowledge the leadership of the Saxon cavalry officers. Pelet has the French officer who delivered the attack order leading the charge. On another field, at Borodino, Napoleon would display less pleasure at Saxon accomplishments by refusing to acknowledge their key role in capturing the Great Redoubt and instead claiming all the credit for the French.

16. Ibid., p. 34.

17. More correctly, Deutsch Wagram and Markgrafneusiedl. For simplicity I am following the French naming.

18. Chevillet, *Ma Vie Militaire*, p. 286.

19. E. Buat, *Etude Critique d'Histoire Militaire 1809 de Ratisbonne à Znaim* (Paris, 1909), p. 218.

20. Ibid., p. 224.

21. Etienne MacDonald, *Marshal Macdonald's Recollections* (London, 1892), pp. 333–334.

22. Ibid., p. 335.

23. Chevillet, *Ma Vie Militaire*, pp. 287–288.

24. Ibid., pp. 293–294.

25. P. Berthezène, *Souvenirs Militaires* (Paris, 1855), 3:252.

26. "Rapport du Duc de Reggio, Général en Chef du 2e Corps, sur les Journées des 5 et 6 Juillet 1809," July 8, in General Koch, *Mémoires de Massena* (Paris, 1850), 6:Appendix XX, p. 412.

27. Exner, *Participation*, p. 36.

28. David G. Chandler, *The Military Maxims of Napoleon* (New York, 1988), maxim VIII, p. 58. Chandler has a slightly different translation, but the sense is the same.

CHAPTER 8

1. Peter G. Tsouras, *Warriors' Words: A Quotation Book* (London, 1992), p. 42.

2. Neusiedel more correctly is Markgrafneusiedl. However, the village's spelling is various, and in a book full of difficult German words, I have taken the easier, but French-ified, spelling.

3. Probably Wagram was the largest battle to date in world history. Ancient battles are notoriously unreliable in their reports of rival strengths.

4. E. Buat, *Etude critique d'Histoire Militaire 1809 de Ratisbonne à Znaim* (Paris, 1909), p. 216, figures Nordmann's remaining strength to be only 6,000 men.

5. Le Coq entered battle with 1,621 men and lost 228 killed, 573 wounded, and 90 missing. Moritz Exner, *The Participation of the Royal Saxon Army in the Campaign against Austria* (Dresden, 1894), p. 86.

6. Edouard Gachot, *1809 Napoléon en Allemagne* (Paris, 1913), p. 265.

7. French accounts have this attack plunging Bellegarde's first line into disorder.

These accounts fail to recognize that Stutterheim's advance guard represented this first line.

8. These were the Scovaux, Putheany, and Brzezinsky grenadiers.

9. French sources say that a soldier in Infantry Regiment #60 captured the eagle, which must be a mistake since that regiment was engaged near Aspern during the morning fight. In all likelihood, a grenadier of the Scovaux battalion took the trophy. One of the regiments contributing men to the battalion was Infantry Regiment #63, and this probably accounts for the confusion.

10. The official Austrian report says that "the enemy, pursuing their victory, had scattered in small platoons." See Buat, *Etude Critique*, p. 249n. 3.

11. Marc Desboeufs, *Souvenirs du Capitaine Desboeufs* (Paris, 1901), p. 109.

12. J. J. Pelet, *Mémoires sur la Guerre de 1809* (Paris, 1824), 4:212. The routed troops certainly included Saxon infantry, Saint-Cyr's men, and probably elements of Legrand's division, although French accounts are notably silent about this latter unit.

13. Exner, *Participation*, p. 41.

14. Baron Lejeune, *Memoirs of Baron Lejeune* (London, 1897), 1:319.

15. Duc de Rovigo, *Mémoires du Duc de Rovigo* (Paris, 1901), 3:174.

16. General Koch, *Mémoires de Massena* (Paris, 1850), 6:315.

17. Baron de Marbot, *Mémoires of Baron de Marbot* (London, 1892), 2:35.

18. Philippe-René Girault, *Les Campagnes d'un Musicien* (Paris, 1901), p. 253.

19. J. W. Ridler, "Ruekerinnerung an Oesterreichische Helden," *Archiv fuer Geographie, histories, Staats- und Kriegskunst* (Vienna, 1811), pp. 201–202.

20. Eugène de Beauharnais, *Mémoires et Correspondance Politique et Militaires du Prince Eugène* (Paris, 1858–1860), 6:8.

21. Gachot, *1809*, p. 275.

22. Exner, *Participation*, pp. 41–42.

23. Dezydery Chlapowski, *Memoirs of a Polish Lancer* (Chicago, 1992), p. 84.

24. Pelet, *Mémoires*, 4:217, provides this detail.

25. Rovigo, *Mémoires*, p. 176.

26. Henry Lachouque, *Anatomy of Glory* (Providence, R.I., 1961), p. 163.

27. René Willems, ed., *L'Odyssée d'un Carabinier à Cheval* (Brussels, 1971), p. 87.

28. Le Baron de Rothwiller, *Histoire du Deuxième Régiment de Cuirassiers, Ancien Royal de Cavalerie 1635–1876* (Paris, 1877), p. 504.

29. A. de Martimprey, *Historique du 9e Régiment de Cuirassiers* (Paris, 1888), p. 137. In this same charge, the 12th Cuirassiers lost 5 officers and 123 troopers.

30. Etienne MacDonald, *Marshal Macdonald's Recollections* (London, 1892), p. 338.

31. Maurice Girod De L'ain, *Grands Artilleurs: Drout-Senarmont-Eble* (Paris, 1895), p. 31.

32. J.N.A. Noël, *Souvenirs Militaires d'un Officier du Prémier Empire* (Paris, 1895), p. 74.

33. Jean François Bon Boulart, *Mémoires Militaires du Général Bon Boulart* (Paris, 1892), pp. 224–225.

34. Twenty-two years later one of his gunners would write a letter that recounted, in glowing terms, Drouot's conduct. This letter is reproduced in De L'ain, *Grands Artilleurs*, pp. 33–35.

35. Jean Michel Chevalier, *Souvenirs des Guerres Napoléoniennes* (Paris, 1970), p. 118.

36. Ibid.

37. Captain Lacombe in a letter to his father on display at the Musée de l'Emperi, Salon de Provence, France.

38. Chlapowski, *Memoirs*, p. 82.

39. Emile Fairion and Henri Heuse, *Lettres de Grognards* (Paris, 1936), p. 112.

40. Lejeune, *Memoirs*, 1:319.

41. Nicolas Planat La Faye, *Vie de Planat de la Faye* (Paris, 1895), p. 58.

42. Among several eyewitnesses, see Jules A. Paulin, *Les Souvenirs du Général Bon Paulin* (Paris, 1895), p. 209; and General Baron de Villeret Brun, *Les Cahiers du Général Brun* (Paris, 1953), pp. 90–91. The timing of his nap is uncertain, but the chronology given seems the most likely.

43. This according to Rovigo, *Mémoires*, who was with him for the entire period.

44. Brun, *Les Cahiers*, pp. 90–91.

45. The divisions of FML Bartenstein and Rohan faced south toward the Russbach.

46. Elzear Blaze, *Recollections of an Officer of Napoleon's Army* (New York, 1911), p. 197.

47. Paulin, *Les Souvenirs*, p. 208.

48. It was also not a "square" with the fourth (rear) side formed by cavalry. Macdonald, *Marshal Macdonald's Recollections*, p. 338, asserts that Nansouty filled in to his rear, which, if true, would have been a terrible tactical blunder. Koch persuasively argues that the cavalry was on the flank in *Mémoires*, 6:432–433 n. 6, and cites Roland, who commanded a carabinier squadron on this sector of the field.

49. The word *volcano* is used by several survivors including General Broussier in his official report. See ibid., p. 415.

50. Macdonald's assertion that they marched 60 leagues (180 miles) in three days is not credible. Macdonald, *Marshal Macdonald's Recollections*, pp. 329–330.

51. Maximilian von Thielen, *Erinnerungen* (Vienna, 1863), p. 62.

52. Seras: "The Army of Italy passed Sussenbrunn with more than 4,000 combatants." Seras's report of July 8, 1809 is provided in part in Gachot, *1809*, p. 280 n. 1. Macdonald wrote to Eugène that he pressed on although "réduit à moins de 1500 hommes," a comment that accurately applies only to Broussier, the division Macdonald accompanied. See Macdonald to Eugène, in Koch, *Mémoires*, 6:427.

53. Macdonald, *Marshal Macdonald's Recollections*, p. 340.

54. Rovigo, *Mémoires*, pp. 178–179.

55. Girault, *Les Campagnes*, p. 255.

56. Maurice de Tascher, *Journal de Campagne d'un Cousin de l'Impératrice* (Paris, 1933), p. 232.

57. Blaze, *Recollections*, p. 125.

58. Marquis de Grouchy, *Mémoires du Maréchal de Grouchy* (Paris, 1873), vol. 3. Grouchy's report to Berthier is on pp. 37–39.

59. P. Berthezène, *Souvenirs Militaires* (Paris, 1855), 3:256.

60. Charles Parquin, *Military Memoirs* (London, 1969), p. 102.

61. According to Pelet, Napoleon told Reille, "Ne vous aventurez pas." See Pelet, *Mémoires*, 4:225.

62. Macdonald, *Marshal Macdonald's Recollections*, p. 343.

63. Two officers and 13 men killed (along with 150 horses) and 6 officers and 57 men wounded. See Capitaine Amonville, *Les Cuirassiers du Roy, le 8e Cuirassiers* (Paris, 1892), p. 184.

64. See Montbrun's report to Davout in Raoul Dupuy, *Historique de 12e Régiment de Chasseurs de 1788 à 1891* (Paris, 1891), p. 163.

65. Gachot, *1809*, p. 273.

66. Parquin, *Military Memoirs*, p. 104.

67. This is the view of his biographer Charles Thoumas. See Charles A. Thoumas, *Les Grand Cavaliers du Premier Empire* (Paris, 1890), 1:41.

68. From an exhibit at the Musée de l'Emperi, Salon de Provence.

69. Noël, *Souvenirs Militaires*, p. 75.

70. von Thielen, *Erinnerungen*, p. 65.

71. Letter on display at the Musée de l'Emperi.

72. Rovigo, *Mémoires*, p. 179.

73. Lejeune, *Memoirs*, 1:322–323.

74. Desbouefs, *Souvenirs*, p. 111.

CHAPTER 9

1. Peter G. Tsouras, *Warriors' Words: A Quotation Book* (London, 1992), p. 313.

2. Paul Triaire, *Dominique Larrey et les Campagnes de la Révolution et de l'Empire* (Tours, 1902), p. 488.

3. Pierre Auvray, *Souvenirs Militaires de Pierre Auvray* (Paris, 1919), p. 31.

4. Elzear Blaze provides this charming anecdote in his *Recollections of an Officer of Napoleon's Army* (New York, 1911).

5. Capitaine Aubry, *Souvenirs du 12e Chasseurs* (Paris, 1889), p. 135.

6. *Correspondance de Napoléon Ier* (Paris, 1866), 19:231.

7. Provided by General Koch, *Mémoires de Massena* (Paris, 1850), 6:286 n. 3.

8. Moritz Exner, *The Participation of the Royal Saxon Army in the Campaign against Austria* (Dresden, 1894), p. 86, reports that the Saxon corps lost 139 officers and 4,295 men.

9. From Molitor's campaign report, MR 664, Chateau de Vincennes archives.

10. "To General Dejean," July 17, 1809 in *Unpublished Correspondence of Napoleon I* (New York, 1913), 3:128.

11. Exner, *Participation*, p. 84.

12. "To the Empress Josephine," July 7, 1809, in *Correspondance de Napoléon Ier*, 19: 217.

13. Eugène de Beauharnais, *Mémoires et Correspondance Politique et Militaires du Prince Eugène* (Paris, 1858–1860), 6:11.

14. Etienne Macdonald, *Marshal Macdonald's Recollections* (London, 1892), p. 346.

15. Boudet's letter of defense, dated July 7, is in Koch, *Mémoires*, 6:Appendix XXIII, pp. 422–423.

16. J. W. Ridler, "Ruekerinnerung an Oesterreichische Helden," *Archiv fuer Geographie, histories, Staats- und Kriegskunst* (Vienna, 1811), p. 197.

17. Capitaine Amonville, *Les Cuirassiers du Roy, Le 8e Cuirassiers* (Paris, 1892), p. 185.

18. Bernadotte's "Ordre du Jour" and Napoleon's refutation are in Raoul de Cisternes, ed., *Journal de Marche du Grenadier Pils* (Paris, 1895), pp. 78–79.

19. General Baron de Villeret Brun, *Les Cahiers du Général Brun* (Paris, 1953), p. 92.

20. J. Christopher Herold, ed., *The Mind of Napoleon: A Selection from His Written and Spoken Words* (New York, 1955), p. 175.

21. Marie Charlotte Oudinot, *Memoirs of Marshal Oudinot Duc de Reggio* (New York, 1897), p. 87.

22. Auguste Marmont, *Mémoires du Maréchal Marmont Duc de Raguse* (Paris, 1857), 3: 255.

23. John L. Pimlott, "Marmont: Friendship's Choice," in David G. Chandler, ed., *Napoleon's Marshals* (New York, 1987), p. 260.

24. Emile Fairion and Henri Heuse, *Lettres de Grognards* (Paris, 1936), p. 109.

25. Captain Lacombe in a letter on exhibit at the Musée de l'Emperi, Salon de Provence.

26. Roger Baschet, *Le Général Daumesnil* (Paris, 1938), p. 90.

27. Henri de Clairval, *Daumesnil* (Paris, 1970), p. 109.

28. See James R. Arnold, *Crisis on the Danube* (New York, 1990), p. 150.

29. Charles Parquin, *Military Memoirs* (London, 1969), p. 104.

30. "Metternich to the Emperor Francis," July 20, 1809 in Clemens Metternich-Winneburg, *Memoirs of Prince Metternich: 1773–1815* (New York, 1970), 2:361.

31. Related in a conversation with Metternich in 1810. See ibid., p. 389.

32. Amonville, *Les Cuirassiers*, p. 186

33. Auvray, *Souvenirs Militaires*, p. 33.

34. *Ordres et Apostiles de Napoléon* (Paris, 1912), Schoenbrunn, August 15, 1809, 4: 84–85.

35. Parquin, *Military Memoirs*, p. 109.

36. Jean Dupin, *Notice Biographique et Historique sur le Général Jean Baptiste Dupin* (Paris, 1851), p. 39. Dupin was on guard that day.

37. Louis de Bourrienne, *Memoirs of Napoleon Bonaparte* (New York, 1891), 3:217–218. Bourienne is not entirely reliable regarding Stapps, certainly confounding dates and probably adding dramatic detail. However, Stapps's conduct on the scaffold is cited in several sources.

38. Jakob Walter, *A German Conscript with Napoleon* (Lawrence, Kans., 1938), p. 175.

39. Lt. Colonel Reiset of the dragoons describes this tactic. See Lt. General Reiset, *Souvenirs du Vicomte de Reiset* (Paris, n.d.), p. 77.

40. Metternich, *Memoirs*, 2:365.

41. Walter Langsam, *The Napoleonic Wars and German Nationalism in Austria* (New York, 1930), p. 139.

42. Ibid., p. 137.

43. Charles A. Fare, *Lettres d'un Jeune Officier à Sa Mère*, (Paris, 1889), p. 209.

44. See "Starhemberg to Stadion," June 6, 1809 and "Stadion to Starhemberg," June 21, 1809, both in Wladyslaw de Fedorowicz, *1809 Campagne de Pologne* (Paris, 1911), 1: 388–393.

45. John G. Gallaher, *Napoleon's Irish Legion* (Carbondale, IL, 1993), pp. 104–105.

46. Brun, *Les Cahiers*, p. 87.

47. William Napier, *History of the War in the Peninsula and in the South of France* (London, 1892), 2:160.

48. "Rapport du général Senarmont," in Claude Marion, *Mémoire sur le Lieutenant-Général d'Artillerie Baron Alexandre de Senarmont* (Paris, 1846), p. 71.

49. Napier, *History*, p. 172.

50. For a French battalion commander's view of the battle, see François Vigo-Roussilon, *Journal de Campagne* (Paris, 1981), p. 249.

51. "Wellesley to Castlereagh," July 29, 1809 in Lt. Col. Gurwood, ed., *The Dispatches of the Field Marshal the Duke of Wellington during His Various Campaigns in India, Denmark, Portugal, Spain, the Low Countries, and France from 1799 to 1818* (London, 1837–1838), p. 506.

52. Napier, *History*, 2:162.

53. "Napoleon to Clarke," August 18, 1809, in Vigo-Roussillon, *Journal*, p. 252.

CHAPTER 10

1. J. Christopher Herold, ed., *The Mind of Napoleon: A Selection from His Written and Spoken Words* (New York, 1955), p. 242.

2. Madame Junot, *Memoirs of the Emperor Napoleon* (London, 1901), 3: 155.

3. Albert Meynier, "Levées et Pertes d'Hommes sous le Consulat et l'Empire," *Revue des Etudes* 30 (1930): table II.

4. Herold, *Mind of Napoleon*, p. 8.

5. Clemens Metternich-Winneburg, *Memoirs of Prince Metternich: 1773–1815* (New York, 1970), 2:376.

6. Elzear Blaze, *Recollections of an Officer of Napoleon's Army* (New York, 1911), p. 46

7. Patrick Turnbull, *Napoleon's Second Empress* (New York, 1971), p. 53.

8. Ibid., p. 57.

9. Metternich, *Memoirs*, 2:465.

10. Madame Junot notes, "All the letters I received concurred on one point—viz., that the Emperor was greatly changed, in every respect." *Memoirs*, 3:210.

11. "Napoleon to Clarke," August 18, 1809, in François Vigo-Roussilon, *Journal de Campagne* (Paris, 1981), p. 252.

12. Herold, *Mind of Napoleon*, p. 209.

13. Lt. Col. Ernest Picard, ed., *Préceptes et Jugements de Napoléon* (Paris, 1913), p. 295.

14. Henry Lachouque, *The Anatomy of Glory* (Providence, R.I., 1961), p. 172.

15. Turnbull, *Napoleon's Second Empress*, pp. 84–85.

16. Herold, *Mind of Napoleon*, p. 17.

17. Napoleon to Eugène, June 7, in Picard, *Préceptes*, p. 39.

18. Picard, *Préceptes*, pp. 30–31.

19. Bautzen is an example of the difficulty of outflanking an artillery-studded defensive line. Recall also that Napoleon rejected Davout's idea to try to outflank the Borodino position because he feared it would take too long.

20. Borodino's total of 33,000, most of whom were killed and wounded, comes close. The three days at Leipzig claimed more than 70,000 men, many of whom were captured. Waterloo cost perhaps 40,000 but again many were captured.

21. Duc de Rovigo, *Mémoires du Duc de Rovigo* (Paris, 1901), 4:121–122.

22. Auguste Marmont, *Mémoires du Maréchal Marmont Duc de Raguse* (Paris, 1857), 3: 241.

23. For the Teugen-Hausen battle, see James R. Arnold, *Crisis on the Danube* (New York, 1990), p. 82.

24. General Koch, *Mémoires de Massena* (Paris, 1850), 6:332.

25. Charles A. Thoumas, *Le Maréchal Lannes* (Paris, 1891). Davout's oration is in Appendix L, pp. 374–376.

26. Marmont, *Mémoires*, 3:228.

27. David G. Chandler, ed., *Napoleon's Marshals* (New York, 1987), p. lvii.

28. Baron de Marbot, *Mémoires of Baron de Marbot* (London, 1892), 2:26.

29. Junot, *Memoirs*, 3:150.

30. Seruzier, *Mémoires Militaires du Baron Seruzier* (Paris, 1823), p. 169.

31. Marie Charlotte Oudinot, *Memoirs of Marshal Oudinot Duc de Reggio* (New York, 1897), p. 86.

32. Marmont, *Mémoires*, 3:243.

33. David G. Chandler, ed., *The Military Maxims of Napoleon* (New York, 1988), maxim XLIX, p. 72.

34. Marbot, *Mémoires*, 2:38.

35. General Count Rapp, *Memoirs of General Count Rapp* (London, 1823), p. 138.

36. Herold, *Mind of Napoleon*, p. 76.

BIBLIOGRAPHY

Tactics can be learned from treatises . . . and so can the various military evolutions or the science of the engineer and the gunner; but knowledge of the grand principles of warfare can be acquired only through the study of military history and of the battles of the great captains and through experience. There are no precise, determinate rules: everything depends on the character that nature has bestowed on the general, on his qualities and defects, on the nature of the troops, on the range of the weapons, on the season of the year, and on a thousand circumstances which are never twice the same.

—*Napoleon*

The following libraries, archives, and museums shared their resources:

Musée Bertrand, Chateauroux.

Musée de l'Armée, Paris.

Musée de l'Emperi, Salon-de-Provence.

Musée de la Poste, Amboise.

Musée napoléonien d'Art et d'Histoire militaire, Fountainebleau.

Musée National de la Légion d'Honneur et des Ordres de Chevalerie, Paris.

Musée National du Chateau de Fontainebleau, Fontainebleau.

Salle du Souvenir du Maréchal Lannes, Lectoure.

Service Historique de l'Armée de Terre, Chateau de Vincennes.

At Vincennes, carton C–2, numbers 88–100 contain correspondence for the Armée d'Allemagne. Numbers 271, 281, and 282 have registers of orders and movements. K1, number 100, has "Notes sur la campagne de 1809"; K2, numbers 2–5 have Gudin's papers. MR numbers 660, 661, 662, 664, 665, 667, 671, and 672 all have battle reports. When using these archives, prepare, if your native tongue is English, for a bewildering bureaucracy and frequent tongue lashings and related humiliations. The bistro across the street serves a restorative pilsner.

PRIMARY SOURCES

Aubry, Capitaine. *Souvenirs du 12e Chasseurs*. Paris, 1889.

Auvray, Pierre. *Souvenirs Militaires de Pierre Auvray*. Paris, 1919. A second lieutenant in the 22d Dragoons.

Barres, Jean-Baptiste. *Memoirs of a Napoleonic Officer*. London, 1925.

Beauharnais, Eugène de. *Mémoires et Correspondance Politique et Militaires du Prince Eugène*. 10 vols. Paris, 1858–1860.

Berthezène, P. *Souvenirs Militaires*. Vol. 3. Paris, 1855. A vivid, tactically detailed account by the able leader of the 10th Légère.

Beulay, H. *Mémoires d'un Grenadier de la Grande Armée*. Paris, 1907.

Blaze, Elzear. *Recollections of an Officer of Napoleon's Army*. New York, 1911.

Bon Boulart, Jean François. *Mémoires Militaires du Général Bon Boulart*. Paris, 1892. Served in the Imperial Guard Foot Artillery.

Bonneval, Général Marquis de. *Mémoires Anecdotiques du Général Marquis de Bonneval*. Paris, 1900.

Bourrienne, Louis de. *Memoirs of Napoleon Bonaparte*. Vol. 3. New York, 1891.

Brun, Général Baron de Villeret. *Les Cahiers du Général Brun*. Paris, 1953.

Cambacères, Jean. *Lettres Inédites à Napoléon, 1802–1814*. 2 vols. Paris, 1973. The second consul who helped Bonaparte secure his position and then served as Arch-Chancellor of the empire.

Caulaincourt, Armand de. *With Napoleon in Russia*. New York, 1935.

Chevalier, Jean Michel. *Souvenirs des Guerres Napoléoniennes*. Paris, 1970.

Chevillet, J. *Ma Vie Militaire*. Paris, 1906. A marvelous account of military service by a trooper who delighted in cut-and-thrust combat.

Chlapowski, Dezydery. *Memoirs of a Polish Lancer*. Chicago, 1992. Entertaining but factually unreliable.

Cisternes, Raoul de, ed. *Journal de Marche du Grenadier Pils*. Paris, 1895. One of Oudinot's men.

Coudreux. *Lettres du Commandant Coudreux à son Frère*. Paris, 1908.

Delmarche, Joachim. *Les Soirées du Grenadier*. Musée de Cerfontaine, 1980.

Desboeufs, Marc. *Souvenirs du Capitaine Desboeufs*. Paris, 1901. A voltigeur in the 81st Ligne. Full of fascinating combat detail.

Desmarest, Pierre-Marie. *Quinze Ans de Haute Police sous le Consulat et l'Empire*. Paris, 1900.

———. *Témoignages Historiques*. Paris, 1833.

Dienst reglement fur die kaiserlich-königliche Cavallerie. Vienna, 1807.

Dupin, Jean. *Notice Biographique et Historique sur le Général Jean Baptiste Dupin*. Paris, 1851.

Dupuy, Victor. *Souvenirs Militaires*. Paris, 1892.

Exercier-Reglement für die kaiserlich-königliche Infanterie. Vienna, 1807.

Fare, Charles A. *Lettres d'un Jeune Officier à Sa Mère*. Paris, 1889. Includes his mother's return letters with their timeless expressions of maternal anxiety for a son at war.

Fouche, Joseph. *Memoirs Relating to Fouche*. New York, 1912.

Girault, Philippe-René. *Les Campagnes d'un Musicien*. Paris, 1901.

Gonneville, Colonel de. *Recollections of Colonel de Gonneville*. 2 vols. London, 1875.

Graham, Thomas. *The History of the Campaign of 1796 in Germany and Italy*. London, 1800.

Grouchy, Marquis de. *Mémoires du Maréchal de Grouchy*. Vol. 3. Paris, 1873. Nominally a biography, it primarily contains Grouchy's writings and reports.

Gurwood, Lt. Col., ed. *The Dispatches of the Field Marshal the Duke of Wellington during His Various Campaigns in India, Denmark, Portugal, Spain, the Low Countries, and France from 1799 to 1818*. London, 1837–1838.

Jacquin, François-Joseph. *Carnet de Route d'un Grognard*. Paris, 1960.

Junot, Madame. *Memoirs of the Emperor Napoleon*. Vol. 3. London, 1901.

Koch, Général. *Mémoires de Massena*. 7 vols. Paris, 1850.

Laborde. *Histoire de la Guerre d'Autriche en 1809*. Paris, 1823.

La Faye, Nicolas Planat. *Vie de Planat de la Faye*. Paris, 1895.

Larchey, Loredan, ed. *The Narrative of Captain Coignet*. New York, 1890.

Larrey, D. J. *Mémoires et Campagnes de Chirugie Militaire*. Paris, 1812.

Lebzeltern, Ludwig Compte de. *Mémoires et Papiers de Lebzeltern; un Collaborateur de Metternich*. Paris, 1949.

Lejeune, Baron. *Memoirs of Baron Lejeune*. 2 vols. London, 1897.

Macdonald, Etienne. *Marshal Macdonald's Recollections*. London, 1892. The memoirs of a proud officer who never made a tactical mistake but was frequently let down by his peers, including the emperor. His version of his assault at Wagram is wrong in at least two important particulars.

Marbot, Baron de. *Mémoires of Baron de Marbot*. 2 vols. London, 1892.

Marmont, Auguste. *Mémoires du Maréchal Marmont Duc de Raguse*. Vol. 3. Paris, 1857.

Metternich-Winneburg, Clemens. *Memoirs of Prince Metternich: 1773–1815*. Vol. 2. New York, 1970.

Montholon, Count de. *Memoirs of the History of France during the Reign of Napoleon Dictated by the Emperor at Saint Helena*. London, 1823.

Napoleon. *Napoleon's Own Memoirs*. London, 1823.

————. *Correspondance de Napoléon Ier*. Vol. 19. Paris, 1866.

————. *Ordres et Apostiles de Napoléon*. Vol. 4. Paris, 1912.

————. *Unpublished Correspondence of Napoleon I*. Vol. 3. New York, 1913.

Noël, J.N.A. *Souvenirs Militaires d'un Officier du Premier Empire*. Paris, 1895.

Oudinot, Marie Charlotte. *Memoirs of Marshal Oudinot Duc de Reggio*. New York, 1897. Compiled from Madame Oudinot's writings; not always accurate.

Parquin, Charles. *Military Memoirs*. London, 1969. A Marbot-like soldier in the 20th Chasseurs à Cheval.

Pasquier, Etienne-Denis. *The Memoirs of Chancellor Pasquier*. Cranbury, N.J., 1968.

Paulin, Jules A. *Les Souvenirs du Général Bon Paulin*. Paris, 1895. Excellent details on the bridging operations by an engineer officer.

Pelet, J. J. *Mémoires sur la Guerre de 1809*. Vols. 2–4. Paris, 1824. A superb source but must be used carefully.

Pelleport, C. *Souvenirs Militaires et Intimes du Général Vte. de Pelleport*. Vol. 1. Paris, 1857. A colonel in the 18th Ligne.

Peyrusse, Guillaune. *Lettres Inédites de Guillaune Peyrusse*. Paris, 1894.

Picard, Lt. Col. Ernest, ed. *Préceptes et Jugements de Napoléon*. Paris, 1913.

Pouget, Général Baron. *Souvenirs de Guerre du Général Baron Pouget.* Paris, 1895.

Rapp, Général Count. *Memoirs of Général Count Rapp.* London, 1823.

Reiset, Lt. Général. *Souvenirs du Vicomte de Reiset.* Paris, n.d. A detailed account by a dragoon colonel of the many vicious fights to secure the French lines of communications.

Roguet, Général Comte. *Mémoires Militaires du Lieutenant Général Comte Roguet.* Vol. 4. Paris, 1865.

Rovigo, Duc de. *Mémoires du Duc de Rovigo.* Vol. 3. Paris, 1901. It is very important to read the French original. The English translation, published in London in 1828, omits text and contains many misleading translations.

Rouguet, C. M. *L'Officier d'Infanterie en Campagne.* Paris, 1846.

Segur, La, Général Compte de. *Histoire et Mémoires.* Vol. 3. Paris, 1873.

Seruzier. *Mémoires Militaires du Baron Seruzier.* Paris, 1823. The detailed accounts of a proud artillerist.

Stutterheim, Général. *La Guerre de l'An 1809.* Vienna, 1811. Before his disgrace and suicide, Stutterheim completed his account through the fall of Vienna.

Tascher, Maurice de. *Journal de Campagne d'un Cousin de l'Impératrice.* Paris, 1933. An officer in the 12th Chasseurs à Cheval.

Thielen, Maximilian von. *Erinnerungen.* Vienna, 1863.

Thoumas, Charles A. *Le Général Curely: Itinéraire d'un Cavalier Léger de la Grande Armée.* Paris, 1887.

Vigo-Roussilon, François. *Journal de Campagne.* Paris, 1981. A battalion commander's Spanish campaign with an excellent historical corrective to the British-dominated view of Talavera.

Walter, Jakob. *A German Conscript with Napoleon.* Lawrence, Kans., 1938.

Willems, Rene, ed. *L'Odyssée d'un Carabinier à Cheval.* Brussels, 1971.

SECONDARY SOURCES

Alville, Alexandre. *Un Suisse Officier d'Ordonnance de Napoléon.* Lausanne, 1956.

Amonville, Capitaine. *Les Cuirassiers du Roy, le 8e Cuirassiers.* Paris, 1892. A regimental history.

Angeli, Moriz Edlin von. *Erzherzog Carl.* 5 vols. Vienna, 1896–1897.

Arnold, James R. *Crisis on the Danube: Napoleon's Austrian Campaign of 1809.* New York, 1990.

Aubrée, Etienne. *Le Général de la Riboisière.* Paris, 1948.

Baschet, Roger. *Le Général Daumesnil.* Paris, 1938.

Bernard, Jack F. *Talleyrand: A Biography.* New York, 1973.

Bessières, Albert. *Le Bayard de la Grande Armée.* Paris, 1952.

Boudard, René. "La Conscription Militaire et ses Problèmes dans le Département de la Creuse." *Revue de L'Institut Napoléonic* #145, 1985–92, Paris.

Bowden, Scott, and Charlie Tarbox. *Armies of the Danube, 1809.* Arlington, Texas, 1980.

Brant, Irving. *James Madison: Secretary of State, 1800–1809.* New York, 1953.

———. *James Madison: The President, 1809–1812.* New York, 1956.

Brinton, Crane. *The Life of Talleyrand.* New York, 1936.

Buat, E. *Etude Critique d'Histoire Militaire 1809 de Ratisbonne à Znaim.* Paris, 1909. A guardedly reliable, detailed account that includes excellent maps.

Camon, General. *La Manoeuvre de Wagram*. Paris, 1926.

Casse, André du. *Le Général Arrighi de Casanova, duc de Padoue*. Vol. 1. Paris, 1866.

Chandler, David G. *The Campaigns of Napoleon*. New York, 1966.

――――. *Dictionary of the Napoleonic Wars*. New York, 1979. A truly useful source.

――――. ed. *The Military Maxims of Napoleon*. New York, 1988.

――――. *Napoleon's Marshals*. New York, 1987. The best modern account.

Chavane, J. *Histoire du 11e Cuirassiers*. Paris, 1889.

Clairval, Henri de. *Daumensnil*. Paris, 1970.

Cole, Hubert. *Fouche: The Unprincipled Patriot*. New York, 1971.

Colin, J. *La Tactique et la Discipline dans les Armées de la Révolution*. Paris, 1902.

Cooper, Duff. *Talleyrand*. Stanford, Calif., 1967.

Criste, Oskar. *Erzherzog Carl von Osterreich*. 3 vols. Vienna-Leipzig, 1912.

Dard, Emile. *Napoleon and Talleyrand*. New York, 1937.

De L'ain, Maurice Girod. *Grands Artilleurs: Drout-Senarmont-Eble*. Paris, 1895.

Doher, Marcel. *Charles de La Bédoyère, Aide de Camp de l'Empereur*. Paris, n.d.

Du Casse, André. *Mémoires et Correspondance Politique et Militaire du Prince Eugène*. Paris, 1859.

Duffy, Christopher. *Austerlitz 1805*. London, 1977.

――――. *The Army of Maria Theresa*. New York, 1977.

Dupuy, Raoul. *Historique de 12e Régiment de Chasseurs de 1788 à 1891*. Paris, 1891.

Elmer, Alexandre. *Schulmeister: l'Agent Sécret de Napoléon*. Paris, 1932.

Epstein, Robert M. *Prince Eugène at War*. Arlington, Texas, 1984. A well-researched account of Eugène's 1809 campaigns before Wagram.

Esposito, General Vincent J., and Colonel John Elting. *Military History and Atlas of the Napoleonic Wars*. New York, 1964. Wonderful maps but somewhat error-prone text.

Exner, Moritz. *The Participation of the Royal Saxon Army in the Campaign against Austria*. Dresden, 1894. A much-needed corrective account of Saxon exploits.

Fairion, Emile, and Henri Heuse. *Lettres de Grognards*. Paris, 1936.

de Fedorowicz, Wladyslaw. *1809 Campagne de Pologne*. Vol. 1. Paris, 1911. Contains the Polish and French documents pertaining to the campaign.

Friant, Jean François. *Vie Militaire du Lieutenant-Général Comte Friant*. Paris, 1857. An uncritical biography written by his son but full of military detail.

Gachot, Edouard. *1809 Napoléon en Allemagne*. Paris, 1913. Use in conjunction with Pelet and Koch.

Gallaher, John G. *The Iron Marshal—A Biography of Louis N. Davout*. London, 1976.

――――. *Napoleon's Irish Legion*. Carbondale, Ill., 1993. A detailed account of this interesting unit.

Herold, J. Christopher, ed. *The Mind of Napoleon: A Selection from His Written and Spoken Words*. New York, 1955.

Holtman, Robert B. *Napoleonic Propaganda*. Baton Rouge, 1950.

Johnson, Ray. "Field Telegraphy in the Austrian Army." *Empires, Eagles, and Lions* 83 (October 1984). The devotion to Napoleonic study shown by editors Jean Lochet and Marc Raiff makes old issues of *EE&L* a wonderful read.

Lachouque, Henry. *Anatomy of Glory*. Providence, R.I., 1961.

――――. *Napoleon's Battles*. New York, 1967.

Langsam, Walter. *The Napoleonic Wars and German Nationalism in Austria*. New York, 1930. A fine, scholarly work.

Loy, L. *Campagne de Styrie*. Paris, 1908. Includes a detailed account of the 84th's engagement at Graz.

McGuigan, Dorothy Gies. *Metternich and the Duchess: The Public and Private Lives at the Congress of Vienna*. New York, 1975.

Marion, Claude. *Mémoire sur le Lieutenant-Général d'Artillerie Baron Alexandre de Senarmont*. Paris, 1846. Contains much of Senarmont's correspondence, including Talavera (and Friedland).

Martimprey, A. de. *Historique du 9e Régiment de Cuirassiers*. Paris, 1888.

Martinien, Aristide. *Tableaux par Corps et par Batailles des Officiers Tués et Blessés pendant les Guerres de l'Empire*. Paris, 1899. An indispensable tabulation.

Meynier, Albert. "Levées et Pertes d'Hommes sous le Consulat et l'Empire," *Revue des Etudes* 30 (1930).

Muller, Paul. *L'Espionnage Militaire sous Napoléon I*. Paris, 1896.

Napier, William. *History of the War in the Peninsula and in the South of France*. Vol. 2. London, 1892.

Ollendorff, Paul, ed. *Souvenirs de Roustam, Mamlouck de Napoléon Ier*. Paris, n.d.

Palmer, Alan. *Metternich: Councillor of Europe*. London, 1972.

Perin, René. *Vie Militaire du Duc de Montebello*. Paris, n.d.

Petre, F. L. *Napoleon and the Archduke Charles*. London, 1976. A classic British work of highly opinionated history.

————. *Napoleon's Campaign in Poland, 1806–07*. New York, 1907.

Puryear, Vernon J. *Napoleon and the Dardanelles*. Berkeley, Calif., 1951.

Ridler, J. W. "Ruekerinnerung an Oesterreichische Helden." In *Archiv fuer Geographie, histories, Staats- und Kriegskunst*. Vienna, 1811.

Rivollet, George. *Général de Bataille Charles Antoine Louis Morand*. Paris, 1963.

Rothenberg, Gunther. *Napoleon's Great Adversaries*. Bloomington, Ind., 1982.

Rothwiller, Le Baron de. *Histoire du Deuxième Régiment de Cuirassiers, Ancien Royal de Cavalerie, 1635–1876*. Paris, 1877.

Saski, C.G.L. *La Campagne de 1809*. 3 vols. Paris, 1899–1902. A compilation of original documents, of special interest because of its influence on French strategic development prior to World War I.

Savant, Jean. *Les Espions de Napoléon*. Paris, 1957.

Serieyx, W. *Drouet et Napoléon*. Paris, 1929.

Sherwig, John M. *Guineas and Gunpowder: British Foreign Aid in the Wars with France*. Cambridge, Mass., 1969. A scholarly work.

Stearns, Josephine B. *The Role of Metternich in Undermining Napoleon*. Urbana, Ill., 1948.

Ternaux-Compans, M., ed. *Le Général Compans*. Paris, 1912.

Thiry, Jean. *Wagram*. Paris, 1966. The standard modern French account, overly reliant on Napoleon's bulletins.

Thoumas, Charles A. *Les Grands Cavaliers du Premier Empire*. 2 vols. Paris, 1890, 1892.

————. *Le Maréchal Lannes*. Paris, 1891.

Triaire, Paul. *Dominique Larrey et les Campagnes de la Révolution et de l'Empire*. Tours, 1902.

Tsouras, Peter G. *Warriors' Words: A Quotation Book*. London, 1992.

Tulard, Jean, and Louis Garros. *Itinéraire de Napoléon au Jour le Jour*. Paris, 1992. What did he do, and when did he do it? This wonderful compilation provides the answers.

Turnbull, Patrick. *Napoleon's Second Empress*. New York, 1971.

Victoires, Conquêtes, Désastres, Revers et Guerres Civiles des Français. Vol. 19. Paris, 1820.

Weller, Jac. *Wellington in the Peninsula.* London, 1962. An entertaining read that misleadingly explicates battles on the basis of column versus line.

Wien Kriegsarchiv. *Krieg 1809.* 4 vols. Vienna, 1907–1910.

INDEX

About the Author

JAMES R. ARNOLD is the author of 10 books on military history, the most recent of which is *The Armies of U.S. Grant*. *Napoleon Conquers Austria* completes his two-volume account of the Emperor's decisive 1809 campaign.